RELENTLESS: THE BLURBS

Slash

Yngwie literally blew my mind when he came on the LA music scene in the early 1980s—the fastest and most articulate, fluid, melodic classical-based rock guitarist I'd ever heard. He's still the best at what he does all these years later.

Steve Vai

When Yngwie Malmsteen hit the scene in the early 1980s, it was as though a monolith had appeared. He was playing electric rock guitar in a way that seemed completely unearthly and had to be seen to be believed.

His tone was pristine and powerful; his vibrato, intonation, and control were stunning; his harmonic and melodic sensibilities were unique; his emotional investment in his melodies was captivating; and his sheer speed and technical command of the instrument were utterly breathtaking, to the point of frightening for some.

Yngwie absolutely set a standard of virtuosity on the instrument that has yet to be matched. He was a breath of visceral fresh air that inspired the movement of a whole new subculture of music. He was always unequivocally and unquestionably dedicated to his passions and delivered without any excuses. And since then, the bastard has just been getting better!

I have had the good fortune of knowing him for the past twenty-five years, and I have stood next to him on stage many times. It always felt as though I were standing next to a mountain—solid, giant, and forever.

A couple of things about Yngwie that some may not know are that he is remarkably intelligent and has a fiery sense of humor that delivers on par with his musical gifts.

Joe Satriani

Yngwie Malmsteen loves to play guitar, and he's really good at it. I know this from personal experience.

I've stood right next to him on many a stage, shoulder to shoulder, trading solos, celebrating our influences, taking chances, playfully testing each other's limits, and putting on a great show for our fans. At the end of every performance, I was sure of two things: Yngwie is an amazing guitarist, and there is only one Yngwie Malmsteen.

Let's face it, every guitarist wishes they could do what Yngwie does with those six strings and a pick, but what he does is not only superhuman, it is undeniably unique and original. There are imitators, some with equal proficiency, but none who can match the heart and the confidence behind his virtuosity.

The last time we played together was at Marshall's 50th Anniversary Concert at Wembley Arena in London on September 22, 2012, and I think it was the best I'd ever heard him play. Yes, he's getting better!

I was on stage just behind the curtain warming up with my guitar as I listened to Yngwie enthrall the audience with his impeccable and furious technique. But it's his passion for music that really lights everyone up in the audience. It's the fire burning in those hands that makes every note scream. He puts all of who he is—no excuses, no apologies—into every note and every sound he makes on his guitar.

There is only one Yngwie Malmsteen.

Zakk Wylde

You have *good* guitar players.

You have *great* guitar players.

Then you have the ones who *change the game*.

Like Jimi Hendrix and Edward Van Halen before him, Yngwie walks among them. It's not just his sheer and utter mastery and command of the instrument that makes him amazing. The phrasing, the vibrato, the tone, and his feel and passion, along with the overall musicality that he brings to the table, are what make him so special and unique. While other guitar players play fast and say nothing, Yngwie speaks. If you've ever wondered what Bach, Beethoven, Mozart, Vivaldi, and Paganini would have been capable of doing if they lived in the twenty-first century, look no further. They all reside within Yngwie J. Malmsteen, and they are smiling.

Richard McDonald, Fender Guitars

The most meaningful endorsements come from artists who truly believe in the products they use. Fender has never embraced a pay-to-play relationship with artists. We are always looking for the quintessential Fender players—individuals who use our instruments to create new, captivating, and inspiring music. Yngwie J. Malmsteen is exactly that kind of artist.

His compositions and playing were so fresh, his technique and sound so different. It represented a new era and a new level of musical sophistication in the heavy rock genre. Guitarists the world over were in awe. Not since Jimi Hendrix in the 1960s had the musical community witnessed such a redefinition of guitar music.

When the idea of "signature artist" instruments surfaced in the late 1980s, we selected two players we thought earned this special acknowledgment. One was Eric Clapton and the other was Yngwie Malmsteen. If you are lucky enough to spend meaningful time with Yngwie, you will quickly understand he is a Fender fanatic, collector, and historian. Not only was it a privilege to design a signature model Stratocaster with him, it was an incredible challenge to reproduce the unique specifications of his guitar. The instrument is still one of our most popular artist models, and it stands as a tribute to his longevity and popularity across a broad audience of players and enthusiasts.

Nick Bowcott, Marshall Amplification

Every once in a blue moon, a rock guitarist comes along who doesn't just reset the bar but turns the whole genre upside down. Such players are few and far between: Jimi Hendrix, Jimmy Page, Eric Clapton, Jeff Beck, Edward Van Halen, Randy Rhoads, Dimebag Darrell—and a six-string supernova named Yngwie J. Malmsteen.

Although Yngwie was first introduced to many people through a "Spotlight" column in *Guitar Player* in the early 1980s, most didn't actually hear his music until the April 1985 issue of the magazine, which contained a seven-inch flexi-disc (remember those now extinct items?) featuring Yngwie performing "Black Star" from his debut solo album. Such was the explosive impact of his playing that I can tell you *exactly* where I was when I first heard it, just as I can recount the location of my initial encounters with Messrs. Van Halen and Rhoads. The result? A new star was born, and sweep-picking and neoclassical playing became the same overnight sensation as two-handed tapping was when "Eruption" was released. And it's all Yngwie's fault.

Yngwie's love for Marshall is well known. The man literally crams as much of our gear into each and every venue he plays at as the size of the stage will allow. And for that we are eternally grateful. As he likes to say, "There are only two man-made objects you can see from outer-space: the Great Wall of China and my Marshall backline!" No surprise, then, that in 2011 Marshall unveiled the Yngwie J. Malmsteen signature YJM100 head—and we do not expect that to be the only project we collaborate on.

Yngwie and the late, great Jim Marshall met in 1984, hit it off immediately as a result of their shared oddball sense of humor, and remained great friends right up until Jim's passing in 2012. During the making of the charity song "We're Stars," one of the members of the fictional band Spinal Tap joked that the only reason Yngwie uses the name "Yngwie J. Malmsteen" is to distinguish himself from all the other Yngwie Malmsteens out there. If truth be told, though, our friend doesn't even need to use his last-name. "Yngwie" is enough for any guitarist on the planet to know exactly who is meant.

Seymour W. Duncan, Chairman, Seymour Duncan Pickups

Yngwie is one of a handful of pioneer players who shook up the world of electric guitar and opened it up to an entirely new way of playing. And he's got some amazing tone!

Evan Skopp, Vice President, Artist Relations, Seymour Duncan Pickups

His guitar virtuosity is renowned. But one thing most people don't know about Yngwie is what a great guy he is. Super-intelligent. Funny as hell. And a family man. He's one of the coolest artists I've had the pleasure of working with.

Paul Youngblood, Vice President, BOSS/Roland Guitar

Yngwie J. Malmsteen is the father of shred guitar. His influence on the guitar and other guitar players is huge. Yngwie is always totally in control and a master. And by the way, Yngwie really rocks!

Walter Rührig, AKG Acoustics

Yngwie Malmsteen is a fantastic ambassador for AKG Acoustics' premium pro audio products. Yngwie's outstanding musical talent and performance deserve top professional equipment support, and we are extremely pleased to have been chosen by him as a partner he trusts.

I'm personally impressed by Yngwie's passion for his music and his incomparable, powerful style when performing live on stage. He fades away, transforms all his energy into his guitar playing, and entertains his fans at a top musical and emotional level. And millions love him for that.

I will never in my life forget when I first met Yngwie in person. When Yngwie left my office, a colleague of mine came in and asked me with great excitement, "Do you know who that was?" And I responded, full of pride, "Yes, my friend, *this* was Yngwie Malmsteen!!"

RELENTLESS

RELENTLESS
the memoir

Yngwie J. Malmsteen

WILEY

John Wiley & Sons, Inc.

Published by John Wiley & Sons, Inc., Hoboken, New Jersey
Published simultaneously in Canada

For general information about our other products and services, please contact our Customer Care Department within the United States at (800) 762-2974, outside the United States at (317) 572-3993 or fax (317) 572-4002.

Wiley also publishes its books in a variety of electronic formats and by print-on-demand. Some content that appears in standard print versions of this book may not be available in other formats. For more information about Wiley products, visit us at www .wiley.com.

ISBN 978-1-118-51771-0 (cloth); ISBN 978-1-118-51773-4 (ebk);
ISBN 978-1-118-51774-1 (ebk); ISBN 978-1-118-51776-5 (ebk)

Printed in the United States of America

For my wife, April, the love of my life,
and my son, Antonio, my pride and joy

Contents

YNGWIE

I like the way he puts Yngwie J. Malmsteen on
his albums—you know, so you don't confuse
him with all the other Yngwie Malmsteens in the
business.

—DAVID ST. HUBBINS, SPINAL TAP

When I was a little kid in Sweden, nobody was named Yngve (or
Yngwie) or anything like that. Pronounced "Ing-vay," it's a
very unusual, very old name. I used to think it would be cool if I'd
been called by one of my other names, Lars and Johann, which are
quite common. That changed when I finally researched what Yngve
means.

I discovered that it's connected to the Swedish word for "young
man," *yngling*. So I assumed that Yngve probably meant something like "young Viking." In any case, I knew it was an old Viking

name of some kind. I further learned that the first name of the Old Norse god Frej was Yngve—Yngve-Frej—who was the god of fertility, sex, and love. I found that the spellings vary—Yngvi, Yngvin, Ingwine, Inguin—but all are names that relate to Yng, an older name for the god Frej.

During this time a certain group of young men dedicated themselves to the god Yngve-Frej and started calling themselves "those who have taken the oath of Yngve." They were the "young men of Yngve," and over time that term shifted to the name Yngling. But the ancient connection with Yngve-Frej is not that well known. It took some digging through histories of Norse mythology and Viking terminology for me to find this out. It stopped me in my tracks when I discovered the origin of my name. I'm sure my mother didn't know it, either—she just liked the sound of the name. The Swedish dynasty of kings grew out of the Ynglings and their allegiance to the god Yngve-Frej.

A thousand years ago, there was no Norway, Denmark, and Sweden, as we know them now. It was all just Northland or Scandinavia. Not all Vikings were warmongers, which is the stereotype. Back in the ninth century or so, some of them were farmers, builders, traders, and so on, with a well-developed culture. In ancient Sweden, there was a little island called Birka, which was the epicenter of all Viking trade at that time. There were a number of chiefs, not kings, with maybe up to a thousand or so followers each. One of these chiefs was Erik the Red, a well-known historical figure who was exiled to Iceland for murdering a countryman. He established a Viking outpost there, and his son, Leif Eriksson, made his way to Greenland and then onto the northeastern coast of North America almost five hundred years before Christopher Columbus.

There were many levels of this Viking culture, which spread throughout the area we call Scandinavia, including the slave class, called *trlälar*. The Vikings kept slaves up until around AD 1100, a fact that many people don't know. As you can tell, I'm fascinated by history. It's my preferred type of reading, because when I'm curious about something, I need to have the whole story, not just a few facts here and there. The subject can be anything that intrigues me, whether it's the history of the Ferrari or the origin of names from Nordic mythology.

Naming boys Yngve wasn't common when I was born, as I said. So it's funny how many times I've heard of fans, often in the United States, naming their kids or their pets Yngwie. I think the first time I ever heard of a fan doing that was when I was in a band called Alcatrazz. I got a fan letter from a girl who told me she had named her cat Yngwie Meowsteen. By now, there are a lot of little boys walking around with the name Yngwie, or maybe spelled Yngve, without a clue where the name really comes from. My son also has Yngwie as one of his names, and he knows what it means.

It means he's a Viking, a Swedish king, like his father.

This is the story that only I can tell—my life, my journey, my failures, my triumphs. This is a window to my soul.

I have been working on this book for six years and now I can finally share it with you.

Enjoy.

FIREBALL

Seeing Jimi Hendrix burning his guitar onstage made me want to play guitar. I swear to God, that was the initial reason. It just looked so fucking awesome.

People ask me why I always come back to places where it's hot and sunny most of the year. Let me tell you something: when I think of Sweden, where I was born and grew up, what stands out the most in my memory is darkness, biting cold, and piles of snow for nine or ten months of the year, contrasted with just a few warm, sunny weeks in the summer, mainly June and July. People who live in Sweden soak up those few weeks when it's daylight twenty-four hours a day, because you know that just when you're getting used to it, the freezing dark is going to come back and hammer you down. It does something to the Swedish temperament, I think. You feel so constricted for so much of the year, then you get let out of prison for a couple of months. You can go boating or hiking or just sit in the sun by the side of a lake and stare at the water. Then it's right back to jail.

If I can sit by a pool with palm trees waving in the breeze overhead and the sun beating down on me, it's paradise. Whenever I can enjoy places like that, whether to record a new album or just take a vacation from touring, it reminds me how lucky I am. That frozen, constricted landscape—and mindscape—of Sweden in the 1970s was a cage I had to escape from. It only made me more determined to have the impossible career and someday sit in my car with the top down, listening to the sound of the surf on the beach in some tropical climate.

I grew up in an environment where adults and older siblings surrounded me. I was born on June 30, 1963, the youngest in a household that included my brother, Bjorn, who was two years older than I was, and my sister, Anne-Louise (Lolo), who was six years older. That's a big difference when you're ten and she's sixteen. Even though I was just a kid, a lot of her tastes and interests made a strong impression on me. I was hanging out with her friends and listening to their talk. It was a very political environment, and much of what they debated and argued over I listened in on. My early interest in politics was kind of secondhand, but these days I have very strong opinions.

The environment of Sweden in the 1960s and 1970s had an extremely socialistic, group-minded slant on what the citizens were allowed to be. You didn't stick your head up above the masses, you didn't aspire to do anything that would make you stand out from the crowd, and you *especially* didn't draw attention to yourself in any extravagant way.

There was a lot of talk in those days that the basic amenities of life should be provided free to all by the government. But here's the catch. In life, there is no such thing as free. When you hear "free health care," or free whatever, it isn't. Somebody has to pay for whatever it is. Money doesn't materialize out of thin air. It's simple: you take money from someone and give it to someone else—this for that. It's called the redistribution of wealth, and in any welfare system there's no way around it. This social process was invented and implemented by the Swedish government when I was growing up in the 1970s. It's the country's social welfare system. The basic mechanism of socialism is simple to understand. Margaret Thatcher put it best: "The problem with socialism is that sooner or later you will run out of someone else's money!" You don't get rewarded if you work hard, but you do get rewarded if you do nothing. Society is leveled so everyone becomes "equal." Unfortunately this "equality" brings everybody down, and you can't elevate yourself by pulling someone else down.

The whole country was like that. The input you got from the media—TV and radio, newspapers, films, magazines, the stuff that you saw and heard every day—drilled this way of thinking into you. To be a musician, a star athlete, an actor, or an artist of any stature—such people were looked down on because they were considered not to be model citizens. We had the occasional Nobel Prize–winner whom the country would officially be proud of, but forget it if you aspired to do something that had even a hint of celebrity to it. Some of the best hockey players now are Swedish, but back then they weren't even professionals. That's why they went to the United States. You'd weld a fucking boat, then play hockey at night.

Anybody who aspired to be a musician had to play it down. You could maybe have a little apartment with a tiny working space where you could play your instrument and so forth, but nothing serious. It was just hobby stuff. I guess that's why I'm such an advocate of being my own person and doing my own thing. I was totally the opposite of the reserved, self-effacing, self-deprecating Swede. By nature, I seemed much more like an outgoing, Mediterranean type of guy—I loved going out on a limb that way, being larger than life and just putting myself out there.

None of the local bands at that time were professional. When I was a teenager, there were maybe a few kicking around, but all the band members had day jobs, and they all played it very, very safe in terms of the music they learned and performed. They were all just doing UFO and Thin Lizzy songs and stuff like that. No one was doing anything extreme or experimental. I don't know if I can express this strongly enough: the Swedish mentality all through the 1970s stifled everybody. If you wanted to stand out above the crowd, it was just a given that you can't do *this*, or God forbid you want to do *that*. It scared away a lot of raw talent all through those years, and now that I think about it, you could even compare it to a really strict religious environment where so many things are taboo. Of course, the society there wasn't religious, but it's the same mindset that tells you "Don't even think about it" if you want to do something outside the accepted behavior of the day. Don't even try.

Yes, it's true that Sweden didn't have the problem of homelessness that you see in the United States. In general, everything was very clean, very proper, and very safe. Sweden was an orderly place, well taken care of. But again, who do you think was paying for all that? College (but not the higher-level university) and technical school training after high school were also free, so it was pretty much a given that to get a decent job you had to have a diploma of some kind.

If you didn't, then you would go on the government dole. You were never penniless. You might get thrown out of your apartment for some reason, but there was always a shelter or a home you could go to, so you were never out on the street for long. But the unintended consequence of the social welfare system was that it basically killed your ambition to try for anything out of the ordinary or to strive to reach higher goals and make something of yourself, because if you did nothing, you'd get taken care of anyway, and if you made something of yourself and got rich, the government would take most of it to pay for those who didn't work.

I never fit into this environment. I was the odd one out, always. I was never part of the mainstream with the other kids—what they were wearing, the records they were buying, or anything. I was on the other end of the spectrum—in every way, shape, and form—as I was growing up, even before I became obsessed with music. So I was branded as a rebel and a troublemaker early on. That continued when I became interested in music.

My home environment had something to do with my inclination to do things my own way. Everybody was very bohemian in my household, unlike in the average Swedish family. That was good for a creative person like myself. My father, Lennart, and my mother, Rigmor, separated when I was around two years old, and then they got divorced, so I grew up without my father. But my brother and sister were close to my father. My immediate household consisted of my mother, Lolo, and Bjorn, who were always in the house around me. We were all musicians, artists, or painters. The attitude was "Oh, there's no dinner ready at six o'clock. Eh, so what? Every man for himself." It was very un-Swedish, I would say. There was a lot of openness and few rules. You could display your emotions without someone telling you to keep a lid on it.

But we weren't bohemian in the sense of being poor or going without a comfortable lifestyle. My mother was able to hold down a well-paying job, although it wasn't what she wanted to do. She was the head of a department that handled import and export for large clients such as Volvo. She really wanted to be a landscape painter, but because she was the breadwinner of the family, she did what she was expected to do. She was the victim of that whole mentality of putting down the artist; she was basically told, "You can't be a painter—you have a family to raise and support, so don't even think about it."

My maternal grandmother was wealthy enough that she owned an entire building in the center of Stockholm. She lived there in her own apartment and had a lot of tenants, which gave her a substantial income, so she made sure that all of us in her extended family didn't lack anything we needed. It was a beautiful building, and that's where I lived as a teenager before I left Sweden.

My mother's brother had a very traditional family. His children grew up very proper, as well-educated, model citizens with model families. He was a civil engineer and an inventor in the research and development department at Philips, the electronics company, and he was quite influential in my life in a different way. I love the guy so much, and I've stayed very close to him over the years. My father had two brothers who were extremely interesting people, too—one is an opera tenor and the other is an illustrator. I got to know them quite a bit later in my life, but they were out of the picture when I was young and rebellious.

You could say I was a rebel with a cause: I did almost anything that would hit up against the expected norms. I got a lot of frustrated support from my immediate family, who would say things like "This is great what you're doing, but you know, it's probably never going to work. It's just not done." It was a given assumption that there was no way you were going to make a living as a rock musician. If you did, then you had to play whatever music was safe and accepted at the time. You had to follow the rules. There was no *American Idol* where anybody could be anything, given a little bit of luck.

FIREBALL

Getting up each morning and going to school was something I didn't want to do, because it was pitch-black outside, with drifts of snow as high as the trees along the roadside. I remember looking outside the classroom windows and seeing a little patch of gray sky that lasted for less than two hours, then suddenly it would be pitch-black again. That was during the school year.

In contrast, my birthday, in June, was the nicest time of the year in Sweden, weatherwise, so I vividly remember every birthday. We were almost always at the summerhouse on the lake. At those times, my life with my mother, my brother, and my sister was the best. It was such a great family group; we were all really tight. There was no father figure per se, as I've said, but my uncle, my mother's brother, was around a lot, and so were his kids.

No one else in the family celebrated a birthday in that perfect, warm, sunny part of the year—I was the only one. Not only did I get gifts (which was nice), the weather itself was a gift: being able to be outside where the sky was so bright blue it almost hurt your eyes.

Many of those birthday gifts were records or musical instruments of some kind. I remember getting one of those music-oriented presents when I was staying in the south of Sweden on my fifth birthday. My family came and woke me up and gave me a big round package wrapped in brown paper. My mother had just been in Poland, and she brought back a guitar. I remember staring at it and wondering, "What am I supposed to do with this?"

They made a little home movie of me running around in the street playing it, but it was more like a toy than anything else. They had asked me what I wanted for my birthday, and I'd said I wanted a dog and a sword. I didn't get a live dog, but I did get a little sword and a toy dog, and this strange Polish acoustic guitar. The year before, they'd given me a mini violin. They were obviously trying to encourage me in a musical direction, but it wasn't really happening—not yet, anyway.

Music really began for me on September 18, 1970. That's the date I learned about the death of Jimi Hendrix, the amazing, iconic-looking rocker from the United States. I didn't really know anything about him, but he was big enough in Sweden that the national news showed a piece on him the day he died. I just happened to be watching it at the time. They showed a brief clip from the Monterey Pop Festival where he set his Stratocaster on fire. You can imagine how that affected me at age seven. It totally melted my mind.

Seeing Jimi Hendrix burning his guitar onstage made me want to play guitar. I swear to God, that was the initial reason. It just looked so fucking awesome. That news program lit the fire in me—a fire that to this day has never gone out.

I used to like to play air guitar to Beatles records by holding a tennis racket when I was five or so. Back then, my biggest musical heroes were the Monkees. They were on TV, and I thought they were the Shit. There was really no Swedish rock music on the air. There was classical music, jazz, and folk music, which actually had a good deal of influence on me in terms of melody and song structures. One of the first songs I ever learned to play was a Scandinavian folk song from the seventeenth century called "The Barkbread Song." It was basically just an A-minor arpeggio, easy beginner stuff.

But after I saw Hendrix, a lot of things changed in me.

A year later, for my eighth birthday, I was given Deep Purple's *Fireball*. It was my very first LP, and I was so proud of it. My sister and my brother had a bunch of records that I listened to, but this one was completely mine. Remember how that album starts? It starts with just the drums—a pounding double-kick beat before anyone or anything else chimes in. To my knowledge, that was the first rock band to open an album that way. Then, after the drum intro, the rest of the band kicks in with a really massive onslaught of sound. I know that most fans of Deep Purple think *Machine Head* is their best album, but I disagree. *Fireball*, for me, was just the very best there was: a true musical revelation. I still have that early piece of vinyl, sort of enshrined in my studio.

I immediately set about learning the songs, sitting in my bedroom listening over and over to the album, following along with my guitar. By then, I had spent the last year figuring out where all the notes were on the guitar and how to play a melody line, so it wasn't that hard to pick up the basic songs. Even as brilliant as the album is, it's basic pentatonic songwriting. I was so intrigued by everything about it. In the liner notes, there was a small black-and-white picture of Ritchie Blackmore, looking all mysterious, and I used to stare at that picture, wondering what he was like and what he was doing now: Was he on tour? Was he recording? What string gauges was he using? And so on. You couldn't just hop on the Internet in those days and track the guy down. All I could do was look at that picture and wonder.

In a lot of ways, that was the magic of it all. That element of mystique, the fact that you didn't know every detail about the person, made him larger than life to you. People often ask me why I was so into Deep Purple instead of Led Zeppelin back then. I didn't know about Led Zeppelin, or Black Sabbath. I was aware of Alice Cooper and, somewhat later, Kiss and Sweet—bands that some of my schoolmates were into. I was intrigued by what I'd heard about the extreme drama of those stage shows, but Deep Purple was by far the rock band that made the biggest impression on me then.

Purple really hit big when *Made in Japan* came out. The band became huge, actually, not long after, and everybody had its records. I was nine then. I would save up my weekly pocket money, my allowance that I got from doing the dishes and things like that, and I would go down to the local record store and say, "Do you have any Deep Purple?" The only album they had at first was *In Rock*, and that album sounds as fresh today as it did then. I can put the CD in the player in my car, and when I listen to songs like "Speed King," "Child in Time," "Bloodsucker," and "Living Wreck," I'm still knocked out by how good they are. To this day, it doesn't sound dated.

I always wondered why those Purple albums weren't bigger in the United States. When you play some of the early Sabbath albums, Tony Iommi's riffs are awesome, but the recording sounds like a demo tape. Not to dis those guys, but it doesn't hold up in comparison. But you put on *In Rock*, and it still melts your head. Imagine what those songs did to an impressionable seven- or eight-year-old kid.

In addition to learning to play guitar from Deep Purple, I learned a lot of blues licks from a couple of records my mother had, stuff like John Mayall and Eric Clapton. But Purple had the greatest effect on me. I managed to pick up most of the songs from *Fireball* quite quickly, but I remember that the solo in "Demon's Eye" gave me a lot of trouble. That was before I knew that you could play the same note on different strings. Then it dawned on me that I could choose where I wanted to play the same notes in the same octave. You could play a note on the high E string or a few frets farther up on the B string, and that way you could actually play the octave without jumping the neck. That revelation opened up the door for me. I thought, "Wow—now I understand. What a cool trick." I already knew how to find the same notes anywhere in different octaves from my piano lessons, but on the guitar you can play the same note in the same octave in three or four different places.

It sometimes annoys me when I read today, "Oh, yes, of course Yngwie Malmsteen plays classically inspired music, because his hero is Ritchie Blackmore." I still adore the guy, and I don't have a bad thing to say about him at all, but my classical style of playing—neoclassical rock, which I'm often credited with inventing—didn't come from him. If anything, Genesis had a much greater influence in pushing me toward classical structures. Tony Banks, the keyboardist, was like a virtual Bach jukebox, with his arsenal of tricks like pedal notes and diminished chords. Because he was the keyboard player, he didn't play with his teeth or do anything visually flashy. It was Peter Gabriel, the front man, who gave the band a face. But Tony's contributions made the band's sound unique.

Guitar is a completely different animal from the keyboard. To produce one note on the guitar (or the violin or any other stringed instrument), you need to use two hands. On the keyboard, you can play much faster because you only need one hand to play one note. Tony Banks' keyboard playing influenced me because of that basic truth. Intrigued, I started trying to figure out what he was doing. When I first started picking out the songs from Purple, it was all just different places on the neck in pentatonic modes, like the solos in "Speed King" or "Lazy" or "Demon's Eye." They were all similar. Once I'd figured out one, I pretty much had the others.

But then my sister brought home some Peter Gabriel–era Genesis records, and they didn't fit the pattern I'd learned. There were inverted and diminished chords and pedal notes, which made the songs extremely intriguing because I couldn't play them right away. I was very self-confident in what I was doing at the time, and this stuff actually humbled me, in a way.

Lolo, God bless her, was probably the most influential person of all on me. She bought records by everyone from Genesis to Frank Zappa, stuff like Weather Report; Savoy Brown; Blood, Sweat & Tears; and John Mayall and the Bluesbreakers, and I would listen to all of it. Lolo was very cool in letting her bratty little brother come up to her room and listen to her albums over and over again. I was like a sponge and sucked it all up.

These initial musical influences all came from her. There were so many albums lying around, and I had a huge range of styles and genres I could listen to.

It's funny how things get associated in your mind. For me, the death of Hendrix is tied to contrasts: that flash of brilliance I saw on the tube and the dreariness of the approaching winter outside. I would wake up around six-thirty or seven in the morning, and it would be unbelievably cold and pitch-black outside. I had to go out and walk through huge drifts of snow and howling wind to get to school. When I got there, I would sit in class shivering. Around eleven o'clock sun would come up and the sky would be all gray, and then around two it would get dark again, and I would have to walk home in the same fucking shit.

Obviously, this forced us to spend a lot of time inside. And if there was something you wanted to spend your time doing, you could get really good at it, because you weren't going to be outside riding your bicycle or whatever—which brings me back to Jimi. I was sitting there, saw him on TV, and right that minute I grabbed my guitar and started trying to play it. I used a coin for a pick. The first thing I did—I remember this very clearly—I played the open high E string, found the third fret, and started playing the two notes that sounded like a little bluesy thing. I kept doing that till my fingers started bleeding, so I put Band-Aids on them and just kept doing it until the first string broke. Then I kept at it, using the second string, until it broke, too. I kept on until there was only one string left.

That forced me to figure out more and more about what notes were located on that final string up and down the frets. I listened to it until it started sounding good. I didn't know how to tune a guitar or how to play a chord—nothing. Bjorn already knew how to play the guitar, but he wouldn't take the time to show me anything. And Lolo knew all the chords and was a really good pianist, but I was so young I couldn't sit still for lessons. I just jumped in and figured things out for myself. Not long afterward, my mom bought me a new set of strings, which I thought was so great—now I had six instead of one.

Every couple of months, we received a catalog called Hobbex, which was like the old Sears catalogs, full of everything you could think of, from heavy tools to small electronics—whatever. For my brother and me, it was like our Bible. We'd spend days looking at this catalog, and in it I found a guitar pickup. I saved up to buy this pickup and could hardly wait. Finally, it came in the mail, and I put it on immediately. I plugged it into an old tube radio, from the 1950s or so, housed in a wooden cabinet. When I cranked it up, I was overjoyed to hear the noise I could make: waves of feedback and shit. I was just a little kid, and this was like only the third week or so after I'd started trying to learn to play, but I was making leaps of progress just by sheer tenacity.

Bjorn was watching me, and I could see it was starting to worry him a little. When I would show him something I had just figured out, he would say, "Wow, all right, that's pretty good," and then go try to figure out some way to top it. He ordered a real solid-body electric guitar from the Hobbex catalog. It looked just like a little Stratocaster. When he got this guitar, he would brag, "Hey, I got the real thing, and all you got is some fucking acoustic guitar from Poland."

He started showing off, with a wah pedal and everything, really rubbing my nose in it. Little did he know that when he wasn't at home, I was playing his guitar like crazy! I remember thinking his guitar was the best. In reality, it was just a cheap thing—but far better than mine. That's when I started figuring out what was going on up and down the neck. I became a fanatic at age seven and went full-speed ahead, almost from day one.

Half a year or so later, and I even made a tremolo bar out of a metal comb for my guitar. It sounds laughable, but it worked. I removed the teeth from the comb and screwed it to the tailpiece, which was separate from the bridge, so I could make lots of noise on my acoustic guitar even though it was a piece of crap.

My brother continued trying to undermine me a little bit. He was jealous. Bjorn was really musically talented and very intelligent, but he was just not focused on one thing. He was a great drummer, playing in a band called Squeeze. But he also wanted to play the guitar, then the bass, then the violin, and then the piano, as well as the accordion and the harmonica—he wanted to play everything. He wasn't obsessed with just one of those things the way I was with the guitar, which is why I was leaving him in the dust.

He would do little things to me like hide the needle for my record player. We would end up in some fights and I'd have to defend myself, which wasn't too good, since he was two years older and a lot bigger. But it helped me in the long run. It just made me more determined than ever to keep playing.

By then, Lolo was picking up on how much I was really getting into this guitar-playing thing. When my birthday came around, she fanned the flame by giving me the Deep Purple *Fireball* LP. About the same time, my mother decided to buy the electric guitar from my brother and give it to me. The two women in the family were my allies, you could say. And I can't forget the influence my maternal grandmother had on me. She was the coolest, best person in the whole world—I owe her everything. She supported me in every way she could. Probably her most important contribution was the studio.

In the late 1950s, my uncle built a recording studio down in the bomb shelter in the building that my grandmother owned. This studio had a control room and wall padding, the whole deal, because he was into that—not as a musician, but as an electronics professional. My grandfather was a Dixieland jazz drummer and had a great drum set, and he used to store his drums and practice down there. He quit playing as he got older, but the drums remained.

Eventually, that drum set ended up at our house. My brother used it when he was playing in his band, until he lost interest, which was cool, because by default the drum set ended up becoming mine. Early on, I played it, too, which is why I've always been a drummer as well as a guitarist.

I would skip school so I could stay home and play my guitar, or I would take the guitar to school, and if somebody said something to me about it or ridiculed me because I had long hair, I would punch him in the nose. Soon I decided I had to have a band. I set about to recruit a few guys and try to whip them into shape.

In my first attempts to recruit a band, I corralled one kid who was sort of a friend at school and informed him, "You're gonna be my drummer." He kind of blinked at me and said, "*What?*" I told him flatly, "You're going to be my drummer, and we're going to practice from [this time] to [this time]." And he said, "No, that's during class." I told him, "No, it isn't—it's band practice time." Then he said, "But I don't have any drums!" "Don't worry about it," I said. "I have a great drum kit." Done. I took absolute control of the situation, and I can't say that I've changed that aspect of my band ethic very much since then.

I taught him how to play "Fools" and "Demon's Eye" and a couple more Purple songs. Obviously, he wasn't into it as much as I was, but we did do a couple of little gigs. I remember the first one was a total disaster. I played through an old amp and it was extremely loud, so everyone was holding their ears. And then I started grinding my guitar against a table, which I thought was hilarious. I figured I'd eventually have to find a bass player, but in the beginning, it was just me and this poor guy I had recruited (forced, actually) to become my drummer. Luckily for him, I joined up with a couple of other guys. We played Deep Purple songs in the beginning but then started doing really loud and long jams. I had a tremolo bar that I would use to make a really nasty annoying sound that nobody liked, so of course I *really* liked it.

By 1974, I'd formed a little band briefly called Track on Earth, for which I'd drawn some posters to put in my school classrooms. Now get this: when I recently played in Stockholm, my third-grade teacher came to the show, and she had with her some of my old drawings, including those very posters. One of them had like a big footprint or something, making a track. I was amazed to see that she'd kept it for the past thirty years. It completely blew my mind to see that old poster again.

RISING

I had never heard of Niccolò Paganini before that, and I had certainly never heard violin playing of that sort. . . . Everything I'd been wanting was all right there. I was losing it while I was watching, yelling, "That's it, that's it!"

I was always on the lookout for ways to make money for what I needed. I grew up in a pretty nice house about ten miles outside Stockholm proper. Our house had two stories, we each had our own room, and outside there was a nice garden with areas to play in when the weather allowed. We also had a little house on a lake where we'd spend the whole summer. We weren't wealthy by any stretch, but we did all right. I learned pretty quickly, though, that if I really wanted something, I could probably find a way to get it, but it wouldn't be free. I would have to do something to earn it.

I got wind of the fact that my mother wanted to have the house painted. Being a two-story house, it was not small, and it had two porches, front and back. Nonetheless, I suggested that if she would supply the paint and the brushes, I would do the job instead of her hiring a painter. It was the only way I could get the money to buy a real Fender Stratocaster, which cost an astronomical sum to me at the time. She gave in and let me do the job. I worked hard the entire summer painting the house, which involved climbing ladders, carrying brushes, cleaning brushes, and carrying paint cans for what seemed like forever.

My mother paid me 2,600 krona, which translated to about $250 in 1975 (about $1,000 today). I remember what followed like it was yesterday. With the money in hand, I went to the guitar store and quickly spotted the guitar I wanted. It was a brand-new Olympic White Strat with a maple neck. I was looking at it, heart thumping—practically beside myself, you know? But it was 75 or so krona more than I had. I was begging the sales guy to please let me have it for a lower price. He wouldn't go down on the price. "This is *brand* new, you know, *not* used," he said.

But then he told me, "Well, we have this one, which is a little less," and he pulled out a 1968 model. I was determined not to leave without a guitar, so I bought that one. And, ironically, now it's the other way around: those vintage late-sixties model Strats are among the most expensive and desired ones on the market. But at the time, I was bumming out because I'd gone to buy a new guitar and came out of the store with an older, used one, which was sunburst and not the shiny new white one that I wanted.

(Here's another irony. Hobbex, the catalog I mentioned in chapter 1 from which I bought my first pickup for my acoustic guitar in 1970 and from which my brother bought his first electric guitar in 1971, now sells Fender Strats. Here is Hobbex's current sales slogan: "Fender Squier Stratocaster, the choice of the greats, such as

Yngwie Malmsteen, Jimi Hendrix, and Ritchie Blackmore"—in that order. Everybody told me, "It ain't gonna happen." But it fucking did.)

I also remember the first time I got a real Marshall amplifier. That was a year or two later—1975 or 1976, I think. In that year, Marshall finally figured out that people really loved the Marshall sound because of how it distorts. But in order to make it do that, you have to turn the volume all the way up, which gets really, really loud. So Marshall designed something called a master volume, with which you could overdrive the preamp and make the guitar distort at any level, so you wouldn't have to actually play *that* loud to get the same effect.

Now this model, which appeared in 1974 or 1975, made all the other amps completely obsolete—you wouldn't even use them for a boat anchor. Nobody wanted them anymore. And guess what? I could pick up these older ones for twenty-five or fifty dollars. I bought about half a dozen of them, so while some other guys had one Marshall onstage, I'd have six or seven; I became known for being over the top, already, even then. *Those* are the ones I still have, plus quite a few more, that you see lined up onstage during my shows now, which led to the running joke in the press that there are two man-made objects visible from outer space: the Great Wall of China and Yngwie Malmsteen's Wall of Marshalls. Those original amps are now worth fifteen thousand dollars or more, if you can even find them. Somebody actually makes reissues of that old design, called the Plexi 1959 Super Lead. Of course I now have my own signature Marshall stack, the YJM 100, which I'm extremely excited about and proud of. More on that later.

Things were now starting to kind of fall into place for me, as far as my basic gear and my sound were concerned. That's where it all began, and it really hasn't changed much since then. When I started out, I wanted a Strat and a Marshall more than anything else, but I couldn't afford new ones, so I settled for older ones. Back then there was no vintage craze. There were a couple of other amps—Vox, Orange, Hiwatt—but nothing in the same league as Marshall. I had decided that Strats and Marshalls were my combination of choice, and I haven't changed my basic gear since then.

I made it into high school, but by that time my focus was not on my studies, you can bet. I joined a band started by a couple of rich kids; they performed mostly Kiss songs. The original rhythm guitar player didn't really fit in, so they got rid of him, and I came in and took over the position of lead guitarist, and the other guy then became the rhythm guitarist. We did quite a lot of gigging during high school. I wanted to play live, and we got paid, which was unusual in Sweden. Not much: sixty bucks or something. I had to show them how to play beyond the simple things they were doing: drum licks, guitar licks, whatever.

The rhythm guitar player's father would make excuses for having parties, just to get drunk and carry on. He'd hire us as a band for the parties and tell us, "You gotta play one Beatles song and one Abba song, and then the rest of the night you can play anything you want." We'd play "Here Comes the Sun" and "Day Tripper" by the Beatles, and "Gimme! Gimme! Gimme!" by Abba. Sometimes we'd have two girls sing.

That was the closest thing to a cover band I ever did, I guess. I have a Super 8 film of that group somewhere. I remember watching it back then. I was wearing all black, playing a black Strat with a white pick guard, and the pick guard was all you could see on the film. I made a decision to play white Strats because they showed up better. It's really amazing to look at now, to see when it all started, but it's even more amazing to hear how much my style had started to gel even that early.

But those guys weren't serious, and they weren't good musicians. I started going into the city to find people to play with. I would go around to all the music stores, places like Sound Side and Music Stock Market. They were all cool stores, and I became really good friends with those people. They'd let me put up ads in their stores for band members. I remember that in 1976 I put up an ad—"Ritchie Blackmore–influenced guitar player looking for Cozy Powell–style drummer"—hoping to find somebody out there who was a totally cool, double-kick-drum drummer, which was pretty ridiculous to expect in those times. But lo and behold, there actually was such a person.

In late 1977, a guy called me up—Michael, I think was his name—and said, "I know all that shit on your ad. Let's meet up." Way cool, I thought. I also recruited a bass player named Bjorn, in addition to Michael the drummer, who was the Cozy Powell freak. I was fourteen years old, and the two other guys were in their twenties or older. But I completely ran the show, even then, and they kind of treated me like a little mad Napoleon.

That's when I took over the basement studio that my uncle built in the 1950s, and it became mine 100 percent. All the recording we did together was in that basement studio in Stockholm. I called this group Powerhouse, and we became quite busy little guys. We would gather down there and play all the time. But the funny thing is, we never did an official gig. We just played together down in the basement for a number of months, recording everything. That was a luxury in those days, believe me.

My grandmother had a reel-to-reel tape recorder, which we had free use of. It worked so that after you recorded one track, you could then record on top of that, and I thought it was the most amazing device anyone could get his hands on. To my great delight,

I realized you could record two different guitars on there. I thought I had invented multitracking right there in my grandmother's basement. It may sound funny now, but at the time I didn't know that's the way that shit was done. For me, it was like discovering a magic wand or something.

I came up with an idea that shows just how obsessed I was. I decided to record the band live with four or five microphones in the room, using a two-track tape reel, and I had my uncle help me build a mixer so that I could wire the microphone to my Marshalls as a transfer from one tape to another. In other words, I'd take the two-track recording of the band and put it onto another two-track recording, and as I was transferring the recording I was putting another guitar on. I know that in these days of digital music and file manipulation this sounds incredibly primitive, but at the time I thought I had come up with a rather clever way of overdubbing. It was a solution to the fact that you couldn't overdub on the two-track recorder. You could on a four-track recorder, but I didn't have that yet. In order to use two two-track recorders, I recorded live to one and then, as I transferred from the other, I would have to play live again—it's a one-shot deal.

I got pretty proficient at that process. I'd record the rest of the band until about 10 P.M., then I'd stay there by myself until 2 A.M. and put on all the solos and overdubbing. When they came back the next day and listened to the tape, they'd say, "Oh, yeah, this is good—really cool shit." I bring this up because these particular tapes started floating around in a sort of underground way. Around that time, a bass player named Marcel Jacob became part of what I was doing. Marre, I called him. We were really close in those early days, almost like brothers. We'd play in my studio until all hours, sometimes staying up for two days straight, just improvising and such. We never did any drugs—let me say that right now. That wasn't part of the scene at all.

RISING

On the contrary, in my own little scene going on in Sweden in the late 1970s, we did other stupid and reckless things. I can remember a time when I was seventeen that I was off the charts in terms of dangerous, but I thought nothing of it then.

There was an unspoken tradition among teenage males in Sweden that you had to attend any rock show as wasted as possible—you couldn't go sober at all, or you would be judged very uncool and not hip. This particular incident was an Ian Gillan concert in Stockholm. I got two bottles of cheap red wine and went to my basement studio before the show. I hadn't eaten anything and was sitting there playing around on the drums, and I chugged the first bottle in just a few minutes—which, predictably, made me feel like total crap.

But I ignored that and got on the subway and headed over to the show. I got to the venue and downed the other bottle, because as I said, it was required that you be completely wasted in order to attend any rock show. I was supposed to meet a bunch of girls there, but some other girl came on to me, trying to make out with me in public. I was too drunk to know what was going on. But then one of my "grouples" saw this and made a scene, slapping me and yelling. I couldn't have cared less, so I headed up to my seat, which was in the first row of the balcony of the theater. I was sitting there, hating the show, the shitty music making me feel worse and worse, and suddenly I started throwing up over the rail onto the heads of all the people downstairs.

That didn't go over very well, so the security guys came and dragged me back downstairs to the foyer of the concert hall. I totally lost my temper and was screaming at the guards, being drunk out of my skull, and I took a swing at one of them. I missed his face and got him in the throat, which immediately doubled him over. He was obviously hurt, so the other guards kicked my ass out the door so that I was standing on the street. The theater had a huge glass window, and in a rage I kicked at the glass, which shattered. The guys on the other side were cut and bleeding.

I had turned into a one-man wrecking crew. Before I knew it, here came the cops, who arrested me and hauled me off to jail. It was the first time I had ever been in the can—but, unfortunately, not the last. I can remember exactly what I felt as I was sitting in the cell: how physically horrible I felt from the bad wine and no food, plus the fact that it was beginning to sink in how I had probably seriously hurt some other people during this little rampage.

This incident only served to ensure my reputation as one of the most volatile, crazy people in my circle of acquaintances. I didn't have a good sense of restraint, you could say, and that little scene was kind of a template for a lot of bad behavior that followed in the next decade. I was as much a danger to myself as to others. I was just a crazy teenager, but I never felt any fear for my own safety, no matter what the situation—which I think, in one sense, is a very Viking way of looking at the world. It's also not too clever, but you live and learn.

But back to what I was saying. Marre became my complete disciple in those days. He was also kind of a rebel, ditching school and so on, like I was. Bjorn and Michael had regular jobs, but the other two of us didn't, so we had all the time we wanted to just record for hours on end. What it boiled down to was that I started recording all the stuff with just him. Bjorn found out and got pissed off, and he took all his gear (which included some of the recording equipment) and left. So then it was just the three of us, and eventually Michael left, too, so it was just Marre and me.

Those very early tape recordings that we made as Powerhouse, from 1977 onward, started circulating around. That was really how people started talking about me there in Sweden. We didn't gig that much; the word of mouth was mostly from these tapes. A lot of local people talked about them. There was sort of a mystique about them. In those days, I didn't worry about piracy or bootlegs—I wanted my stuff to float around through whatever means. There was, of course, no Internet to disseminate your material over, but these "basement tapes" went far and wide, let me tell you. They became legendary in certain circles of fans, who talked about this weird kid who played with a dark neo-classical sound with a technique far beyond his age of fourteen or fifteen.

Once Michael left, Marre and I went on a serious quest to find a drummer. Ian Haugland (of the band Europe) was in the band for a little while, but he didn't really fit in because he had a regular job as a bakery delivery boy and didn't play at the freak-out level that I did. I decided I didn't want anybody who wasn't totally committed to the cause. We wanted somebody who was wilder and on the edge, which was how we saw ourselves. It became us against the world.

I look back on those years with a lot of fondness now. We were such rebels and so uncompromising in our goals and aims. If people think I'm single-minded and uncompromising now, they should have seen me then—it was insane, the level to which I was unswerving in my vision of how things should be. Marre was a willing disciple in all of this, and he learned to play exactly the way I wanted him to.

We started auditioning a bunch of drummers, and we found a guy we nicknamed Josef Göring, who was a freak if ever there was one—worse than we were, if you can imagine. He introduced me to the area called Uplands Väsby, where there was a little enclave of musicians and bohemian thinkers. But he wasn't that good a player and didn't last long. Then along came an interesting guy named Zepp Urgard, from the Balkans or somewhere—he wasn't Swedish. He was also *very* weird and thus fit right in with us.

A quick aside: At that time, around 1979, when I was fifteen, I saw a Strat in a store called the Amp Doctor. It was a cream white with a maple neck, and I really wanted it. When I went back to get it, though, the guitar was gone. I was disappointed, but it wasn't the end of the world. About three months later, when Zepp answered our ad for the drummer slot on the phone, he said that he was really a guitar player more than a drummer. I asked him what kind of guitar he had, and he said it was a Strat. I asked him what color and he replied, "It's kind of yellow." He agreed to bring it along.

When he showed up and sat down at the drums, he played like a freaking monster—like some Barrie Barlow–style player. He was so good, but he didn't want to play the drums; he wanted to be a guitar player. Still, I offered him the gig as a drummer, and he took it. I also convinced him to sell me his guitar. It was the one now known as the Duck (because of a Donald Duck sticker I had put on the headstock years ago) and was, in fact, the one I'd seen in the store window in 1979. That's how I got the Duck (which some fans also know as the Play Loud guitar, from a sticker on the body). It remained my main guitar for many years.

During my Powerhouse phase (the band was also called Rising, and eventually Rising Force), I'd write a few songs one week and we'd record, then maybe I'd write none the next week and only a few the next. Some were done intensely, in one long session. It was kind of hit-and-miss. One place we used in January 1980 was Northern Studios, which was very nice. It was an eight-track studio, which was a big deal to me.

Some of those old Powerhouse tapes are still floating around; they've been bootlegged extensively, along with the Varney demo tapes. There are similar versions of the same basic songs on both. That main riff of the song "Rising Force" was on there, as well as the basic riff for "Krakatau," among others. There was only a year and half or so between the making of these two tapes, but there was a universe of improvement between them in terms of sound, playing, composing—everything.

That was the lineup that made those fabled demo tapes: me on lead guitars and lead vocals, Marre on bass, and Zepp on drums. Versions of those tapes have been floating around for years and years and are the source of the CD I put out in 2002 called *The Genesis.* Zepp pretty much left the scene after that. He was a bit unstable, in terms of his commitment to the music, and didn't last. Eventually I replaced Marre, too, with the bass player from a band that later became Europe.

Even though I was just a kid, fifteen and sixteen, I was so fucking serious that people complained that I was hard to work with. Listen—music was my only real job. Others had day jobs, like my former drummer Mike, who worked in the train yard during the day hooking train cars together in freezing weather. But I would demand that he work his ass off to learn to play what I wanted him to play.

It was ridiculous. I insisted these guys follow me unswervingly. These days, I pay people's salaries, so of course I'm the boss, period. Back then nobody was getting paid, but that didn't matter. It was my way or the highway, even then. I don't think most of the kids that I played with thought they would end up doing it for life. But for me, there was no option. It was this or nothing. Do or die.

By then, I was completely fixated on my music and had pretty much stopped going to school on a regular basis. High school was kind of a gray area for me: I was at school physically, but mentally and emotionally I was light-years away. For some reason, the principal must have seen something in me, even though I was a complete rebel, and he cut me slack in a lot of ways. I would do crazy stunts, wouldn't come to class, and was just generally unruly. I would ride my motorcycle inside the school, because I didn't want to park it outside—and sometimes I'd ride it up and down the staircase, too.

I was not part of the crowd. I did my own thing, and sometimes people made fun of that. That usually didn't go over so well. At the beginning of a school year, somebody might say something to me, and I'd have to put him in his place. Also—and I didn't really understand it then—girls liked me. They thought I was cool because I had long hair and I was by myself with my guitar. I think that's why some of the jocks didn't like me. But I didn't realize that. I just wanted to do my thing. I had grown up with an older brother, so I knew how to take care of myself. I wouldn't start fights, but anything could set me off—one wrong word and that would be it. I'd take care of business. That's the way I was. It was really kind of bad, but I can't deny it.

In Swedish high school, you can choose some subjects you want to study, while others are mandatory. English was required, but I had learned it long before I started having to take classes in it, mainly from watching English-speaking programs on TV and working my way through things written in English that my mother and others brought home. I used to correct my English teacher all the time—probably to his lasting annoyance. Lucky for me, this teacher doubled as the wood shop instructor, and better yet, he was a guitar player. He wanted to build his own guitar, so he befriended me very early on. That was quite a break for me, because it gave me unrestricted access to the woodworking tools and shop and allowed me to spend a lot of my time at school doing what I really wanted.

At my high school, there was a big cafeteria-type room at the end of a hallway that had a raised stage at one end, so the room doubled as an eating facility and a community center of sorts. At the other end of this corridor was a little storage room that the school administrators gave me for my own use. In addition to that, they gave me a key to the school, which allowed me to use that little room twenty-four hours a day. I also had a key to the wood shop classroom, thanks to my guitar-playing wood shop instructor, so I had access to all the machines and tools that would let me work on my guitars.

Remarkably, the school administrators let me do all that even though I gave nothing in return, such as trying to actually do any schoolwork—*of course* I wasn't going to go to class when I had the choice to work on my guitars instead. It was a really good break for me, though, and as I remember now, it seems amazing that they let me do it. I assume that the school let me get away with murder probably to keep me out of trouble, but now it has become like a shrine to me. They even have my desk labeled THIS WAS YNGWIE MALMSTEEN'S DESK. I have to laugh about that.

By the time I hit eighth or ninth grade, I said to myself, "I can't freaking do this shit anymore." I knew I needed to immerse myself in music full-time. By the way, believe it or not, I had very good grades for the classes I did attend, such as art, history, science, and English. In that sense, my academics were not suffering, and I felt like my education was complete, probably from my growing up around much older people who taught me a lot and forced me to think on a more adult level than my peers in school did. I just didn't want to sit in class anymore. The school officials offered a compromise. They told me, "What you can do, instead of coming here, is to go do an apprenticeship at a luthier shop." I thought that sounded kind of cool, so I agreed to do it.

I was taken on at Tord's Guitar Verkstad, a very famous luthier shop, which is where stringed instruments are built and repaired. That's where I first saw a guitar with a scalloped neck. A scalloped neck has a fret board with concave depressions between the fret wires. (My signature Strats have fret boards like this.) I was so intrigued by this that I tried it out on an old neck of mine, and I was pretty amazed at how you could control the notes with the left (fretting) hand. So I started scalloping all my guitars.

Many years later I learned that Blackmore also scalloped his guitars, albeit in a different way. (He didn't scallop under the bass strings.) How ironic is that? Where would I have gotten that information back then? By calling him up? Looking his gear up on the Internet? Not likely.

I learned a lot from those old guys, but it didn't last. They started bossing me around and using me as a kind of errand boy to go off and get bakery buns for their coffee breaks, which pissed me off. I put up with it for awhile, but it ended when I was told I also had to clean the toilet. I told them to clean their own fucking toilet, and I was out of there.

Under Swedish law, students are supposed to attend at least nine grades. I was trying to stick it out, without much success, and then the school officials came up with another plan. They said, "We have this special chance open to you, because we know you love music. It's a scholarship to a music conservatory." Once again, they were trying to keep me in school and find something that would interest me, but I wasn't going along with much of anything. They actually got me into the conservatory, though, where most of the students were in their twenties and I was only fourteen. I agreed to try it, and I did go for a little while, but that ended up as a complete disaster.

Thinking back, I can't believe they got me into this conservatory in the first place. I would wear a black top hat like Ritchie Blackmore's and all black clothes, and my hair was really long. Yet here I was, sitting next to all these very proper guys who had finished all their academics, high school and college, and were studying music exclusively, to become performers and conductors. They looked at me like "Who the fuck is this?"

I didn't know what the hell I was doing there, either. It was horrible for me, because the teachers would spend hours dissecting the compositions of people like Franz Schubert and Robert

Schumann, discussing just two bars of a piece and how the composer's life at the time may have caused him to write a C-sharp here instead of just plain C. They would discuss it in depth, debating why he would do that. I sat there listening to them, going crazy. But they were being good little Swedes and following what the society dictated you should do if you wanted a career in music: you went to a conservatory and studied the composers' lives. I don't know what good it may have done them. I've never heard of any of them since.

To be sitting in those conservatory classes at age fourteen was very bizarre. To this day, I'm not really sure how I got approved to enroll there. I remember being given a piece of paper (my entry form, I suppose) that I gave to somebody else in this gloomy old eighteenth-century building that had gargoyles and such on it and long black marble corridors, like in a horror movie. This wasn't like any school I was used to. It was a quite well-known establishment, supported by the Royal Academy of Music. It wouldn't surprise me if it's still there, looking exactly the same as it did then, as though it has been there a million years already.

One of the things the teachers did was to test for perfect pitch. To take this test, you had to sit and listen to a chord played on the piano and then write down all the notes. I was okay with that; it was challenging, but I could do it. But other than that, the classes I went to didn't have much to do with actual music playing or performing. It was all theory and analytical discussion. You can imagine how well that went down with a fourteen-year-old.

I didn't come away from there having learned anything I thought was useful. I had already figured out basic music theory, such as chord structures and key signatures, before I got there, so there wasn't much else the school had going for me. A good bit of my musical theory knowledge came from my sister, who knew the proper terminology for things I was discovering on my own just by playing and exploring on my guitar. I also did a lot of personal studying. I would go and buy books on harmony, composition, relative scales, and things like that. I would figure out how the relative scales—like the majors and minors, harmonic minors, Dorian, Mixolydian, Phrygian, and so on—all worked together. And I realized when I started reading about it that I already knew all of that—I just didn't know the proper musical terminology for it.

I could hear in my head how each of these scales sounded. For example, B Phrygian is relative to E harmonic minor. They consist of exactly the same notes, but depending on which key you're in, the scale has a different name. The notes you play in E harmonic minor are the same notes that you would play in B Phrygian, such as F-sharp minor and C-sharp Phrygian, respectively. These things are rather simple, and you can figure them out just by playing and using your ears.

To harmonize, if you want to do a melody line in A minor, for instance, whatever the melody line is, you do exactly the same one as in C major, starting on the root note. It's very simple, but if you haven't been shown this, it might take a little longer to figure those patterns out for yourself. It's all relative, and it's very mathematical. As it turned out, my instincts were right. I just didn't have all the terms to refer to what I could hear in my head.

I had to relearn all of the musical vocabulary when I came to the United States because the scale names are different. For example, the note B in the Swedish scale (and in German, for that matter) is H, and B-flat is B. The sharps and flats have different names because the names of the actual notes change—they're not called *sharp* or *flat* anything. It didn't take too long for me to make the switch, and to be honest, most of the musicians I encountered during those early days didn't know any of that shit anyway. They played a few simple chords, and that was the extent of their music theory.

Needless to say, I quit the conservatory in utter frustration, and when that ended, I guess the school administrators just gave up trying to figure out what to do with me. I left school at fifteen, and that was that.

I think that much of what you can learn has a lot to do with the kind of home environment you grow up in. If you're the youngest child in a household of adults and older siblings, you're going to soak up what they know and what they're interested in, as well as developing your own interests. If being intellectually curious about things is encouraged, and all the older people around you are that way themselves, you're going to learn things because you want to, not because you're sitting in a classroom with a teacher threatening to fail you if you don't pass a test or do your homework.

My uncle (my mother's brother) was a great influence on me in that way. His oldest son must have gotten those genes, because he's now some sort of engineer, very highly educated in electronics and physics. I learned quite a lot from talking and hanging out with my uncle and his family. That's really how I got my education—a very unorthodox method, but it seems to have worked. I don't think I learned too much from the Swedish school system, to be honest.

While all these attempts by school officials to keep me in class were happening, I'd been spending a lot of time in my uncle's little studio in Stockholm, so I just moved there on a permanent basis. I had been more or less living at my grandmother's apartment building anyway, and it just made sense. Until then I slept at my mother's house, but otherwise I was mostly never there.

I would get up, freeze while waiting for the bus, catch the bus to the train, stand on the outdoor train platform shivering my ass off, and ride into Stockholm. I didn't waste time during the train ride (about thirty-five minutes); I took my guitar out of the case and played very intensely, both coming and going. I remember there was a little hot dog stand I'd pass when I was walking from the station to my uncle's studio, and I would buy a mug of hot chocolate and carry it to the studio with my hands wrapped around it to keep my fingers warm. Then I would get to the studio, start playing and recording, and stay there until the last train, which was at 2 A.M. When I got home, I'd play till 5 or 6 A.M., then crash for a few hours, wake up, with my guitar still on me, and do the same thing all over again.

That's a pretty strict schedule, but it just shows how serious I was then—obsessive, really—about being a musician. That was when I started putting bands together and advertising for other like-minded musicians in the area. I did some of that at the same time that conservatory nonsense was going on, which to me was like a parentheses in time. I went there, but I didn't really do anything. I was biding my time until I could escape.

Not long after that, I suddenly stopped in my tracks and became very anti-Purple and anti-Rainbow, turning my back on my early heroes. It's kind of strange the way that happened, but I guess it was my way of declaring my musical independence. I suddenly didn't want to do anything like that at all. What took its place?

To answer that, let me back up a little to the time when it was just me and Mike the drummer and a couple of different bass players: we were doing Blackmore-influenced stuff—the songs were mine, but the sound was very Rainbow and Purple. Then my sister brought home those Genesis records I mentioned earlier, the ones with Peter Gabriel. When I listened to some of them again just a few days ago, I realized what a strong effect that music had on me, because eventually those albums led me to raid my mother's classical records (mainly Bach, Vivaldi, and Beethoven), which was what I heard on the radio a lot, too.

Although I loved the edge and hard sound of rock music and never wanted to get completely away from it, what I heard in Genesis started creeping more and more into what I was writing. Arpeggios slowly but surely started working their way into the mix; then they became two-stringed arpeggios, then three-stringed, and then a very important thing happened.

I was watching one of the two available channels on TV when I was twelve or thirteen, and a Russian guy came on. What he did was a true revelation for me—right up there with seeing Hendrix light his guitar on fire. The program was an hour long, and I taped it by putting a portable tape recorder in front of the TV (no VCRs or DVD recorders back then). The music was incredible, but I didn't know what it was, which meant that I couldn't run right out and buy it. The more I listened to it, the more I was thinking, "Man, what is this?"

What really freaked me out was that I heard from his violin *exactly* what I heard in my head when I was composing. It was exactly what I'd been wanting to pull from the guitar but didn't quite know how. I had never heard of Niccolò Paganini before that, and I had certainly never heard violin playing of that sort. What solidified it for me was the flowing, linear rush of notes, the singing vibrato, and the amazing arpeggios spanning two or three octaves. Everything I'd been wanting was all right there. I was losing it while I was watching, yelling, "That's it, that's it!"

Now, to get that sound through a Marshall stack with a Stratocaster guitar was a different story altogether. But that became my all-encompassing quest. It wasn't that I wanted to copy Paganini exactly. No, it was a new sound and a new direction that I got from watching that performance of Paganini's 24 Caprices for Solo Violin. I didn't want to do something that was a note-for-note reproduction of the classics. Instead of just playing a piece exactly as written by a classical composer, I wanted to play guitar music *in that style* but composed by me. I wanted to emulate that violinlike sound on the guitar, although even I couldn't fully imagine at the time how far that adaptation could be pushed.

Seeing that Russian violinist that day, and wanting to adapt the violin sound to my guitar playing, was exactly what I needed to inject a new element into my playing to take it to the next level. I had already gotten pretty damn good by then, and I was looking for something that would allow me to expand my music to greater heights. Up until that moment, the things I had been playing were, to me, pretty good, but they were lacking something because they weren't what I heard in my head. For so long the door had been only cracked open a tiny bit, giving me faint glimpses of something new and different. What I really wanted to do was just bash it wide open, and Paganini showed me the way.

My philosophy about music during my developing years was unorthodox. I never practiced in the sense that when you're learning something, you practice it by playing the same scale or riff or whatever over and over and over. I didn't do that because I simply couldn't accept the approach of trying to learn a specific set of notes by screwing them up continually and practicing over and over until you finally got them right. I had to be at peak performance every time I picked up the guitar, even though I might be by myself and no one else would hear it. In my mind, I was performing, not practicing. That's why I was so adamant about recording everything: it was so I could have a reference point from which to push myself further. When I was living in the moment, I didn't look at it as practice or even analyze it that way. I never was thinking, "Okay, if I do this, maybe I'll get better at that." No, I had to be right then and there, the absolute best I could be.

I forgot to eat, ignored sleeping, and was in a pretty run-down condition a lot of the time in my early teens. Looking back, I seemed to be like a tortured artist, but at the time I wasn't thinking of my obsession in those terms. I was just completely consumed by the desire to play and expand myself. I got rather malnourished for a while. If it hadn't been for my grandmother, who made sure I ate something, I would have blown away. I was pretty pale, got nose-bleeds, and caught pneumonia when I was sixteen from walking around with an unbuttoned shirt when it was freezing cold, twenty below zero, with no coat on or scarf around my neck. Luckily, I came from very sturdy stock, especially on my father's side, and I managed to come through that period with no permanent damage.

You have to understand, this was a competition with myself. I didn't have a person or an idol I was trying to copy, or even a goal so that I could say, "Okay, that's it, I've done all I wanted to do." It was an ongoing desire; every time I picked up the guitar, I had to blow myself away. By doing that, I couldn't settle for something I had done previously. For example, I had figured out the diminished scales, I knew how to achieve arpeggios on two or three or more strings, and I could rip them off to a point where they might sound mind-boggling to the average person, but it wasn't enough for me. I then had to throw myself over a cliff like Wile E. Coyote, not worrying about whether there was a net below. I did that because that was a way to break another barrier or reach another level.

I would not accept anything less than mind-boggling playing. Stuff had to come out of each recording session that would make me say, "Holy shit!" I'm not really sure why I was like that. Most of the people who would hear what I was doing would just shake their heads and say, "What is this stuff? Where are you going with it?" This was in the late 1970s, and there was nobody playing like this on the guitar. Randy Rhoads hadn't teamed up with Ozzy Osbourne yet, and Eddie Van Halen had made his big break just about that time in the United States, but he wasn't doing what I was doing. He was truly great, by all rights, and what he was doing was quite new: the whole tapping thing was brilliant, and his sound was unique. When he came out with that, it was like a fucking bomb dropped—it was killer and everybody loved it.

But what I was after was in a completely different headspace; I wanted to invent something that didn't exist, and I was trying to push myself beyond any limits and barriers. So practicing was out of the question. It was a waste of my time. I was trying to create music from scratch, not practice something that already existed.

Here's the other thing that affected my playing. In the late 1970s, cassette tapes were coming on the market, but not every cassette recorder played at the exact same inches per second as another. Then the various manufacturers, such as Philips, came to an agreement that cassettes should be recorded and played back at a uniform speed, such as 7.5 inches per second. Some very high-end players had a variable speed control, but most people didn't own one of those. I had a cassette player at my mother's house and another in my uncle's basement studio. I would record every day at the studio, and every day, when I played the results back on the player at my house, it was a tiny bit faster—maybe an eighth of an inch per second, or a quarter note faster. At first I'd think maybe the guitar was just out of tune, from transporting it in the cold weather or whatever. Then, I'd go back to the studio, having heard what I'd done the night before on my home player, and think, "Okay, that was good, but somehow I have to top that." And every day, those tiny increments got higher and higher.

Another thing came out of that. People who heard this stuff always said to me, "We've heard a lot of guitar players who play fast, but we've never heard anybody play so articulately, isolating every single note out there like your life depended on it." I was extremely adamant that the execution of every note had to be crystal clear, the way it sounds on a violin. That's one of the things I love about the violin: the clarity and sharpness of the notes.

People used to say to me, "I can't believe you have no distortion on your guitar." Let me tell you something: I had and still have more distortion in my sound than anybody, but it's just that I play so that every note has a small breath of space before it and after it—no note blends into another. In a lot of fast guitar playing, the notes sound blurred, and I was damned if my playing was going to sound that way.

I've also been asked why I didn't just learn the violin, if that's the sound I was after. That's misunderstanding completely what I was trying to do. I didn't want to just play the violin; that wouldn't be something new. Besides, I had already developed so much technique on the guitar that it was clearly my main instrument. My brother played the violin well, and he tried to show me a couple of things, but I could see that it was going nowhere. What I really wanted was to take the sound and technique of violin playing and transfer it to the guitar—in particular, the electric guitar. My aim was to just go further and higher than what had already been done, by me or anybody else. Because of that, I had a cult following even back then.

I know I must have seemed completely insane to everyone around me with my obsession that if I did well yesterday, today must be even more extreme. I would never allow myself to slack off or have what others might call an off day. No, no—that could never happen. I approached every day like it was the last damn chance I had on earth to excel. That mind-set became so ingrained in my psyche that I do believe it's one of the reasons my drive to achieve hasn't slowed down yet.

THE BIRTH OF
THE SUN

It was quite possible that I would find myself right back on a return flight to Sweden after a week, so I took almost nothing with me: just one guitar, my toothbrush, and an extra pair of jeans packed inside my guitar case.

In Sweden, as I've said, it's like this: Don't stick out. Don't do or say anything out of the ordinary. Don't be bombastic. Don't buy anything expensive.

I'm the exact opposite. My whole life philosophy is that more is more. I'm not going to have a couple of Marshall amps, I'm going to have more fucking Marshalls than *anybody*. I'm going to play faster than anybody. I'm an extremist. That didn't sit well with Swedes, ever.

There was a constant nagging from relatives about what I planned to do with myself once I moved out on my own. At seventeen, I moved into an apartment in my grandmother's apartment building, right on top of my studio. (Sweet.) There was much less noise about my finding a respectable job after that. When I turned eighteen, it was like "Well, you're on your own, baby." It helped immensely that I could live in my grandmother's apartment building if I needed to, and I was actually making enough money to pay my own way. I played my guitar in subway stations and did odd jobs in music stores. Right around this time I started gigging more and more around town, and my name was getting much more well known. They would talk about this crazy kid who played the most insane stuff with loads of Marshall stacks and smoke machines and lit his guitar on fire and so on. The gigs didn't pay much, but it was something.

I wouldn't say my mother kicked me out. But she made it clear that I was an adult now and would have to make my own way in the world, although I knew that if something desperate happened, she would be there for me. The basic message from the family was "We've let you play for nearly eighteen years, and now it's time for you to grow up." The wife of my mother's brother was the most vocal about it. She's a lawyer and very practical-minded, and she told her husband and my mother, "Look, you've got to straighten this kid out."

At eighteen I also got drafted into the army. Service was compulsory, and at eighteen you had to report for duty whether you wanted to or not. When you got drafted, the army recruiters basically took off all your clothes, put a number on you, and tested you for every physical and mental condition they could think of. Then they decided what to do with you, like whether you were officer material or should just be put in the infantry at the front lines (as cannon fodder, essentially). They made me a corporal. Big mistake.

Of course, I had no intention of serving in the army, because that would be a *huge* impediment to my career plans. I considered trying to flunk the exams or make them believe I was a mental case.

When I think back on that experience, it seems funny now, but while it was happening, it was just totally bizarre and unnerving. First you had to pass the physical test, which I did with no problems. They had you do all kinds of weird stuff like "Put your foot in here and press as hard as you can" to measure your calf strength or whatever.

One of the worst things during my physical happened when they hooked me up to an EKG to monitor my heart. The two guys who were operating the test were bored and decided to fuck with the results, making it look like my reading was off the charts, which scared me to death. I was thinking, "Damn, I'm gonna die!" It had me worried for about a month, but of course there was no problem. It was just these guys screwing with my head, which wasn't hard, given my state of mind.

After the physical test came the intelligence test, which was a three-day affair. This thing was unbelievable—and timed, of course. It had questions like this: "In the following paragraph, underline every third vowel in every other sentence that starts with a *B*. Then put a circle around every consonant that is followed by a verb in the sentences that precede the ones that start with *B*," and so forth and so on. I mean, it was just ridiculous stuff to numb your brain. And, of course, it had all sorts of mathematical questions and mind-tiring wordplay problems. Unfortunately, I passed that as well—too well, as it turned out.

As much as I tried to do everything I could to get out of being drafted, like trying to convince them I was psychologically unstable, I decided, on an ego level, to do this one test really well, just to see what I could score. I actually had pretty surprising results. The possible scores ranged from 1 to 9, with 6 being sort of normal,

7 pretty high, 8 a genius, and 9 never happens. I scored 9—maybe it was luck, I don't know, but the testers were suitably impressed. Then they made me take a telegraph test, because the more clever they thought you were, the more likely it was that you could be useful as a telegraph operator or even a code cracker or something.

Miraculously, I did manage to finally convince the recruiters that I was an unsuitable candidate, test scores notwithstanding: I sort of blew a gasket in front of a colonel, which convinced them they did not want to trust me with a loaded weapon—so that was that. The military and I went our separate ways. I didn't receive my discharge papers, however, until after I was already in the United States.

In my early days, I wrote most of my stuff around the guitar solos rather than the vocals of a song. Today, I write songs that the guitar solo has to add something to. But when I was fourteen, I'd have four lines to sing and then there'd be a guitar solo for twenty minutes. But once I started recording with drums and bass, songs and riffs came around that I thought sounded really good and heavy, beyond the insane solos I was putting on top of them. I would play the drums and put down a groove to tape, do the guitar and bass over it by myself, and then begin to work it into a defined piece of some sort.

I was working on developing my compositional skills as well. The first song I wrote was called "Burn the Wizard," and then I wrote one called "Hunted," probably around age ten.

My idea, even though I was a really young guy, was never to be just a guitar *player*. That was never my only goal or a way I wanted to limit myself. I was always after something much broader and more expansive. I considered myself a *musician*: a composer and an arranger as well as a player. I wanted to write songs for my albums as well as have instrumental interludes and solos woven into them. My managers and the artistic development guys at the record company totally missed the point of what I was doing, because they wanted to market me as an over-the-top player, which meant focusing on long extended solos to the exclusion of everything else. But that was what I spent the least amount of time working on.

I always spent more time on writing and composing whole songs than actually "practicing," or playing the instrument itself. I was writing complex, interesting songs on a variety of topics that drew from history, literature, and mythology—with modern rock settings. I thought that all these songs should be heard on the radio and that given the chance, the listeners would like something a bit different from the usual brain-dead stuff played day after day. But the stations were afraid to play anything not on their record company–approved lists of songs that were being promoted, so only some of my best songs ever made it into heavy rotation on the radio, which was okay, except for "Heaven Tonight," one of my least favorite songs.

A number of the songs I was writing were radio-friendly, at least to my ears, while also being a little off the beaten path. But there was certainly a strong resistance among the industry people toward my being a songwriter and a composer, and this resistance transferred to rock music fans as well. A lot of it had to do with the media and my handlers wanting to promote me as just a guitar hero and nothing else. That was what wowed people in the beginning, and they didn't want to see me as something other than that.

Many people have asked me how I compose songs and what steps I go through to create the music I record. The answer is not as straightforward for me as it is for some songwriters. Everyone's approach to writing music is different, obviously, and mine probably isn't the way I would recommend for everyone. My approach has also changed somewhat over the years as I've gained experience and gone through changes in my life. But to answer that question, let's go back to the beginning, when I was starting to embrace music as my passion.

Wolfgang Amadeus Mozart said, "Music is melody, and melody is music." Paganini said, "One must feel strongly in order to make others feel strongly." Here's what I say: "Improvisation is the genesis of composition." What I mean by this is that everything I have ever composed that's worth anything has sprung from improvisation.

When I first got interested in the guitar, I was also taking lessons on the piano, the flute, the trumpet, the drums, and other instruments. These all relied on a somewhat rigid teaching structure in which I learned a little set piece and practiced it exactly until I could play it perfectly for the teacher, then I would move on to the next little bit.

In my piano lessons, for instance, the teacher might say, "This is your assignment for next time," and it might be four bars of a little minuet or a set of scales or something like that. "It must be learned at this tempo, this velocity. Practice it every day, and when you come back, I want you to play it perfectly, just like it's written on the page, note for note, in this time signature." Now, obviously that's one way to learn to play the piano, but it's a method I never liked—playing something somebody else wrote exactly the same way, day after day.

In terms of my own career, I'm sure that people who have seen me live in concert have said something like "Wait, that's not the solo that's on the album. Can't he play the solo the way he wrote it for the album?" The reason it's somewhat different is that the recorded solo on the album was improvised, too. I never write a solo note for note before I record it. I always leave myself room to improvise and elaborate on a basic solo key and tempo for all the songs I record.

The only time I tried to actually reproduce a recorded solo note for note was for the two songs my band Alcatrazz made videos for. I wanted my hands to be visibly doing exactly what you were hearing on the audio. It worked, but I found it very tedious and didn't like it at all, and after that I just decided to hell with it if it doesn't match. It's not going to be the same onstage, anyway.

There may be times when there is a phrase or a little piece of a melody inside the improvised solo on a recording that's so catchy I'll play it just like that every time. But the longer solo in which that little phrase is embedded will be improvised and *not* be exactly the same as what's on the record. That's just the way I work.

From the beginning, I've always tried to impress myself. I try to blow my own ass away, and that's difficult. I was playing at Wembley Stadium in London not too long ago, and I was surrounded by guitar players: Zakk Wylde, Joe Satriani, Glenn Hughes, Steve Vai, and a bunch of others. I knew that all these guys were there, as well as fifteen or twenty thousand people in the crowd, and the only thing I could think of as I was playing was to impress myself— to be able to say, "Wow, that really is fucking amazing." In order to do that, I can't play something that I've already sort of figured out. I have to throw myself over a cliff and really take risks, including the risk of kind of blowing it.

I know what I'm doing. Music is like mathematics. The equation is the equation; you can't change that. But the numbers you put in are going to change the outcome. I know exactly what's going on. I would never play a wrong note in a scale. That's just an automatic function. But within that, I try to come up with something that, for a moment, is completely brand-new to me and impress myself with that. That's how I approach it every time I'm onstage, every time

I'm in a studio, and every time I go on TV and play. I never play it safe. Never. I never give myself a break, either. Most of the time I say, "Well, that was all right; could've been better."

That's how it's been from the very first time I started playing. I could impress the shit out of my friends by playing Deep Purple's "Strange Kind of Woman" exactly the way it sounds on the *Made in Japan* album—I mean, *exactly*. But once I could do that, I became very adamant about wanting to lift myself to higher levels.

One day I saw an announcement in the newspaper that said, "If you have a tape or a recording, or you sing in the fucking bathtub or whatever"—it was very casual—"send it in." The first prize was twelve hours at Swedish CBS, a proper sixteen-track studio. I sent my tape in, not expecting anything to happen, given my success rate so far. The tape, the recordings that later became *The Genesis*, had already made the rounds of all the record labels in Sweden, and nobody had the courage to sign me. "It's great, but it's not safe, it's not in the format." they'd say.

But despite that, I won.

I used the studio time to record two songs—"Far beyond the Sun" and "Now Your Ships Are Burned"—for which I ended up doing all the drum tracks myself. The drummer I had there wanted to do another take, but I told him, "If you don't just shut up, you can leave." And he did. That's how I was back then. I thought the session went pretty well, and I had high hopes for the recording. But nothing came of it because the record company guys wanted me to sing the lyrics in Swedish. I wanted the songs to be accessible to a global audience. We couldn't agree, so the tracks were never released.

THE BIRTH OF THE SUN

In the beginning, I really wasn't playing out that much. I was mostly in my studio down in the basement. But I would go to music stores and bother people, play loud, break the fucking tremolo bars off, and shit like that. Everybody around knew who I was. I think people had a soft spot for me, thinking I was maybe a little nutty because I didn't follow anybody's direction. People called me "that hippie kid" because of my long hair and because I didn't play all the normal cover songs that other bands played. But there was no encouragement—all I heard was "Yeah, dream on, kid."

Fate has a way of intervening, or maybe rewarding unrelenting persistence such as mine. Somehow, and to this day I don't know how, I got added to the bill of a big festival that was held on the south side of Stockholm. It was in the summer, I remember, because it was right after my birthday in 1980. The organizers called it Woodstockholm, and the bill included a number of regional and national bands: not heavy metal or hard rock, but more pop rock and a mixture of commercial stuff.

The festival started at 2:30 P.M. and went till midnight or later for several days in a row. The whole thing was pretty casual. We (that is, Rising Force) didn't have a sound check or anything; we just went out and started playing. Our lineup consisted of a bass player, a drummer, and me, and I did the singing. We played five songs and had a blast. This was one of the biggest gigs I ever did in Sweden before I left. I had played for schools and stuff like that before, but this was really big, and I thought just maybe it could be important for me.

We did the gig and went partying afterward, and that was that. The next day I got up and went to the convenience store to buy something unimportant. I just happened to catch a glimpse of the newsstand, which had the two main newspapers—*Espressen* and *Aftonbladet*—and the one in front had a huge headline that said something like CONCERT OF THE YEAR in big letters. I thought,

"Yeah, cool." I looked at it a little more closely, and then I saw it: on the cover of the country's biggest newspaper was a picture of a guy with long hair, wailing on a white Strat, and I was thinking, "Hey, that dude looks familiar"—and I realized it was me.

I opened the paper, and inside there was a full-page picture of me, with the drummer and the bass player in the background. Not only that, there was this huge fucking write-up that called Rising Force "Stockholm's Deep Purple." Needless to say, my mind was blown to hell and back. There we were, a struggling trio with no record deal or anything, being called the next Deep Purple, while bigger bands that had played in the show got little or no write-up at all. It was insane.

It was a moment I'll never forget. I bought every damn paper that store had, because I'd never been in the newspaper before for anything. But here I was on the cover and on a full page inside. I was freaking out, and I showed it to my family. It was amazing publicity—the kind you'd kill for today—but it still didn't get me a record deal. By this time (I was seventeen), I was trying really hard to get my music career off the ground. In my mind, I was already fully accomplished in my abilities and was way past ready to be out there, making my way as a musician, and I thought, "Cool, this is it." But no. I had made a momentary splash, but then nothing came of it—again.

I bought *Guitar Player* every month because that was the only guitar magazine of that type available in Sweden at the time—there weren't any others that covered what was happening in the music industry outside Sweden. Besides *Guitar Player*, which was imported from the United States, there were a few music-oriented periodicals, like *Melody Maker* and *Sounds*, which were more like newspapers than magazines. Around the time I left Sweden (1983), the British magazine *Kerrang!* started coming out as well. It was brand-new then and focused on heavy metal—dangerous stuff, edgy and very cool, which greatly appealed to me.

From 1979 to 1982 or so, the new heavy metal scene was going on basically underground, fueled mainly by bands like Saxon and Iron Maiden. They were making it really big elsewhere, and I was just starting to see kids walking around in leather jackets like the ones Saxon's Biff Byford and Bruce Dickinson of Iron Maiden wore. The times were slowly changing, which brings me back to *Guitar Player*.

In one issue, I saw a column called "Spotlight" written by a guy named Mike Varney, and I thought, "What's this?" It said that three noteworthy but unsigned lead guitar players would be spotlighted every month, and the magazine would choose you if its editors liked your recording. What did I have to lose—the postage? Honestly, in my wildest freaking dreams I had no illusion that anything would come of it. I really didn't.

Frustrated that nothing had materialized either from the fleeting front-page splash of nearly a year ago or from the CBS recording session, I decided to make a composite demo tape using stuff from three separate tapes: the live performance at Woodstockholm; the "Now Your Ships Are Burned" recording from the sixteen-track session at Swedish CBS; and a recording I had made in my uncle's basement studio on which I played all the guitars, drums, keyboards, and bass. In that particular session, I had recorded "Black Star," which immediately became one of my most recognizable signature pieces, especially since the long sustained note in it is so exciting to do onstage.

I remember clearly how "Black Star" came about. I had just gotten a new mixer and microphones. My regular drummer wasn't there. This may sound bad, but I probably had everybody who played drums in Sweden in my band at some point, so I don't remember his name. But I remember he had a red double-kick drum set that was sitting in the studio. I started to play a groove for a drum check and went into a very distinctive beat with no idea what would go on top of it. With that drum rhythm, I put on the bass and then the keyboard with the E minor and C chords over it. Then I thought it would be cool with a twin lead melody and came up with the signature riff on the spot. I was mostly happy with the sound, because it was so good on the new mixer board.

I sent the composite tape to Varney at *Guitar Player* for the "Spotlight" column, and the picture that I sent with the tape was the photo taken by the official newspaper photographer for the Woodstockholm concert. I figured the magazine would want to have a good, professionally shot picture. I finally managed to get a little bit of mileage out of that Woodstockholm gig.

I sent my stuff off to *Guitar Player* thinking it was a really long shot, but what the hell? I estimated that my chances were as good as anybody else's to be one of the three guitar players chosen from the submissions coming in from around the world. But I have to laugh now at the way that tape sounded, because instead of a fancy cover letter listing all my so-called accomplishments or whatnot, I just sandwiched a running narration between the songs on the tape itself: I began with "Hello there, my name is Yngwie, and I play a Fender Strat, and here's this song called 'Black Star,'" delivered in a hyper, fired-up tone of voice. The music started, then I broke in again, saying, "Yeah, man, that was 'Black Star,' and this next one is . . ." Well, you get the idea.

Varney thought I was a madman, but he also thought the tape was cool and the music extraordinary. He had recently established a record company called Shrapnel and was working with a little band called Steeler. He wondered if I might want to come over and make an album. Indeed.

When I sent that tape out into the wide world in 1982, I didn't really know what might happen. I didn't know my life was about to change permanently. I threw that demo tape in the mail and then forgot about it. But before I knew it, I started getting all these strange phone calls from overseas, from the managers of bands like Night Ranger and Kiss.

Can you believe it? Kiss's manager called me up and said something like "We hear you're the new hot thing on guitar," and I was like "Huh? Okay." He went on about how they were looking for a hot player, and my head was spinning—the whole thing was so alien to me, and I was also conducting this conversation in English. I was proficient in English, but it still felt weird, trying to follow some of the American slang and such.

"We need to know a couple of things," the guy said to me, "like, are you six feet tall?" I had no idea. I knew how tall I was in meters and centimeters (I'm actually six foot three), but I had no idea how to respond when he asked me that. I guess I didn't give the right answer, because I never heard back from him. But that was just as well, because other offers started coming in.

For a while, I thought about going to London. It wasn't that far away from Sweden, and I had some friends who had been there and claimed it was a happening place. Maybe even more convincing was the fact that all my music heroes from my childhood (like Ritchie Blackmore) were from England. But Varney told me, "You gotta come over to America," like I was just next door or something. He said, "You gotta get yourself over, man," and I replied, "Okay, where are you?"

"California," he informed me. And I actually asked, "Where's that?" I didn't know anyone who'd ever been to the United States, much less anybody *from* there. In the 1970s and the early 1980s,

Swedes would go on vacation to Greece and Spain, but virtually nobody went to the United States, at least among the people I was acquainted with, so I knew nothing, zilch, about the music scene over there or which end of the country was which. The West Coast, L.A.—these were like places on the moon to me then.

Before I knew it, I was getting a bunch of PR from a band called Steeler. From what I could tell, it sounded like these guys were the kings of L.A., but I didn't even know what "L.A." was. I had no clue what the scene there was—which clubs were popular, what kinds of gigs were happening—because there was nothing for me to compare it to. It was like thinking, "I wonder what the weather's like on Mars."

Obviously, I didn't find out until a good bit after this what it was *really* like, but that story comes later. I was torn about getting these offers, because I was somewhat established in Sweden at that point and had a life going for me. I really had no idea whether this would be my big break careerwise or another dead end, but I strongly felt the gut-level impulse to go, no matter what happened. I figured that the worst that could happen would be that I'd stay a few days or so and then just come back home, because there was no guarantee of anything—it was an offer over the phone from people I'd never even heard of. It was completely like jumping off a cliff.

Word got out that I was leaving for the United States, which was a huge deal, both for my family and for the Stockholm press. There were a couple of stories about me in the newspaper shortly after my departure, one of which I remember very clearly: "Young Yngwie Malmgren [*sic*] does great success in the United States." It wasn't a great success in my mind, because all I was doing was possibly making a record with this mystery band called Steeler, but it did get me out of Sweden. Ironically, from that point on, the floodgates were open in Sweden as far as hard rock and heavy metal bands were concerned. But I was gone by then and never looked back.

THE BIRTH OF THE SUN

When I left for the States, I really could have used a crystal ball, because there was no way for me to guess what I might be in for. I mean, it was quite possible that I would find myself right back on a return flight to Sweden after a week, so I took almost nothing with me: just one guitar, my toothbrush, and an extra pair of jeans packed inside my guitar case. People have the impression that I was a destitute, starving artist because I arrived in L.A. that way, but that's not quite accurate.

Among the things I left behind was an entire production setup. In the Rising Force band at that time, I had a singer whose parents were very wealthy: he had a van and lots of equipment (a PA system, lights, smoke machines, and flash pot pyro). So even though he wasn't a total shit singer, I took him into the band for obvious reasons.

Right around this same time, I had just met the musicians Anders and Jens Johansson. I had done some odd jobs in a music store called the Amp Doctor. The guy who owned it would buy up a bunch of bad guitars below cost, I'd fix them up, and he'd sell them for full price. I became good friends with a couple of guys from the store, and they told me about a group playing in the south of Sweden. I had heard some of their tapes and liked the keyboard player. My pals said, "You know who that is? That's Jens Johansson, the son of the famous jazz musician Jan Johansson." His brother Anders played drums. About two weeks before I went to the United States, I flew down to Malmö for a week and ended up recording some of my new songs with them: "Evil Eye," "As Above, So Below," "Anguish and Fear," and others.

The fact is, I actually had it pretty good around the time I left. I had a full life: I had a wide circle of family and friends, plenty of girl "friends," my uncle's studio, a band (an early version of Rising Force), six or seven Strats, many stacks of Marshalls, cool clothes, and a cat. My name was pretty well known around Stockholm, and

I was managing to make ends meet solely on my music. I wasn't living on the street, as some stories about me seem to imply.

I left all that behind when I got on the plane for the United States. I cast my fate to the wind, as they say, like those Vikings who set sail into the fog, not knowing where they were going to end up and hoping that Odin would give them safe passage.

When I left Sweden for the United States, it was a pretty emotional scene. My mother, my sister, my stepfather, and I had driven back and forth from my grandmother's apartment building in Stockholm to my mother's house outside the city, moving all my Marshalls and other equipment into storage at her place. It was very early in the morning when we headed out from my mother's house to the airport. I remember it being dark and cold (as usual), in the middle of winter, when we arrived at Arlanda International Airport in Stockholm. The whole scene was very surreal, almost like a wake.

When I think back to that time, Sweden seems like another dimension, almost, like an ice planet or something, because here I sit now in the perfect climate: beautiful sunny days with palm trees all around me. Maybe I was born in the wrong place by mistake or something. All my friends growing up in Sweden never minded playing out in the snow, building snowmen, and having snowball fights, but I have loathed the cold ever since I was born, I think. When I got to the airport on that pitch-black, freezing cold morning in February, I was overjoyed to be leaving that dark frozen world behind, regardless of what might be waiting for me on the other side of the world.

The whole departure ordeal was very hard on my mother. She was so dejected that morning when she put me on the plane, but she was valiantly keeping it together. On the one hand, she was happy that my rebellious nature hadn't allowed the Swedish social system to kill my own dreams and plans, but on the other hand, it must have been very painful, because I was leaving her behind for a very distant and completely unknown place.

Everyone who knew us had pretty much said that it was a nice fantasy to run off and become a rock musician, but it was never really going to work—I would eventually have to get this rock music stuff out of my system, knuckle under, and get a real job. But I can tell you, for me it was *do or die*. There was no way I was going to work in the local burger joint and play guitar for a hobby.

In contrast, my mother was a good example of someone whose artistic talents could be pursued only as an avocation and not as a vocation. Her true artistic calling in life went unfulfilled, and it caused her a lot of pain. She did have some outlets, though. She sang in the prestigious choir called Schola Cantorum, which was founded at Storkyrkan (the old Stockholm Cathedral), specializing in Gregorian chants of the thirteenth and fourteenth centuries. I think that may be the origin of my love for choral music, which I incorporated fully into my *Concerto Suite* album some years later. I used to go see her perform with the choir in various churches, and I especially loved the shows at Christmas when the choirs would perform pieces such as Johann Sebastian Bach's *St. Matthew Passion*. She was also a jazz singer in the style of Ella Fitzgerald and would sing with bands at a well-known jazz club called the Fashing.

My mother also took us on vacations to Paris, Lisbon, Madrid, and other places where she could paint landscapes and indulge her artistic side. Some stories about my departure for the United States have given the impression that I'd never been outside Sweden before I landed in L.A., but that's not accurate. Before going to

America, I had traveled a bit to other parts of Europe on these vacation trips with my family.

One of my strongest memories is from 1976, when my family went to Greece for our summer vacation. It was me, my mother, Bjorn, and Lolo. That's where I fell in love with Rolex watches. We were on the island of Rhodes, and the place was just so beautiful, all sun and green-blue water. I saw a Rolex Submariner in the dive shop window, and I thought, "Oh, man, I'd love to have one of those." Even at age twelve, I'd become a collector of watches, and I'm afraid that fascination continues to this day. I'm a bit obsessed with wanting to know how things work, and I love to take the backs off some of the watches I have and tinker with the mechanics. Maybe I should have become a watchmaker.

Greece was wonderful at that time of year. What makes that memory so particularly special to me is that my mother got to paint some beautiful landscapes while we were there. She was so talented, but as I've said, that talent got stifled because there was no outlet for her to become an artist professionally, and she spent most of her energy working in an office to support the rest of us. But that trip to Greece was such a beautiful interlude. We went to a lot of rural places, rode donkeys, and visited some of the Roman ruins. I have great mental snapshots from that trip that have stayed with me all these years. So I wasn't completely new to traveling outside Sweden, but I'd never been as far away as the States.

In contrast to these occasional sunny moments, I remember my mother's working life as a big source of much of her depression, a recurring atmosphere of unhappiness around her while I was growing up. I mention this because it was all brought home to me as I was making my escape on that dark, cold morning. I'm sure the metaphor of escape wasn't lost on either of us. Everyone was teary-eyed, and I could hardly keep from crying myself. In my mind I saw a melodramatic image of my mother standing on a cliff, looking over as I was flinging myself into an invisible abyss. It was exhilarating and terrifying at the same time.

My mother was trying to hold it together, and I kept saying, "Don't worry, don't worry," but I was kind of worried myself. I didn't really know what to say, because in truth I had no idea whether what I was doing was going to be a good thing or a disaster. That scene and the intense emotions I felt are crystal clear to me, even now, decades later. It was a perfect example of the old saying "If you love something, let it go," because she was just destroyed by having her baby going so far away, into the unknown. But she knew that I would do anything to grab this chance, that there was nothing she could do to stop it, so she made it happen for me. I had done everything I could where I was; I had exhausted the limits of how far I could go in Sweden.

The enormity of what I was doing didn't really hit me hard until I was on the plane, sitting by myself, realizing there was no turning back now. I had no idea how long I would be gone. In fact, it was three years before I went back to Sweden again. After a somewhat rocky start with the Steeler guys, which involved a very steep learning curve, I quickly found my footing and became a fish *in* water. My English was fluent (I used to correct my high school English teacher all the time, remember?), and once I began to understand both the vernacular and the scene in L.A., there was no question of turning around and going home. I'd left the cold and the dark behind me for good. I was pretty sure that I would go back to visit eventually, but I would never live there permanently again.

When I had told my friends about this offer from a rock band in the United States, they had been pretty excited for me. Although they were playing in bands, they all had day jobs. Music wasn't something they were doing 24/7. They drooled over the promo pictures of Steeler that band member Ron Keel had sent me, which looked like the group was playing in Madison Square Garden or something. I was pretty impressed, to be honest, until I heard the band's actual music. My first reaction was "Oh hell, this is not gonna work," but then I thought I could just go over to the States and try to get them to do something else. Shows you how naive I was then.

It turns out that these guys had recorded a 45 single when the band was in Tennessee (where they started out), and then they shopped it around in L.A. At the same time, Mike Varney was forming his own heavy metal label called Shrapnel Records and putting out compilation albums in which a bunch of local garage bands would each have one song on an album. The idea I got from Varney—at least, this was what I believed at the time—was that if I would become a member of Steeler, we'd all get signed. Varney was a guitar-playing kind of guy, and that's what he was really after. I don't know if he realized how smart that move was—I certainly didn't—by putting me with a sort of local band whose music was pretty unremarkable. What I mean by this is that here was a band that totally fit in with the type of predictable, acceptable rock that was the staple of the club scene there, and if you added to the mix an insane classically trained guitarist from Sweden, it would kick the whole act out into left field. I don't know whether that was his plan, but it definitely created a monster that had everybody talking. That was Varney's role in jump-starting my career in the States.

It was a monumental decision, a tremendous risk. I thought if I could just get my foot in the door in the United States, I might be able to make something happen. And that was precisely the way it played out. I was in Steeler for only a few weeks before I decided to move on. When the record titled *Steeler* came out, I had already left the band for Alcatrazz. By then, not only my foot but also my whole body had made it through the door, and my career was launched.

THE GOLDEN DAWN

I looked out the dressing room window of the
second floor before the gig, and on the street
there was a line of people stretching down the
whole block. I thought, "Wow, I wonder who's
playing tonight." I asked one of the people in the
backstage area, "Who's the big draw tonight?"
The guy looked at me and said, "You are."

I'd gotten the invitation to join Steeler in the United States, but
the band's managers didn't offer to pay my way there. Instead,
my mother paid for my ticket to L.A. I suspect it was the cheapest
ticket available, because the routing to get me from Sweden to
L.A. was just ridiculous. It was a circuitous route that took me
through at least three different countries. It was also my first
transatlantic flight, and I was completely unprepared for the jet
lag that followed. I felt like I really *was* on Mars.

I remember that at the start of the trip, I had a really long layover in London. I had no idea where to go or what to do during such a long layover. It was probably only the second or third time I'd ever been in a big international airport, and I had certainly never been at Heathrow before. I wandered around waiting for the connecting flight, which was to Brussels, and thought, "What have I done?" It involved a lot of stops and hassles with Customs in several different countries for a kid who'd never taken a transatlantic flight before. To say that I was in a very confused state of mind when I got to my final destination is putting it mildly.

From London, I took off for Brussels, where there was another layover, and from there I flew on to Chicago. That stop wasn't too bad, but I remember thinking, "Holy crap, I'm actually in America!" From there, my next flight was to San Francisco. Everything had been going fairly smoothly up until then, but when we came in for a landing in San Francisco, the huge Pan Am jet that had just taken us cross-country almost crashed, nearly ending my career before it got started. The plane developed some kind of engine problem at the last minute and came down so hard that it triggered all the oxygen masks to come down. I didn't even know what they were—I was totally jet-lagged by then and had no clue what was going on.

It was very surreal. I was wondering whether this was the end and I'd made the biggest mistake of my short life. And, of course, it was doubly unreal because I had no idea what was waiting for me if I ever got safely onto the ground. Most times when you travel, you know where you're going, who's meeting you, and so on. But for me, the whole trip was in Neverland to start with, without even considering the possibility that I might die before I got to see the land of my dreams.

And once I finally got safe on the ground and made the short hop to L.A., I found out that what was waiting for me was even more bizarre than I had imagined.

THE GOLDEN DAWN

It was February 3, 1983. I was nineteen and was stepping out into the unknown. I'll remember that moment forever. There was no way to predict what would happen. It might lead to disaster or world domination—anything was possible.

The Steeler guys met me at the airport, and then the shit really hit the fan. It was like a scene out of a bad movie. I was totally jet-lagged, which I'd never experienced before and nobody had warned me about, and because of the time difference, it was nine hours earlier than in Sweden. I didn't know left from right or which end was up, which was maybe just as well. The guys drove me to their so-called dwelling, which was in the middle of a fucking ghetto. Right away, my perceptions of what to expect took a monumental shift downward. Going from very low-key Sweden—where there was practically no crime in the streets (and the most dangerous person had probably been me, ha ha ha)—to the slums of L.A. was an intense culture shock.

Now, you should know that when I agreed to join Steeler, I'd been told that the band members lived in a mansion, which I thought sounded cool. And you have to understand that in Sweden in the 1970s and early 1980s, the cities were so clean you could practically eat off the streets. The water coming out of the tap was pure, like Evian, and there was no air pollution or devastation of natural resources.

So you can imagine my dismay when I was immediately confronted with smog, stifling heat, and bad smells everywhere. I didn't know what to think, really. I've always been a very strong person in the sense that I'm extremely resilient and it's almost impossible to knock me down so hard that I can't get back up and dust myself off. This trip was the ultimate test of that, because when I got to L.A., *nothing* was like it had been described to me.

Not only was Steeler not the band I had thought it was, the place they were living in was indescribable. Heading home with the

Steeler boys, I discovered that they all lived together in a warehouse—which they'd bragged to me was their private rehearsal space. It was not a mansion, not a house, not even an apartment. It was a warehouse without rooms, a big cave, on the corner of La Brea and Washington. This is as bad an area as it gets—it was like stepping into a war zone. But I had no clue at the time, of course, because I knew nothing about where things were located and what parts of town you should avoid.

It was really hot and humid and was raining like hell, and I could see that the roof was leaking inside. Instead of having actual beds, the guys slept in hammocks made by tying sheets from one post to another. They told me they had reserved the best space for me, which turned out to be what looked like an old boiler room or something where a waterbed was set up. I told them that was cool, and then I noticed a couple of baseball bats and machetes near the door—"in case of break-ins," they said. I also discovered, when I turned on the faucet to brush my teeth, that brown water came out. It was so disgusting. My brain was going into overload and near meltdown, resetting all my expectations.

I decided that what I needed immediately was some beer and cigarettes, so I asked them where the nearest convenience store was. They told me to wait until the morning and we'd all go together, but I insisted I wanted to go *now*, even though it was nighttime. And the guys were losing it, yelling, "*No*, no, no, no!" I had no idea how dangerous the neighborhood was.

"Don't worry about it, I'll be right back," I said. I went outside and looked down the street. It was exactly like something you'd see in the movies: a backstreet with burning oil cans on the street corners and bums lying around. Exactly. It was totally bizarre to me, who had never seen such things. But I just shrugged and thought, "Whatever."

As I started walking down to the convenience store, groups of black guys were staring at me and yelling, "Hey, rocker!" They were showing me the insides of their jackets, just like in the movies. I have no idea what they were trying to sell me. I was really just too amazed to be concerned about my safety. I got to the corner store, managed to buy cigarettes and beer, and started walking back. When I got back to the warehouse, the Steeler guys were sweating bullets on the other side of the door and yanked me in as soon as I knocked.

They started telling me tales about how dangerous it is—like the night before, the bass player's girlfriend had stopped at a phone booth to give him a call, and when she went back to her car, there were two guys inside the car with a gun. She managed to fight them off, and one of the guys accidentally shot himself in the leg, so they ran off. She was unharmed, thank goodness, but I was amazed at the stories they were telling me, because things like this apparently happened every day on the streets. And here I was, from a country where we often didn't even bother to lock our front doors at night. Needless to say, my mind was blown to shreds.

Musically, it was just as bad, or worse. To me, the essential things for playing gigs were guitars, mikes, Marshall stacks, and smoke machines—you just had to have that shit. I have a motto: No smoke, no Marshalls, no show. When I said, "So where are the Marshalls?", they kind of looked around without looking me in the eye and replied, "They're not here." I asked, "Okay, what happened to them?" Then they admitted, "We had to sell them." I wanted to know how they rehearsed without equipment, and one of them told me, "Well, what we do is, the drummer drums and I kinda hum the song, and we rehearse the moves."

I remember standing there in disbelief, thinking, "This is a fucking nightmare!" But then my self-reliance kicked in, and I figured, "Okay, I'll just play along and give it a shot." What did

I have to lose? I fell in with them and started to blend into the L.A. scene, reserving judgment.

I'd been in town only two days or so, when the guys got all excited and said, "Hey, let's go to the Rainbow." I had no idea what the Rainbow was, so I just went along. I found out that the Rainbow was a pizzeria and club where everybody who was anybody went to hang out. And who was in the corner on my first visit there but Ronnie James Dio himself. It was like seeing God hanging out at a club. Even more amazing, he came over and started talking to me, and later he came to see me play. I eventually ended up going over to his house and jamming with him a number of times after I left Steeler. He was the first "important" guy I met in the rock music business, and we continued our friendship for many years, until his death in 2010.

When I arrived in L.A., I had long straight hair, like a hippie. The first thing the band did was drag me off to a hairstylist to get it all layered and poufed out, and that became my look. But here's something weird: after my car accident several years later, my straight hair went permanently wavy. I have no explanation for that, but it's a fact—I haven't deliberately curled my hair in over twenty years.

But hair was just the beginning of my L.A. makeover. The band members made me wear makeup, too, which to me was just beyond strange. I didn't know what to think about that shit—eyeliner and mascara and all that. Then they made me shave off my little mustache. I just gave in to it all, thinking I'd do whatever they wanted as long as I got to play my music onstage. I was kind of having fun with it, too, and I just decided to enjoy going along with the craziness because it was so alien to my scene back home.

THE GOLDEN DAWN

At lot of work went into image back in the 1980s, when I landed in the L.A. scene. When you were photographed, you had to look a certain way, your hair had to be a certain way, and so on. It was part of your mystique. When I was still a teenager in Sweden, there really wasn't any way to know much about the guitar heroes whose albums I collected, aside from album liner notes and occasional photos and articles in magazines. I had no idea about their personal lives or what they were like offstage. That was their mystique, and you filled in the missing pieces from your own imagination. I didn't want my heroes to be normal—if anything, I preferred them to be larger than life. Take, for example, my Ritchie Blackmore idol phase when I was around twelve years old. I'm very glad that I never met him then, because it might have dispelled the magic that surrounded him in my young mind.

For me, charisma is part of what it's all about—you either have it or you don't. It's not something you can put on. It's just there, and it's part of what I mean when I refer to maintaining a certain mystique. I'm not one to hang out with the audience before or after a show. It's not that I think I'm too good to hang out with my fans—not at all. I think it stems from my early years, when I was very antisocial in a lot of ways, and I never wanted to ruin the image I had in my head of my heroes by meeting them and having them turn into ordinary people, warts and all, so to speak.

I would rather give 120 percent of myself to my fans while I'm onstage and then leave them with that larger-than-life image while I go backstage or out to the bus, get out of my sweaty clothes, drink a soda, and put my feet up. When I was reading up on Paganini, I found it interesting that he was described the same way. He would never show himself before he went onstage, and he didn't hang around with the audience after he'd performed. He wanted to leave people with the magical experience of his performance.

Here's another aspect of it. When I go out in public, I look the way I do not because I'm trying to put on a persona of some kind. I know some people complain that I haven't changed the way I dress and look in twenty years. What you see is the real me—this is a look that feels comfortable to me. It is who I am. It's what I like, and I don't want to be any other way. I always wear black jeans, black shirts, and a certain kind of boots because I feel most comfortable in those clothes—it's what I like.

There's no mystery to it, no persona I'm trying to achieve. It's just what I like. Albert Einstein is known for having had more than a dozen identical sets of clothes—suits, shirts, pants, socks, even shoes—in his closet because didn't want to waste his time in the morning choosing what to wear. I completely understand that, and I have applied it to my own routine.

Anyway, once I was properly made over, we—the Steeler guys and me—played our first gig at the Country Club, opening for Hughes/Thrall. Only thirty or so people showed up, but I couldn't have cared less. I was in the United States, I was playing in a band for a live audience, and I was ripping it up, totally into it, running around the stage doing my thing.

The second gig was at the Troubadour a week or so later, and I'll never forget it—it's like it was yesterday. I looked out the dressing room window of the second floor before the gig, and on the street there was a line of people stretching down the whole block. I thought, "Wow, I wonder who's playing tonight." I asked one of the people in the backstage area, "Who's the big draw tonight?" The guy looked at me and said, "You are."

I was speechless. This was after just one gig! I was! We were the classic overnight sensation. Only then did I realize that news was all over town about the insane kid from Sweden doing this "new" thing. I'd been doing this stuff for years back in Stockholm, and nothing even remotely like this had ever happened. But suddenly here I was, the toast of this huge town, where the whole 1980s metal thing was just getting launched. Ratt, Quiet Riot, and other well-known bands were still just clubbing it. This was long before Bon Jovi hit it big and the huge "glam rocker" thing went through the stratosphere.

It was all embryonic when I landed in L.A. in February 1983. At this time, most of the bands that we know as big names from the 1980s were still unsigned. I remember that Mötley Crüe had made a record, and it was right on the verge of breaking out big. I did a few gigs with all these bands, and you could feel the electricity in the air, like we were all just waiting for something really big to gel and take off. I'd clearly landed on another planet, but I was breathing the atmosphere like a native by then and was ready for anything.

I went to the clubs with the Steeler guys and saw all the bands that were popular at the time. Luckily for me, this was *the* time and *the* place to be. It was such a musically fertile environment that it almost felt like the stars were aligned to get me there at just that point in time, when the rock music scene in this very permissive culture was exploding in all directions. Think about it. Van Halen was making its mark, Ozzy Osbourne was king, and then Randy Rhoads died, changing the guitar scene yet again, and all the time, as soon as something became familiar, players were pushing to see what would come along next. And right at that moment, that next big thing was me.

It was both flattering and funny to find myself mentioned in the movie *Spinal Tap*, which is now the all-time classic rocker's road movie. In it, David St. Hubbins, the Spinal Tap guitarist, was quoted as saying about the *Rising Force* album, "I bought the album the other day and I threw the guitar out. I said, 'Why bother? Why bother?' Use it as a coffee table, you know, because I can't play the thing like that. He's great. I like the way he puts Yngwie

J. Malmsteen on his albums—you know, so you don't confuse him with all the other Yngwie Malmsteens in the business." That was pretty funny, because at the time there was nobody on the scene who even remotely looked or sounded like me.

The problem with this so-called scene that was ballooning in L.A. was that all the bands looked and sounded the same. The record companies had a formula that worked, and everybody was doing basically that same thing. Some of those bands became really huge, no doubt about it. But nothing was climbing out of the box, musically. The timing for me couldn't have been better, because I didn't fit into anybody's box. Of course, it didn't take long for the Yngwie clones to appear.

When you think about it in retrospect, that whole L.A. music movement was actually pretty intimate. Everybody knew everybody else; it was all happening on one street, where the action was. There were three or four bars where people played, and then there was the Rainbow, which is pretty funny because it was actually a pizzeria, but it became the place to hang out at. I bumped into all kinds of musicians whose names I'd heard, like Don Dokken, Ronnie James Dio, the guys from Ratt and Quiet Riot, Metallica, Mötley Crüe—you name it. It was a very cool but weird world that I found myself tossed into.

A few days after I had moved in with the Steeler guys, they decided they didn't want me in the band because they were sure I was the devil or one of his minions. I thought this was quite funny, because, to me, words like *satanic* and *devil worship* spiced up magazine features or newspaper stories about rock musicians, and pentagrams made promo shots look cool, but it was all just part of the show. I never was a devil worshiper. But I *have* had an interest in the occult and the unexplained from a very early age. Let me jump back in time a little bit, and you'll see what I mean.

When I was eleven or twelve, I attended art school during the summers, which was totally different from the disastrous music academy my high school teachers had sent me to. The art school was on a lake, and the surrounding landscape was just gorgeous—idyllic, really. The classes were held in a very old Gothic manor house that was right out of a horror movie. These were private lessons, tutored out in the country, for mostly older students. It was an academy for gifted students of a wide age range, and I benefited greatly from it. I attended those sessions for about four summers.

Some of the students at this summer school used to gather at night and tell ghost stories, which scared the shit out of me at that age and in such a scary setting, but it also fanned my interest in the occult for some years to come. We did many séances during those times, and I met some very unusual people. There was a guy from Iceland who was extremely metaphysical in his beliefs and was always pulling stunts on me. He said to me once, "I can levitate." I said, "Well, that's cool, man, let me check that out." I sat on the carpet in a room with him, watching him meditate as he sat in the lotus position and chanted whatever—mostly for atmosphere, I think—with candles and shit going.

I was thinking, "Okay, this is kind of cool" and was just watching. Nothing was happening, and this continued for quite some time, so I finally decided that maybe he had gone to sleep and I should just get up and sneak out. I looked away for a few seconds, and when I looked back, he was in the air. Yes, really. I assumed I must have been influenced by the surroundings and very tired from just sitting, and perhaps I had slipped into some kind of hypnotic state—I don't know. But what I *do* know is that I ran out of there. It was one of those things you just put in your mental X files, you know?

I've experienced a number of things that can't be explained properly. For example, I'm pretty sure I've seen a UFO at least once. It happened while I was waiting for the bus as a schoolkid. Yeah, I know that sounds stupid, but here's what happened. It was back when I had my band Burn, when I was in seventh grade. It was a classic sighting, the kind you've read about hundreds of times, I'm sure.

It involved me, the bass player, and the rhythm guitar player in my high school band, and we were standing on a road that stretched so far that you could see the timberline at the end. We were standing at a bus stop, waiting to catch the bus into town. It was late afternoon in the summertime, so the sky was clear and the sun was shining low from an angle, and we saw something shiny above the timberline. We didn't think much about it at first, because we were talking and not really paying attention to it. There was a small local airport not far from there, with mostly propeller planes, but this didn't seem like any typical aircraft, because there was no engine sound. It just hovered, unmoving, in the same spot above the trees. I said to Niels, "Do you realize that that thing isn't making any noise?" And they agreed, a little spooked.

It wasn't a weather balloon, because we could see that it wasn't the right shape, and besides, it was shiny like metal. We could see the sunlight bouncing off the surface of the classic disk shape. But it wasn't a blimp, either, because I knew what that looked like, and there wasn't any little gondola underneath or a propeller. All three of us saw it quite clearly, maybe a football field's length away, for the longest time while we were standing there waiting, maybe twenty minutes or more. We kept talking about it, wondering what the hell it could be.

Then suddenly it just took off and disappeared in a flash, like snapping your fingers. There were no rainbows or atmospheric effects of any sort, and there was a totally clear blue sky all afternoon. We all kind of looked at one another like "What the fuck?" We were mystified, but not really afraid, I guess. I started getting more into the whole UFO thing when I got to the States, where there's a lot of interest and speculation about such things.

My home environment contributed to my love of the occult as well. Back in the summer of 1972, on Wednesday nights, there was a TV channel that would show classic horror movies: werewolf movies, Frankenstein movies, you name it—old classics like Lon Chaney's *The Wolfman*. This was a big deal to me then, because we had only two channels, and they had rather sparse programming. But every Wednesday night I could see these great old horror movies, mostly in black-and-white. I would buy the books the movies were based on and read them again and again. That's where a lot of my interest in horror fiction came from, I guess.

This led me to read the books of H. P. Lovecraft around age eleven or twelve. I read all of Whitley Strieber's books, too, like *Abducted*, as well as Alistair Crowley's *The Golden Dawn*. A lot of my early imagery came from sources like that. My sister and I and some friends would hold our own private séances, with candles and such. I got really heavily into that stuff, especially during those summer art classes.

When I was a teenager, I hung out with some friends from Uplands Väsby who were also really into that shit. It's an area outside Stockholm, forty kilometers (about twenty-five miles) away from Arlanda airport, and much farther away from my little homestead—not even in the same county as Stockholm. It's an isolated little town; not many people bother to go into Stockholm from there.

The original bass player of the band Europe, Peter Olson, was really heavily into the occult. We would entertain ourselves by having séances, sitting around together in the dark making up spells and incantations. We managed to scare ourselves a couple of times, probably from our overactive imaginations. It was never anything really bad, though, compared to some other people we knew about.

All these things had a big influence on me. I wanted to know all about the occult and its origins, so I immersed myself in studying it. By *immersed*, I don't mean playing at devil worship or pretending to be some kind of black magician. To me that was childish. I was after the historical angle and read everything I could get my hands on, from extrasensory perception to alien abductions to reincarnation. I had an encyclopedia that I particularly liked, called *Natural/Supernatural*, which contained entries on everything related to the occult. One favorite was Erich von Daniken's *Chariots of the Gods*. That book makes perfect sense to me.

On a few occasions I tried doing some spells of my own, but of course I never went as far as the stuff that was in Crowley's books. I was, however, into pushing the boundaries of what accepted reality was. By the time I was fifteen or sixteen, I had delved heavily into the history and written lore of the occult, and I had a few friends who were knowledgeable as well. The entire field was hugely fascinating and intriguing to us. Everybody had his own occult stories to tell. For me, the whole subject was very interesting and intriguing, an intellectual pursuit.

I admit to doing some stupid things with that group. We used to wear pentagrams and such, which looked really evil—but we weren't, of course. The pentagram right side up is a symbol of God, and it's not bad at all. In fact, many Wiccans and practitioners of other earth religions consider it a positive symbol of the divine nature.

As my interest in all this expanded, my songs started getting darker, and I was using the typical esoteric imagery. I suppose it was inevitable that people would assume I actually believed in all that stuff, since it was showing up in my lyrics all the time. The truth is, I just liked the kind of power it gave to the songs. That was all well and good in Sweden back then, because nobody took it really seriously. It was pretty well understood that this was all just stage drama. But in the United States such things were a totally different story.

I used to scare people when I came to the States, because I talked openly about all the knowledge I had of occult history, so they thought I was actually going to cast spells on them. The guys in Steeler, especially Ron Keel, who was a good old boy from Tennessee, were completely freaked out by me. They thought I was Damien or the devil incarnate and that I was going to put a hex on them or something. They acted like I had sold my soul to the devil in order to get my virtuoso playing ability. That was so silly. Some of them said to Mike Varney, "This kid is really scary and dangerous." It was so different from Sweden, where there's no religious superstition. But in the United States, it was just the opposite, and I spooked a fair number of people pretty early.

In addition to that, Varney was a very religious man. Here I had been in the States for only a week, and they were already talking about shipping me back. They reacted like I was evil incarnate. And I talked in my own typical way, which is kind of to joke about such stuff, but they were taking me at face value, and I guess they began to think that I was going to curse or jinx them in some way. I think they were actually scared of me. I would jokingly point out omens to them: if we saw a dog going to the gig, it meant something bad; or I'd say, "A lightning bolt nearly killed me, and it took a piece of wood out of my guitar." One night, the flammable stuff I put on the guitar wouldn't ignite, so of course that was ominous.

I'm laughing about it all now, but it was pretty serious back then. Varney called me up and said, "Hey, what's going on? Are you, like, killing goats down there or something?" I had to allay his fears and convince him I was just a regular guy, so to speak, but all the while I'm thinking, "Fuck, I just blew my first gig in the States." Of course, my association with Steeler didn't last all that long, anyway, so that was just a funny story that was part of my introduction to American culture.

I realized that people in the United States took the occult far more seriously, in terms of religion. People here are way more religious than in Sweden. Even though everyone in Sweden automatically belongs to the Lutheran Church, which is the state religion, nobody goes to church very much. As for the concept of being afraid that the devil is going to get you for straying off the path, so to speak, there was nothing like that in the Sweden I grew up in. But I confess that I did like the imagery associated with the occult, so I used that on a superficial level, like wearing a pentagram and writing songs like "Disciples of Hell," which was on my *Marching Out* album.

The Sweden of my childhood was very insular from the rest of the world—not at all like it is now. There was less immigration, so it was also not very racially or ethnically integrated. There were Serbs, Finns, Greeks, and maybe some Arabs, but even in Stockholm these groups weren't very evident. Religion was mostly an institution of the state that you used for baptisms and weddings and such. Occasionally there would be cultural festivals of one type or another, but I never really participated in them. When I got to the States, I had no preconceived ideas about race or religion in terms of it making people acceptable or not. I was brought up with the understanding that everyone should basically be treated the same and that Sweden didn't have class divisions or race divisions as there were in the United States. There was nothing in Sweden like the kind of religious fervor you see in the States. That was a rude awakening for me.

When I played gigs with Steeler, the guys would let me have a really long solo every night. That was good for me, because it gave me a showcase in a band setting. When we were playing Steeler songs live—which were really basic, two-chord songs, for the most part—I would throw in diminished scales, harmonic minors, pedal notes, arpeggios, and other shit, which really didn't fit at all. But my thinking was "Okay, it's my turn to solo, so here's what you're gonna get." It was outrageous, but they didn't stop me or tell me I couldn't play that way.

The album *Steeler* was recorded outside San Francisco in a barn on a farm, if you can believe that, on a very tight budget. Varney told me that Steeler had a recording budget of two thousand dollars, which didn't mean much to me, since I didn't know how much anything cost in U.S. dollars. I remember Ron Keel telling me when we were living in that little farmhouse during the recording of the *Steeler* album that he could see the future, which was me. He meant that I would introduce a new style, the way Van Halen had done a few years earlier.

I think they all knew that I was not going to be in the band very long. But that album, *Steeler*, has developed a cult following over the years, mostly because of the long extended solo tacked on to the end of the fairly banal song "Hot on Your Heels." They wouldn't let me use a separate title for that solo because it would have cost more in terms of publishing to add it (they had a deal for only ten songs on the album). I just said okay and shut up about it, then I did what I had to do, which was to let them append that solo onto an existing song. I didn't care, as long as it got on the album for people to hear, because it was my musical statement and a shot fired across the bow of the boat, kind of the way "Eruption" was for Eddie Van Halen.

I recorded all my tracks for that first album in one day, because that's all the time I had. When it came time to record the album, Varney had made arrangements for us to record in rural California, in the middle of nowhere. The place he picked was more like a barn than a farmhouse, another rude awakening. I slept on a pool table in a huge room, and every morning I'd wake up with a moose head that was nailed to the wall looking down on me. Every morning I'd go into the chicken coop to get some eggs for breakfast, and the chickens would put up a barrage of squawking. Then I'd walk through the field to the farmhouse.

One morning I had gone through my ritual of getting the eggs and walking across the field to the farmhouse. I put a frying pan on the stove, and when it was sizzling hot, I cracked the egg into the pan. But instead of an egg yolk and egg white, there was a tiny bird—beak, feathers, and all. Needless to say, it didn't survive, and I threw it all out. The whole experience was completely unnerving, but at the same time it was like a cartoon or something. It was very surreal.

With this kind of situation as a backdrop, we were supposed to come up with an album of heavy metal rock music. The guys worked on writing the lyrics for the ten songs, but I couldn't do anything until my work permit came through. I remember that the other three guys were working every day while I just sat around doing nothing, just hanging out while they were laying down their tracks.

Finally, on the last day, Varney turns up and says, "Okay, it's your turn now. You got one day to record all your parts for the whole album." Luckily it was all simple stuff, so it wasn't difficult for me to do. The long solo I mentioned earlier took probably a couple of hours, but for the rest of the album I didn't break a sweat.

And then it was time for me to go. This was March 1983. In the beginning, it felt kind of weird to be playing songs that weren't my own and that to me were so banal compared to the kinds of songs I'd been writing. But in hindsight I can see now that being part of Steeler was a good choice. The other option offered to me by Varney had been to just do a solo album with other free agents like bassist Billy Sheehan—just rip it up, basically, with no band or group. Looking back, I don't think that choice would have had the same effect as being associated with a band that went on tour and played gigs. Just recording one solo album with other solo players didn't seem like it would get me to where I wanted to go, and maybe it wouldn't have. I don't know.

In any case, I went my own way once the Steeler album was done.

HIROSHIMA, MON AMOUR

I'd never been to Japan, and I didn't have a clue what the rock music scene was like there. My mind was blown. When we got there, it was like the fucking Beatles had landed.

While I was gigging around with Steeler, a lot of musicians came to the shows—Gene Simmons of Kiss, Ozzy Osbourne, Ronnie James Dio, and a lot of others—as well as music industry people. One night we played in a really bad club somewhere out near Long Beach, and Phil Mogg, the singer from the band UFO, was there. I talked with him a little bit, and he invited me to his house the next evening for a barbecue to discuss the possibility of my joining the group.

Early in the morning I got a phone call from someone named Andy Trueman, who turned out to be the manager for Graham Bonnet, who replaced Dio in Rainbow, sang with Michael Schenker's band, and also had a solo career. Andy told me they were putting together a supergroup and wanted to see whether I would be interested in auditioning. So I'd just scored another possible offer, in addition to two auditions I had already lined up for spots in other bands. I couldn't believe my luck.

I got directions and headed out to a big warehouselike studio, and there was Graham Bonnet in the flesh. I was stoked because I'd known about him since I was fifteen. I figured he and Andy would want me to play something, to see how I would fit in with their plans, so I asked them what kind of material they had, and they told me they didn't have any songs yet—no musical direction, nothing at all. But then they also told me I had gotten the gig without playing a note. I know they couldn't believe it, but I told them I needed to think about it. These guys just laughed; I guess they thought I was joking. But I said I had another offer, and I just needed to think about it.

That evening, I went to Phil Mogg's house and was shocked. He was a total mess, drunk and falling over, and there were no band members around and no sign of a barbecue. I asked him what he wanted to do, and he said, "I wanna play music." I asked him what kind, and he slurred, "I wanna play *good* music!" He got up on a stack of books and told me I'm too tall. "I used to be tall," he wisecracked, and offered me a cigarette. "No, thanks," I said. He said, "I'm trying to start!" He was acting like a comedian or something. I decided right there to split that scene and go with the guys I'd met earlier, who would eventually become Alcatrazz.

I called them up and told them I would accept their offer, but only if they'd change the drummer. The initial idea had been to put together a band with the guitar player from Nazareth, the drummer from Jethro Tull, the keyboard player and the bassist from New England, and Graham Bonnet. The drummer and the guitar player backed out, so the others got a drummer from a band called Detective, which was semihot at the time, and then approached me. I didn't think the drummer was all that great, so I said, "I'll join your thing here if you'll get another drummer."

They weren't too happy about that, but when it looked like I was walking away, they said, "All right, done," and that guy was out of there. And I was in, without playing a note for them. They just said, "He's the one"—no further questions. All that happened in just one day, and my fortunes went from a rat hole in the ghetto to a beautiful house overlooking Laguna Beach, which was where my record company, Rocshire, put me up.

We started auditioning drummers, which was really interesting. We tried out Aynsley Dunbar, who had played with Journey and many other big groups. We had guys who had played with Jethro Tull, Frank Zappa, and Robin Trower, and we had a bunch of others, including Clive Burr from Iron Maiden. Then along came the drummer from Alice Cooper, whose name was Jan Uvena, and I really liked him, both the way he played and just as a person.

In the end, it came down to two. The other guys wanted Clive because he was famous, but I insisted on Jan because he was the better drummer. It finally came to the point where I said, "It's Jan Uvena on drums, or I'm out of here." He came into the band, and I stayed.

When we started recording the album *No Parole from Rock 'n' Roll*, I wasn't thinking about looking for a solo career, really, because I expected to pretty much control the musical direction of the band, since it was starting from scratch. It was the perfect scenario for me. I could write songs and play to my heart's content, and I liked all the guys in the group. The only thing that I wasn't happy with was the image of the band. I was hoping to get a strong Gothic vibe going, but the band didn't want that.

In fact, these guys didn't want a strong cohesive image of any kind. They were happy performing in just the clothes they hung out in, like jeans and T-shirts. I was hoping for something with a little more flash. I wanted the band to be called Excalibur. But the other guys wanted Alcatrazz, so they could call our first album *No Parole from Rock 'n' Roll* as a cute joke. I thought that was the corniest thing I'd ever heard, and I was still hoping to push the band in a dark, Gothic direction. One look at Graham, though, and I knew that it wasn't ever going to happen. So I gave up on that.

Originally, Alcatrazz was meant to be Graham's band. When I came into the group as a guitarist, because it had no songs, no name, no direction, and basically no idea what its music was going to be like, I sort of invaded the whole thing. Graham wrote the words and I wrote the music, including the vocal melodies. Some of the songs, like "Too Young to Die," I had already written during my creativity-starved Steeler stint, in the backyard of Steeler's warehouse in east L.A. Once I got rolling, writing new songs for the album and taking over the process, the others just said okay, so we ended up using all of my material. For anybody who knows my way of writing and playing, it's very easy to tell it's my stuff. When I left and Steve Vai took my place, there was no trace of me—it became Steve's band with his musical stamp on it.

In the beginning with Alcatrazz, I was happy with the way things were set up, but after a lot of touring it became pretty clear to me that this wasn't going to be a long-term gig. I must say that Graham, on tour, wasn't in the greatest of shape: he wasn't eating well, and he was drinking a lot, which made him unstable. One day he would be really happy and fun to hang out with, and the next day he would be suicidal. He had no concept of being professional in the sense that the show must go on because people had paid to come see you and you should fucking deliver.

We toured a lot, and the first trip to Japan was a watershed event for me. Here I was, nineteen years old and on my way to Japan with a really good band. I'd never been to Japan, and I didn't have a clue what the rock music scene was like there. My mind was blown. When we got there, it was like the fucking Beatles had landed. It was unbelievable. I came back from there with a gold album (the actual gold disc you get when your album goes gold in Japan), and I was just shaking my head. It was all escalating so fast.

Then I was offered a solo record deal from Polydor K.K. It was supposed to be a side deal for the Japanese market that I would record in between shows and recordings with my main band, Alcatrazz. It was not intended that I leave and form my own group.

But things were seriously eroding inside Alcatrazz. Graham is a nice guy, but when we were in the band together, he had a very serious drinking problem, to the point that he would be nearly unable to remain vertical and perform. I used to go over to his house quite a lot, but he had often been drinking too much and wasn't good company. We had a strange relationship. We kind of liked each other, but there was a tension and rivalry that set everything on edge. With Alcatrazz, I was definitely asserting myself, and he had to claim his territory as well.

In retrospect, I really hate to say anything bad about him, but his personal problems made it difficult for the band machinery to work. Alcatrazz toured so heavily that if you weren't on top of your game night after night, it was all just going to fall apart. We started touring in 1983 and continued straight into 1984. We toured with Heart, Loverboy, Eddie Money, and Ratt, and then we did some of our own headlining shows.

One of the first big tours we did was with Ted Nugent—at hockey arenas every night, no clubs. I learned a lot from him. One thing that Ted taught me was how to play to a crowd. I thought I really had the showmanship thing down. To me, showmanship has always been part and parcel of what I do anyway. I've never been the kind of guy to just stand onstage and play. I do every fucking thing there is: kick, play with my teeth, whatever. Ted had a great thing with the audience.

I thought he was beyond cool, and I absorbed a great deal from watching him and talking with him about touring and just working with music industry people in general. Ted's a really great guy, and although we were incredibly different musically, we worked surprisingly well together on tour. He has remained a good friend over the years.

Before launching on our long stretch of touring, we recorded the first Alcatrazz album, *No Parole from Rock 'n' Roll*, which went pretty painlessly, compared to the experience I'd had with Steeler. It was done in Rocshire's big studio, which was light-years away from that farmhouse setup in northern California.

I had a new place to live as well. It just felt bizarre at the time, but now I realize how incredibly lucky I was, going from the warehouse on the corner of La Brea and Washington to a three-story beach house in Laguna Beach, overlooking the water. It was a stunning place and was owned by Rocshire, which decided something like "Let's put the kid in there." I couldn't believe it. I was living in such luxury, and I'd only been in the United States for one and a half months.

Rocshire had what seemed like an endless stream of money, but it didn't have many big acts. For a business-savvy person, that would have set off alarm bells, but I had no clue. I remember one big-name act it did have was Eddie and the Munsters, which featured Butch Patrick: Eddie from the TV show *The Munsters*. I attended a release party for the band and met all the characters from the show. It was weird but fun.

The recording complex Rocshire owned had a huge arena-style rehearsal room, a PA system bought from AC/DC, and a full recording studio with all the latest equipment. It also owned a tour bus and a fleet of limousines, not to mention beach houses and more. I was completely amazed by this unbelievable show of wealth, and there was never any shortage of cash. If you needed something, you got it.

The company was founded by a couple, Rocky and Shirley Davis—hence *Rocshire*, a combination of their names. You know how it feels when you meet somebody and you suddenly get the creeps, like somebody had walked over your grave or something? These people were like that. Rocky had a disability, an amputated foot or something that had been stitched back on, and the rumor was that he'd gotten all his money from his insurance claim. I believed the stories at the time because I had no reason not to, but I heard later that Rocky and Shirley were allegedly embezzling money from Hughes Aircraft, which was fueling their adventures in the record business. I didn't learn all that until I was already out of there, though.

Rocshire funded Alcatrazz very well. We had lots of different producers coming in, and some pretty big names like Eddie Kramer and Andy Johns were involved. We were building our musical repertoire, and I coached Graham to sing the melody lines and minor scales I wanted for the songs I'd composed while he wrote the words. Recording with him was a real struggle, as I recall, because he would come to the studio well on his way to being drunk. He'd record a few lines, at most, and keep drinking, to the point that he'd have to go back home. We couldn't get the album done quickly because of that, but everything was pretty smooth with the rest of us.

Andy Trueman, a very charismatic English guy, completely ran the show as our manager. He had figured out that Graham Bonnet was a very big name in Japan, because anybody who had anything to do with Rainbow or Deep Purple was an automatic winner there. And Graham had also worked with Michael Schenker, who was big in Japan at that time. Andy figured that, by association, the Japanese audience would assume that if Graham had sung with Schenker and with Ritchie Blackmore, then this new guitarist must be just as good as they were. Japan was handed to me on a platter.

All this sudden notoriety descended on me in a whirlwind. When we were in rehearsal to go out on the road, Andy would bring in Japanese magazines and fan letters, mainly from girls who would do drawings of the band with me out front with my guitar in hand like a samurai warrior. It really blew my mind to suddenly have rabid fans of that nature.

When I was in Alcatrazz, everybody else in the group was much older than I was. I mean *much* older: some even twenty years or more. They had common interests that didn't include me all that much, especially their ideas about touring, which they'd done a lot of in the States. I was just starting out and was looking for adventure. They had already had their adventures.

But looking for adventure almost ended my career before it started. We were opening for somebody in the Midwest. We had finished our part of the gig and were hanging out after the show. I suggested we go into town and go exploring, find some action of some kind. None of them wanted to go, so I got a cab and took off for a bar. I was just nineteen, or maybe barely twenty, and full of nervous energy—no way was I staying around and just hanging out after the show.

I ended up at a bar, and a woman started chatting me up. She found out I was with a band and got real cozy, and, eventually I went back to my hotel room with her. It was a Holiday Inn or something like that, where they all have the same floor plan. When you open the door and step into the room, there's a small foyer, on the left is the bathroom, and on the right is a closet with a louver door that's made of wooden slats like blinds.

This woman and I were getting it on when suddenly there was a loud pounding on the door. I leaped out of bed buck naked, ran to the door, and looked through the peephole, and there was a guy with a shotgun. He couldn't see me, but he started yelling, "Come outta there!" I also then noticed that he had a little girl in tow, maybe four or five years old. My guess was that this was the rest of the woman's family. She obviously recognized the voice and headed for the door like she was going to open it. I asked her what the fuck she thought she was doing. I was completely freaking out, thinking this might be my last moment on Earth, that I'd be killed by a jealous husband.

I jumped in the closet, still completely naked, while she got dressed and then opened the door. Because of the slats in the closet door, I could see the guy come in, holding the shotgun not a foot away from me. I could see every detail of it, and him, very clearly through the door. I stood really still, holding my breath, trying not to make a sound. It was just like being in one of those Hollywood slasher movies. He was yelling, "Where is he? Where is he? I'll kill him!" while she played totally dumb, saying stuff like "Huh? Who? There's nobody here."

But he kept yelling at her, with the little kid there, too, and I was totally convinced that this was the end, that there was no chance in hell that he wouldn't jerk the closet open and have a look. But miraculously, she convinced him to leave, and they all went out. I waited in the closet for what seemed like a long time, but there was no more sound of them and they didn't come back, so I got out, got dressed, and with a sigh of relief went to bed.

I have no idea how the guy knew where we were. It was a small town, and maybe somebody who knew him saw her leave with me at the bar, or maybe he was following her when she went to the bar, or maybe somebody at the hotel who knew him saw us. Who knows? It just shows that touring can have its dangerous side and that it's easy to get yourself into a risky situation when you're out on the road in a strange place.

That kind of exploring used to be my typical thing to do in those really early days. I didn't want to hang with the guys in the band after the shows, so when we'd play out-of-town gigs, I'd just go off on my own afterward to explore and see what kind of nightlife I could scare up. I'm a pretty fearless guy, but a jealous husband with a shotgun was the last thing I expected to encounter. I was a little more cautious after that, but not much.

We went to Japan for a big tour after playing only a small number of gigs around the States. We were playing at Osaka Festival Hall, a very famous venue (where most of Deep Purple's *Made in Japan* album was recorded), and I remember taking the wrong exit or something trying to get to the sound check. All of a sudden, I was surrounded by hysterical, mostly female fans. Now, I had always had fans at my shows, even in Sweden, so I knew what that was like, but this was totally different. These fans were screaming, jumping up and down, and pushing too close for comfort. There was no security or anything there, but I had my guitar case with me and kind of kept it in front of me. It was so strange; I'd always been amazed at those kinds of scenes when they involved other bands, but I never imagined it happening to me.

I had gone to Japan expecting the shows to be just another gig, and I never imagined the reception we were going to get over there: it was the difference between being a musician in a band and being a rock star, which I did not see myself as. The fans fell in love with me as soon as I played the first show there—it was like an immediate love affair. Part of it was that we were riding the whole Ritchie Blackmore wave of guitar-based melodic rock that was very popular in Japan, and part of it was that I was so young. It was like they thought they were launching me on my career or something, that they appreciated what I was doing more than anyone else did. I just did what I'd always done when we were onstage, and they ate it up. It can't be denied that something instant happened when I went to Japan for the first time.

We played a lot of sold-out shows there, some of them very big and getting bigger as word spread. And the magazines fed into that. I was on the covers of all the music magazines, and suddenly Alcatrazz was being talked about as though it were my band rather than having originated around Graham Bonnet. That wasn't my intention and never had been, but it happened anyway.

Because of that, the Japanese record company Polydor K.K. immediately decided that I needed to do a solo album. A lot of people were of the opinion that making an instrumental guitar album was a cool thing, and it became rather common for several years for rock musicians to do instrumental guitar albums. I didn't want to do that. The record company people twisted my arm to get me to do it. They explained that having vocals would interfere with Graham Bonnet and the fact that I was in Alcatrazz. After all, it was just supposed to be released as a side project in Japan, on the Polydor K.K. label, capitalizing on Alcatrazz's success in Japan.

You can see some of the band's wild following in the video shot for the live album, *Live Sentence.* I didn't know there was going to be a live album at the time or that the footage from that show would end up being a concert video. I wasn't ever told that we would videotape and record the second show there at the Nakano Sun Plaza in Tokyo, and I was quite perturbed about it when I found out. The video shoot was just thrown together, but that's what record companies did when they had a hot property and needed to get some product out there for the fans. They just wanted to milk the hot property for as much money as they could, for as long as it lasted. But I guess for the fans it's kind of good.

We also shot promotional video clips for "Island in the Sun" and "Hiroshima, Mon Amour," which was done on the set of the Clint Eastwood movie *Escape from Alcatraz.* It was actually very cool doing it there. I really liked those videos and thought they were well produced. (The video director, Michael Miner, went on to do *Robocop.*) This was the first time I'd ever made a music video to promote an album. I didn't enjoy the process—that is, lip-synching to a recording of the music and pretending to play when I wasn't. But I realized that this was part of the entertainment industry and I'd better take the chance that was offered to me.

We did some live TV, too, which led to some great moments. I remember one in particular. While I was being interviewed, I showed the interviewers how to put two strings into one slot on the nut of the guitar, but I was careless and slit the end of my picking finger really badly. Everybody was horrified, but I glued the wound together because I had to play live the next day on one of those late-night TV shows in L.A. During our gig, my wound broke open and started bleeding all over the guitar. At the same time, Graham was so shitfaced that he dropped the microphone into the stage smoke (we had smoke machines going) and was crawling around on all fours trying to find it. To me, it seemed like a complete train wreck of a performance, but apparently it was a big hit.

Alcatrazz toured all over the States for months and months, and throughout all this Graham was very uneven. I have to admit that I was kind of unforgiving of this behavior, because I demanded the best of myself and believed that this should apply to everyone else as well. So if he sang out of tune, for example, I would let him know. He would mumble something and put himself down or whatever, and I just couldn't understand it. I would tell him how great a singer he was, and I really meant it, but it didn't fix things.

Because of that, eventually his shows began to evolve into my shows. It wasn't meant to be that way, but he was not a strong leader, and in fact he was liable to crumble at any given moment, so I just took control. It also became clear that people were coming to Alcatrazz shows to see me, the crazy alien guitarist from Sweden. He became quite bitter about this, and there was really nowhere for the band to go in this situation. I hadn't intended to take over the band or cause its demise or anything—I had just joined to play my music. But as I said, the dynamics of the band brought this situation on, and I know Graham became very frustrated about that.

Here's how my departure went down. We'd been having some arguments all along, and some of them became somewhat physical, even, so the vibe wasn't good. And every time the band had a day off, I would pack up one Marshall and one of my guitars and fly back to L.A. to record tracks for my solo album. Graham kind of knew this was going on, but not the full extent of it. I did play some of the solo material for Jan because I'd gotten close to him.

It came to a head one night when I accidentally knocked out the front teeth of my guitar tech (who'd left Steeler to come with me). I handed the guitar to him offstage in the dark, and it hit him in the face. He had to go to the hospital, so obviously he was no longer able to tour with me. I felt really terrible about it, but as I've said, the show must go on. That left me on my own, with no guitar tech for the rest of the tour. I had to change my own strings and do all the things the tech does for you to keep the show moving.

We had a gig at a bar in Oklahoma, and what happened during that show made the whole situation go straight to hell. This particular bar had a set of steps behind the stage so that you could go from the bus to the stage in just a few steps, and it was pretty easy to go back and forth. Since I had no tech at this point, I had to get all my guitars tuned up before the show. Before the doors opened, I was sitting at the bar with the guitar up on the counter so I could change the strings myself. Once the show got under way, my extended guitar solo would come about halfway through. It was a very big part of the show for the audience, which expected to see it every time.

Graham had made it very clear to me that he didn't like it. "Nobody wants to listen to that fucking drivel," he would say. He told me he used to tell Ritchie Blackmore the same thing: that guitar solos are rubbish. But our routine was that immediately after my solo spot in "Kree Nakoorie," the focus would shift to him, and he would get his time in the spotlight.

We got to "Kree Nakoorie" and I was onstage all alone, about to go into my solo, when out of the corner of my eye, I saw Graham heading back behind my Marshalls. And as I started to play, the sound went dead. Now, granted, it could have been a bad tube, a bad cable to the preamp, or something else. Who knows? I had no tech to try to figure it out on the spot. But for some strange reason I just knew that the speaker cable in the back of the Marshall must have become disconnected.

I immediately thought that Graham must have tripped over it and so that's why I didn't hear sound coming out. I went behind the amp, and I was right. I connected it back up, the guitar came on like gangbusters, and I really ripped into my solo. I ended with the old flanger white noise, the crowd went mad, and that was that. Or so I thought.

I changed guitars, ready for Graham's big part of the show, and started with the chords to "Since You Been Gone" for his entrance. But the sound died again. Then I saw Graham coming out from behind my amps, and it became clear to me that he had pulled the cable out during my solo and that here he was, doing it again, only now it was his *own* song he was sabotaging. Not only did he try to fuck *me* up, he was doing it to himself!

I couldn't believe it. I yelled at him that I wasn't putting up with any more shit, and I told him, "I'm outta here!" He yelled back, "Fine, we didn't want you in the first place!" And all this was taking place *onstage*. He took his microphone and poked me in the stomach with it like a spear, and that was the last straw. I punched him hard, and he went down. I walked off, and that was my last gig with Alcatrazz.

I went straight back to the bus and sat there wondering what the hell was going to happen now. And then the rest of the band and the crew came crowding onto the bus. Jan was crying, Graham was crying, and the others made it clear they weren't on my side. Plainly, it was time for me to move on.

For anyone who has ever wanted to know the Malmsteen version of why Alcatrazz broke up, that's the story. I did stay in touch with Jan, and we became very good friends, but I didn't really talk to the other guys for many years afterward.

I AM A VIKING

It was truly unbelievable how destructive we
were, like one huge uncontrollable wrecking crew.

From the wreckage of Alcatrazz, I flew back to L.A. from Oklahoma, already forming a new band in my mind. My intention
after leaving Alcatrazz was that Rising Force was going to be my
band, with playable songs that we would perform in concerts and
which would serve as a vehicle for my instrumentals. I would be in
control again, as I had been in Sweden.

I wanted Barriemore Barlow, who had done the drum tracks for
the solo sessions I had recorded, but he was in Jethro Tull at the
time, so he wasn't available. When I arrived at my home in Canoga
Park, California, Anders Johansson was hanging out in my pool
and kind of invited himself along for whatever was going on. I
already had Anders' brother Jens on keyboards, and I planned on

recording the bass tracks myself and hiring a touring bassist. That left the drummer slot open. Anders said, "I can play drums," so that was that.

Having Jens and Anders around all the time added a certain loose-cannon element to the situation. Soon the big black Cadillac convertible I was driving became a casualty of theirs: they drove it off a cliff. This was when we were living in Topanga Canyon, which was overrun with coyotes that ate my cats. The brakes on the Cadillac weren't very good, and by that time I didn't really want the car, anyway, because I'd just bought my boyhood dream car: a Jaguar E-Type convertible with a V12 engine. So I gave the Caddy to them. Since Jens and Anders were known to be destroyers of cars, I figured it wouldn't last long.

Sure enough, Jens and Anders came bursting through the house one day yelling, "Yngwie! We almost died! The brakes failed on that car of yours, and we had to jump out before we went into the canyon!" Knowing them, I said, "Yeah, you probably just pushed it over to watch it fall." They both protested very loudly about how they had nearly died and had just scrambled out of the car moments before certain death, but I remain convinced to this day that my interpretation of that event was much closer to the truth. That was a typical day back then.

It was all very tumultuous in those days. Here's something I'll never forget. I was in Rocshire's big studio with Jens, and Andy, my manager, called and ordered me to "get your guitars, take all the tapes, all your gear, and leave now!" I'm like, "Wha-a-a-at?" And Andy just said, "Leave now!" We grabbed everything, threw it all in the trunk of my car, and drove out of the complex.

At that moment, a fleet of police cars with sirens blaring like a scene from the movie *The Blues Brothers* came pouring in and seized the whole fucking place. If I hadn't gotten that phone call, everything related to that first solo album would've been confiscated, and it probably would never have seen the light of day. We found out later that all the embezzling the owners had been doing had finally been discovered, and Rocshire was completely shut down. With all the tapes for that first solo album under my arm, we moved to Record Plant. (Gene Simmons of Kiss was working next door, recording and producing, and I got kind of friendly with him. He was such a cool and intelligent guy. I liked him right away, and I still do.)

I was completely out of Alcatrazz, but I still had the same manager as before, the notorious Andy Trueman. Everybody from that era in the music business had tales to tell about him. I remember sitting in the back of his stretch limo—everybody traveled in stretch limos back then; it was a little *Spinal Tap*-ish, but that's the way it was—and I was talking with him about putting my new band together. I said, "I hope this is gonna work." He assured me that he had no doubts. Alcatrazz had the gold album by then, and my name was known. I felt pretty good about the whole situation, because I was finally doing what I had really wanted to do in the first place, which was to make my kind of music, on my own terms, just as I had been doing in Sweden, only for a much bigger audience in a vibrant musical environment.

I already had Jens and Anders, and then I brought in my old buddy Marcel (Marre) Jacob as the bassist. We didn't have a singer, although we had a mountain of audition tapes from many different people. I had originally thought about doing the vocals myself, but I didn't want to be tied to the mike stand in performance. I started listening to the tapes and auditioning singers, but I wasn't hearing too much that I liked. Then Jeff Scott Soto came in, and the songs he did for that audition actually went right onto the album—that's how good he was. The Polydor K.K. people expected me to deliver an all-instrumental album, but I managed to get two songs with vocals on it, anyway.

Jeff just clicked into place as soon as he started singing for his audition. We got on really well with each other, even though we were very different in temperament. He didn't drink, didn't smoke, and didn't do wild and stupid things for entertainment, and I did all of that. Jeff was a very interesting fellow. He seemed like a wild man onstage and certainly looked the part, but that was his stage persona. In ordinary life he was reserved and quiet—not timid or anything, but just a very laid back and low-res kind of person. And I was just the opposite. You wouldn't think he would fit in very well with the mad Swedes—me, Jens, Anders, and Marre—but somehow he did.

With the addition of Jeff, my Rising Force band was well under way. After I finished mixing the *Rising Force* album, I went straight into the studio and began working on *Marching Out*. There was no touring or live performances between the two albums, because *Marching Out* was supposed to be my first record to be released worldwide.

But several unexpected things happened. The original deal for the *Rising Force* album had been Japan only, which back then was quite common. Contracts in Japan demanded exclusivity in a lot of ways: bonus tracks, deluxe packaging, release before other countries, and so on. According to my deal with Polydor K.K., this was to be an exclusive release for Japanese fans, even though I was still a member of Alcatrazz. And in fact *Rising Force* was released in Japan long before I was even finished with the *Marching Out* album. It got released in the United States as an import with no promotion or introduction at all, and guess what: it landed on the *Billboard* charts at number forty. Once word got out about this album, fans started ordering it from record stores, and pretty soon it was in big demand.

Then Polygram Worldwide decided it had better put this album out everywhere, and the upshot of that was that the album got nominated for a Grammy. Now *Rising Force* is regarded as the blueprint for instrumental guitar. That somewhat branded me as an instrumental virtuoso, which had the unfortunate side effect of many people not seeing me as a songwriter. I had to fight that misperception for many years afterward.

I'd deliberately decided I wanted a certain sound for *Marching Out* that was a little more commercial, with songs that were more radio-friendly and no long instrumentals. Maybe the fans who had scarfed up the *Rising Force* album weren't too happy about that, but that was just supposed to be a little side project. My intention with *Marching Out* was to give the bands like Dokken and Ratt some competition, with solid songwriting *plus* insane guitar playing. I was doing a commercial project, but I was doing it *my* way. This album still had some songs from my old Swedish days, like "Soldier without Faith," "Anguish and Fear," and "Don't Let It End." I still think the latter is a very good, catchy song that didn't get enough attention.

I couldn't entirely leave my northern Gothic roots behind, and I think "Disciples of Hell" was just my way of reminding people that I like that kind of thing for its dark, scary imagery and drama. It was received somewhat differently in the States, though, where people are much more religious and take that kind of thing much more seriously than I did. It might have even been a slight poke at religion in general, at people taking their beliefs to such an extreme that it's ridiculous. The irony, of course, was that most people took that song as proof that I was a devil worshiper, which I found quite funny.

The song that describes me much better was "I Am a Viking," which I wrote on the plane as I was leaving Oklahoma and heading back to L.A., after the bomb dropped on my last show with Alcatrazz. The lyrics "By my sword you shall die" kind of described how I felt at the time—not that I intended any physical violence to anyone, it just demonstrated the level of frustration that erupted from my final confrontation with the band. That song was my declaration of independence in the strongest terms I could come up with. The opening riff was from my Swedish days, but the lyrics were completely drawn from the fury of the moment that I felt when I left Alcatrazz.

"Overture 1383" was just a little melody I liked. I had played around with it and decided to include it on the album. The big joke was the title. Everybody asked me what's the significance of the number, and I would just laugh and look mysterious. The actual fact is that it's the number stamped on the bottom of the old Löwenbrau beer bottles. (No Kabbalah secrets at all!) The overture sort of became an intro to a song that was one of my favorites on that album, called "Anguish and Fear." I really liked the opening riff, which was another old melody from those Swedish years, back in Malmö in 1981.

I've been asked a lot what "Anguish and Fear" was about, so here's the truth. Ever since I was a little kid, I've been interested in the sound of words, especially pairs or groups of words, regardless of what they mean. The phrase "anguish and fear" is a good example. "See the light tonight" is another. No deep meaning there—sorry. That was true of a lot of the lyrics I wrote in the early days, but it's not true now. These days I sweat blood over the lyrics to my songs, to the point that they have multiple meanings, very symbolic and metaphorical. But back then was another story. "Soldier without Faith" actually did refer to something real: I wrote that when I had to go into the army.

Another song on that album, "On the Run Again," had lyrics written by Jeff. I'd written the riff back when I was in Steeler, but it never got used, so it ended up on *Marching Out*. The final instrumental, "Marching Out," was just me fooling around with modes and experimenting with the sound. The root mode was B minor, but everything was played in the A-major scale, which produces a weird but pleasing tension. It gave that whole piece a suspended feel, which was enhanced by just letting it fade out like that. The piece has a great vibe, but I could play it a lot better now, I think.

My new band now had two albums to tour with. The solo album became my band's first, even though it had only two songs with vocals on it. The song "As Above, So Below" was done right on the spot, there in the studio as Jeff was trying out for the singer slot. I would say, "Here, can you sing this?" and he'd say okay and do it, and then I'd ask him to sing something else another way, and he'd do that. I liked his ability to do the songs the way I asked, so the job was his.

This Rising Force lineup toured the United States and Europe, then we went to Japan, where we got a huge reception. It was working amazingly well. But then Jeff came to me and told me straight out that he planned to leave the band to pursue a different opportunity that had come up. I told him I thought he was making a mistake, but if that was his decision I wished him all the best. It was a very friendly parting.

I started searching for a new singer and found Mark Boals, who completed the tour with us. The record company wanted us to shoot a video for "I'll See the Light Tonight" using the back-lot movie set from *Conan the Barbarian*. It had a huge set of stairs leading up to a dragon's head, which I managed to destroy by throwing my guitar onto it. It was papier-mâché or something like that and got totally wrecked. Then Anders somehow walked away with some of the wigs and makeup that the actors were using for the movie.

It was truly unbelievable how destructive we were, like one huge uncontrollable wrecking crew. I'm not saying this to brag about it—far from it. As I look back on it, it seems incredibly stupid and a waste of so much time, money, and energy, but I want to paint an accurate picture of the way things were in the L.A. music scene of the mid-1980s when I was making my early albums.

By the way, on that video, it's Jeff's voice from the recording and Mark's face miming the audio. I know that has been a point of confusion for fans, who saw different singers doing videos for that album, but that's why. We started the tour off with Jeff and ended up with Mark.

And here's the really funny part. Eleven years later, in 1996, I was on tour with Mark again, this time to support the *Inspiration* album. We got to New Jersey and the record company wanted to shoot a video for "Carry On, My Wayward Son." On that album, Mark sings a lot of songs, and Jeff Scott Soto and Joe Lynn Turner sang just a few. Wouldn't you know it, though, that of all the songs that could have been chosen for a video, they chose one with Jeff's vocals on it, which meant that once again it was Jeff's voice and Mark's face? Unbelievable. I remember Mark saying, "Can't we just rerecord it?" But once again, Mark had to sound like Jeff on the video.

The way Mark came into the band is a tale in itself. When Jeff informed me that he'd decided to form a band with bass player Rudy Sarzo, I really tried to convince him that it was a big mistake. Don't get me wrong—I love Rudy, he's a real sweetheart, but Jeff was already in a sure thing, and I didn't think he should walk away from it. But he was determined, so I sat down with my manager and we went though hundreds of tapes of singers, and one of them was Mark. He had such an amazing voice, I freaked out when I heard it. It was nothing like any of the other audition tapes I'd ever heard. It was a soaring voice with an unbelievable range. His résumé said he'd sung with Savoy Brown and Ted Nugent, so we were expecting a real powerhouse.

When Mark came to the rehearsal studio, he wasn't at all what we expected. He was short, going bald, and really looked just the opposite of the typical 1980s rock singer. The immediate reaction from the rest of the guys was that he wasn't going to fit in. I told them I appreciated their opinion and all, but it was my band and I was going to bring the guy in, looks or not. Believe me, it was the right decision, because he would come to rehearsals and be flawless, every night. I couldn't believe how good his singing ability was—he was a complete natural.

And in performance, Mark was the same, even under tremendous pressure. The first gig he sang at with us was a huge outdoor event with a hundred thousand people. And he sang as pitch-perfect as ever.

Right after Mark joined, I signed to go on tour with AC/DC. What an unbelievable tour that was. To this day, twenty-five years later, people still come up to me and tell about seeing me there. That was such a great tour; the guys in AC/DC were just beyond cool to me. I got along so well with them and learned a lot about how a properly run tour should function.

When the 1985 tour (the one where Jeff quit and Mark joined us) was done, I went back to the studio to begin working on *Trilogy*, and Mark recorded all the vocals. But there was yet another twist. We finished recording *Trilogy* and headed out on the road. Mark was let go midway through the tour; he had started acting strange, doing all this weird shit, and his singing wasn't good enough. Guess who stepped in to fill the singer slot to finish out the tour? Jeff Scott Soto. Luckily, he was quite willing to stay for the remaining gigs, although it was sort of agreed on that he wasn't going to rejoin the band. I kept in contact with him throughout the years after that, and I still work with him on occasion.

My career was in full gear, and my hard times in Sweden were a distant memory. You know how it's said that the older you get, the quicker time seems to pass? There's a reason for that. It's the increments in which your life span is measured. When you're five, a year is a fifth of your entire life, whereas when you're fifteen, one year is a fifteenth of your life—and so on. By the time I was twenty, I felt like I'd been living this kind of life forever. And when you look back at how early I started to play music, I *had* been doing it for a long time. When I left high school to pursue music full-time, I thought that if I didn't manage to have my name on a piece of vinyl before I was twenty years old, then I would have failed.

I ended up having my name on three.

I'M MY OWN ENEMY

It's like the media all picked up on the idea "Hey,
this cat's really controversial—let's push his
buttons and see what kind of story we can sell."
And I became the guy they loved to hate on paper.

I want to address my relationship with the press at that time,
because dealing with such intense media attention wasn't something I was used to at all. In Sweden, the only time I was actually
noticed by the press was for the Woodstockholm event. But there
wasn't an interview; it was just an article about the show and a
couple of pictures. The caption had called us "Stockholm's Deep
Purple." The editors didn't even know that I used to be into
Deep Purple or anything else about me. I was thinking, "Yes! This
is it!" I knew next to nothing about how one deals with the press
and whether so-called exposure is good or bad.

Then, all of a sudden, I was in the States and I was the next big thing. People wanted to know everything about me—some of it good and some not so good. And what I didn't tell them, they just made up. I'm basically a very trusting person. If you treat me straightforwardly, I'll do the same with you. If you stab me in the back, watch out. I'm also a very transparent person. I'll tell you what I'm thinking without sugarcoating—it's my opinion, and the world's entitled to it. I guess it's safe to say that after just blurting out exactly what was on my mind during an interview, whether it was my opinion of somebody's playing or singing or the state of rock music in general, and having some things taken out of context, I slowly figured out that I had to be more guarded in what I said and to whom.

The first real interviews I did were for *Guitar Player*, *Guitar World*, and *Guitar for the Practicing Musician*, which is now called something else. I tried to be open and forthcoming, but almost from day one, my words got twisted and repeated out of context, and the effect was to paint me as a "bad boy" on the rock scene. For example, I was asked what I thought of Jeff Beck, and I answered honestly, "I don't know, I've never heard him play." In print, my answer was turned into "Jeff Beck who? Never heard of him," which, of course, came across as extremely arrogant.

I'll grant that occasionally that kind of attitude was probably true, but a good part of the image wasn't. I did learn that when being interviewed for a magazine that's sold nationally, and maybe internationally, you shouldn't always tell the whole truth. It took me many moons to get that one down. It's like the media all picked up on the idea "Hey, this cat's really controversial—let's push his buttons and see what kind of story we can sell." And I became the guy they loved to hate on paper. I was continually baited, especially in the British and Swedish press; they were the worst of all. There was one reporter in Sweden whose name I won't mention.

He was a scheming little worm, always looking for the grimiest, dirtiest angle to hang a story on and twist it around.

There were also some journalists on the other end of the spectrum: they wrote truthfully about me, and I consider them to be my friends. But I had never encountered the way the press can just lay your personal life open to the world and flay you to bits so that you have no way to counteract it. When I asked one of the journalists who wrote shit about me for years, mostly lies and fabricated stories, why he did that, why he wrote things that never happened, he shrugged it off and said, "I need to sell a story, and people are not interested in good guys. The more controversial I can make up the story on you, the more newspapers I will sell." It was a rude awakening, to put it very mildly. But then, 99.9 percent of the really bad stuff, which I consider outright lies, was *never* about my music—it was always personal attacks. I guess it is easy to justify dishonesty if you make your living from it. Greed always plays a major role.

It used to get to me when I'd go on tour and do press events before or after the shows, and the reporters would always ask me the same boring questions, like "Who's your favorite guitar player?" I'd say something like Paganini or Bach, and they'd think I was crazy. Or, worse, they'd ask questions that had nothing to do with my music. I hated talking with them and trying to explain my personal life to them for their magazines and newspapers just as much as I loved performing and connecting with the fans in the audience.

It was the public me versus the private me, and in this business the media seem to assume that when you become a celebrity, it automatically gives them access to your private life as well. It was very hard then, and to some degree it still is, to make people understand how separate those two aspects of my life are for me.

Let me explain it another way. To be on stage is the most natural thing for me. It's effortless, I enjoy it, and when everything's flowing and I'm in the moment, I'm giving myself to the audience completely. It gives the fans their money's worth, and that experience feeds me as well, because I have to feel that I've done a really good job. Being an entertainer in that sense has always been totally natural to me, like breathing. This was true even when I was only ten years old in shows at school.

Stage fright? Never heard of it. I mostly just couldn't wait to get out there and connect with the audience and do my thing. But then I realized that to survive in this business, you also have to become a politician, you have to talk to people you don't want to see, and you have to be nice even though you loathe the person in front of you. It was also difficult for me to convince people that what they saw onstage was the real me and not just some act or phony persona.

I wanted people to understand that what they see in my shows, as bombastic as it may come across, is purely my expression of being in the moment with the music. I swing the guitar around my body, I play with my teeth, I drop-kick picks into the audience—it's all part of the experience of the show. It's not something fake, like lip-synching in a video, which is quite phony. Pretending to play, pretending to sing, acting out little scenes, or doing whatever in a video—I always hated those things. But filming a live performance for a video? Absolutely, because what you see in the show is the genuine article. It can't be misinterpreted. It's not diluted. It's just me.

I can understand people wanting to know more about someone who's famous or in the spotlight, to try to understand that person a little, I guess. But I've always believed that some things should just remain private. You don't need to know everything about a performer, because in a way it dispels the magic. But the Internet has changed all that. If you are a celebrity, there are no secrets anymore.

This fact was brought home to me not long ago when an incident during a flight to Japan in 1988 finally made its way onto the Internet a few years ago and gained new life. Jens and Anders had decided to start playing head games and pranks. Jens went to the bathroom, got some sanitary napkins, poured a Bloody Mary drink mix on them, and began throwing them on the other passengers' food trays with the first-class filet mignon. One woman got totally pissed and dumped ice water all over *me*. I had been trying to ignore Jens's shit and get some sleep, and that caused me to yell those now famous words: "You have unleashed the fucking fury!"

That's really all there was to it, but in the retelling of the tale over and over since then, it has acquired its own mystique. It briefly caused a flap in the press and among online bloggers. But in the end I turned it to my advantage, using the most infamous line from that bootleg-taped incident as the title for my next album, *Unleash the Fury*. Free publicity!

When I first hit the scene, I had a need to prove myself, and I was lacking a certain sensitivity in the social department, you might say. I just told it like it was and said things the way I saw them. That kind of honesty didn't go over very well, and instantly an opinion of me was formed in the press and among fans who didn't know what I was all about. "Outspoken" was the mildest label pinned on me, which made me the favorite guy to interview because it was easy to generate controversy by baiting me and pushing my buttons.

It took a long time for me to fully grasp how perfectly I was playing into the reporters' hands and giving them fodder that they could sell in their tabloids. I was trying to express an honest opinion, but the things I said would often get taken out of context, or the reporters would latch on to just a single phrase and run with it. Once it finally dawned on me that maybe I should give a little thought to my answers and try to sound a little more diplomatic, the damage had already been done. In magazines like *Kerrang!* or the Swedish entertainment newspapers, nothing I did was ever reported in a positive way. It was all bad press, over and over.

It is only now, some twenty years later, that the press treats me well. It's almost like I had to earn their respect the hard way. These days, the Swedish press either says good things or is just neutral about me. There's not much of the old let's-rip-him-to-shreds action anymore. And the American press has been very supportive, especially since my career resurgence.

I had to tough it out all those years, but these days all that seems very long ago. What's happening now, though, with the Internet is something very different. Anybody who's got a computer can set up a blog and become an instant music critic. There's *so* much of it now, it's not even worth keeping up with it. What it has done for me is that I no longer care about any of it, whereas I used to read the awful things about me in printed magazines and fume over them or whatever. These days it just doesn't matter—not one iota. Now that's freedom.

Many of those music magazines have since folded, and the rest have gone online, so the 1980s' absolute requirement of a rock group having the cover feature of at least one of the "big three" guitar magazines to launch its new album is a thing of the past. Online zines and blogs have as many readers, or maybe more, these days. Again, it's a whole new ball game. The stuff online is all over the map, too, depending on who's doing it.

I know that I was famous for having a volcanic temper years ago, but these days it takes a lot, if anything, to make me snap. I think part of it was that when I was young, I had a kind of survival mentality: I had to look out for myself, and if it meant yelling or punching somebody to make my point, I would. I came from an environment where I had to fight for every fucking inch every fucking day, and all of a sudden everything was almost easy for me. It took me a little while to learn how to deal with the realization that I didn't always have to fight anymore.

That was a wrong approach, obviously, and I think now how much energy I wasted being combative and confrontational when I could have maybe gotten better results some other way. But as I've said before, I feel like that all happened to somebody else—that's just not the way I approach dealing with people and situations anymore.

FURY

Those *Marching Out* and *Trilogy* years were
all about excess: how much alcohol you could
consume and remain standing, how many chicks
you could get into your hotel room after the
show, how much damage you could inflict on your
surroundings, how fast you could drive your
sports car down the freeway, and on and on.

By no means have I ever been a choirboy, that's for sure. But I'll say this: at least 50, if not 60, percent of my reputation for being completely out of control is courtesy of Jens and Anders Johansson. Jens was like the mastermind, always scheming some new hell to inflict on the world, and Anders was like the wrecking ball that put it into motion. They'd pull the fire alarm in a hotel in Canada, and five thousand guests would have to stand in the snow in the middle of the night. I fell somewhere between the two of them. As you can imagine, when the three of us were together, the mayhem that could follow was unbelievable.

I rented a little house in Canoga Park, California, which wasn't a very good area. But it was okay, and it had a little swimming pool. It was kind of a plain, working-class neighborhood, but we didn't care. We'd set the drums and stuff up to rehearse, because we were professional musicians, right? I would turn up the Marshalls at fucking stadium volume inside this tiny unsoundproofed house in the middle of this ordinary neighborhood and lift the roof off every house on the entire block. It may have been bad for the neighbors, but it certainly wasn't bad for us, because I wrote "I'll See the Light Tonight" during one of those 3 A.M. sessions.

I also had four cars at the time: a Jaguar E-Type V12 convertible, a Triumph TR6, an MGB, and a black 1967 Cadillac Coupe de Ville convertible. The Cadillac was the hugest car I'd ever seen, and we'd ride around in it, yelling and acting like crazy people. We'd stay up all night drinking beer, jumping in and out of the swimming pool and going completely crazy—then at 1:30 A.M. we would fire up the whole backline of Marshalls and just go insane. It goes without saying that this did not go over very well with our neighbors. We even started getting death threats from them. One day we came home and found a note taped to the door that read DEAR ALCATRAZZ, WE KNOW WHO YOU ARE, WE KNOW WHERE YOU LIVE, WE CAN MAKE YOUR LIFE A LIVING HELL IF YOU DON'T TURN THAT SHIT DOWN.

I wasn't too worried about it, and Jens thought we should just up the ante, so to speak, so we started throwing eggs at their houses and shit like that. It could have gotten really nasty, even worse than it currently was, but we decided to move out of there, leaving a trail of destruction in our wake. It was a totally out-of-control scene for us in those days. I guess we thought of ourselves as some sort of merry pranksters or maybe the Droogs gang out of

A Clockwork Orange. We were pretty oblivious to the distress we caused to anybody who crossed paths with us, and there was really no limit to what we were willing to do.

Yet the funny thing is that during this time, people started thinking of me as some sort of lord living a very proper and elegant life in a manor somewhere. They were inventing a background that would fit with my very precise and classical way of playing. The truth, of course, was the complete opposite of that fantasy. However, *now* I *do* live in an extravagant mansion with suits of armor, chandeliers, and so on like what they imagined, but the music I make is even more outrageous and intense.

By the time I started working on *Marching Out*, a lot of distractions began to get in the way, like alcohol, women, and cars. I became very unfocused in 1985 and 1986, and the tours we did then were just a complete blur in my mind. The whole scene was completely out of control, but it was the typical rock 'n' roll thing that a lot of other bands were doing as well. We certainly weren't the only ones leading a very risky and dangerous lifestyle. We were leaving trashed hotel rooms, trashed backstage areas, trashed tour buses, and wrecked cars in our wake. We'd bed all the chicks and drink anything with alcohol in it.

I can remember getting wasted and watching videos of myself in performance. The experience was very surreal, but in another sense it was normal, because to get completely wrecked and then go play a gig was standard operating procedure. Of course, going onstage and not remembering much of the show or what happened afterward is hardly functioning. It was a very typical over-the-top, excessive 1980s rock band scene, which wasn't reflected at all in the music I was creating. The music itself was very serious and demanded playing at a high level of skill—I mean, even the most sing-along songs would have five key changes, diminished chords, and odd time signatures. It was only after I became completely sober years later and performed clearheaded and totally aware of every note and every part of the show that I realized how dysfunctional we all were.

I remember being on the road with Billy Sheehan and his band, Talas, when it was the opening act for Rising Force. For my twenty-second birthday, Jens, Anders, and Billy bought me a gallon of Southern Comfort, a disgusting drink if there ever was one. I drank as much of it as humanly possible, and I was predictably a mess afterward. But that was standard behavior for the rock tour scene. Most people expected you to behave like that.

Then there was Miami, 1985. That was on the tour with AC/DC I told you about, when I was promoting *Marching Out*. It was at this very large gig in Miami that my bass player, Marre, decided not to show up. Let me take this opportunity to talk about Marre and my complicated relationship with him.

Marre was a strange cat in many ways. He was very arrogant, very smart-ass about everything. He would always contradict whatever you had just said whether or not it was true. If I said something sounded really cool, he'd say, "No, actually it's shit." After a while, I just ignored him, because I knew this was what he did.

Marre was in and out of my band all the time during my early years in Stockholm. I'd tell him to get lost, and he'd come back; I'd fire him again, then hire him again. It was a real revolving door with him. By the time I got the call from Mike Varney, Marre had been ousted and was not part of my band. I went off to the States and did the Steeler and Alcatrazz things. It wasn't until I got to *Marching Out* that I decided to call him up. I invited him to come to L.A. and join the band as the touring bassist and travel the world with us. He took me up on the offer and flew out to L.A.

Rising Force went out on the road with AC/DC, and he was the bassist. Since he didn't bring anything with him when he came to the States, I gave him one of my bass guitars for the tour, which he evidently didn't appreciate at all, because he threw it out into the crowd one night. That was only one of the really annoying things he did on that tour. But the worst thing came after we'd taken a short tour break and were due to all meet up again for the very large gig in Miami.

After the break in L.A., I flew out to Miami to start the tour again, and I went to the arena for the sound check. Everybody was there but Marre. Nobody had seen or heard from him, and we had no idea where he was. I found out that when I had flown to Miami, he had taken a plane to Stockholm without telling anybody he was quitting the tour.

Let me backtrack a little bit. At an L.A. show, we had choreographed a silly little Judas Priest kind of stage move that we would do together. It was intended to look cool, but he messed it up (whether accidentally or deliberately, I don't know), and I blew my top. I told him, "After this tour, you're done. That's it—you're outta here! You are given the opportunity that thousands of people want, and you behave in this manner."

We did the first part of the tour with AC/DC, then we took the break. That was when he decided to split, but he never said a word to me, knowing we'd be in trouble once the tour resumed in Miami. Once the tour was over and I got back to my house in L.A., I discovered that not only had Marre split for Stockholm, he'd taken all of my recording gear with him as well, not to mention copies of certain tapes we'd done in Sweden around 1980.

This infuriated me but didn't surprise me, because I knew the kinds of things he was capable of. For example, when I left for the United States, he formed a band called Power with a guitarist who was such an Yngwie Malmsteen clone that he even wore a pair of my pants that someone gave him—a stunt I found very pathetic and disturbing. But his attempt to wreck the gig in Miami and then steal from me was beyond forgiveness. Our friendship ended right there.

I didn't contact him for a long time, and later I wrote the song "Liar," which pretty well described how I felt about the whole affair: "You came to me / You said you're my friend / I shared my art and my mind / You found it easier to steal than create / Then call it yours, though it's mine," and so on. It took a good ten years before I would speak to him again.

But eventually he did come back—to my house in Miami with Jeff, I think—and he played on one track on the *Inspiration* album, the covers record I released in 1996. As a result of that, I agreed to do a small number of shows in Sweden with him, Anders, Mark, and Mats. But I later found out that he sneaked all the receipts from the shows, essentially hiding the money the promoters gave us. I basically told him that our relationship was over and it would never be mended. Don't even bother ever contacting me again, because this time I was really, *really* done with him. But he wasn't done with *me*.

He then took it upon himself to release all my old demo tapes from the Sweden years that I'd recorded in my grandmother's apartment building studio, even though he had no copyright ownership or legal permission to do so. In 2003, I sued him and sent him a cease-and-desist order. But when I returned to Sweden, I was met with a countersuit by him, essentially suing me for preventing him from releasing *my* shit. It was beyond ludicrous.

After that, I stopped all communication with him, but I heard from others in Sweden who knew him that he had developed mental problems of some sort, which may have eventually led to his death. He took his own life in 2009. I don't really know what was going on with him in those last few years, and I don't want to speak badly of the deceased, because we did have some good times in spite of all the bad shit he pulled. The fact remains, however, that some of the ways he repeatedly screwed me over are documentable and can't be undone, and it colors the way I remember him.

That brings me back to the gig in Miami, after he had taken off. I refused to go onstage without a bass player, but the tour manager was begging me to go on anyway, which would mean playing in front of ten to fifteen thousand people every night without a bass player. The stage manager was pleading, "Go on stage, just go on stage," while I was yelling, "I don't have a frigging bass player!" And Jens was saying stuff like "No problem, I have two hands, I can play the bass part, too."

It was a scene straight out of *Spinal Tap*. I grabbed the tour manager, who was practically crying by then at the idea of me not going onstage at all, and I told him that in a city as big as Miami, there had to be somebody who was a professional bass player. So he found bass player Wally Voss.

What a lifesaver he turned out to be. Wally stepped in and just nailed all the songs with practically no rehearsal. And he was so easy to get along with, I couldn't believe it. I remember talking with him in the hotel room. I played a bass line from "I Am a Viking" that is very demanding and asked whether he could do that. He played it back to me note-perfect. He might have known the song already, but it was good enough to convince me.

I asked him, "What are you doing now?" And he mumbled around a bit, saying he didn't have any real plans. I said, "Pack your bags, you're coming with me." Once again, it seemed the rock gods were smiling down on me. Wally joined the band halfway through the *Marching Out* tour and stayed through the *Trilogy* tour. I believe he's also in the videos we made for some of the *Trilogy* songs. He died from Hodgkin's lymphoma in 1992. God bless him. He was a fine musician and a really good person.

We finished up the *Marching Out* tour in good shape and returned to L.A., where I started writing songs for *Trilogy*, including "Liar," which allowed me to vent about Marre. As I look back on that whole period now, it just seems so totally undisciplined and out of control. We were all involved in very serious alcohol consumption that was so much a part of the scene that people hardly even gave it a second thought. It was just how you functioned (or not): you drank, you wrote and recorded music, you went out on the road and performed it in an even more wasted state, you did photo shoots and magazine interviews that were a blur, and then you came back and started the whole cycle over again.

I really had no idea what was going on with my career on the business side. For example, I had no idea whatsoever that *Trilogy*, after it was released, had been receiving awards and was critically acclaimed or that it was selling extremely well. My manager, Andy, gave me spending money, and I had a nice car and rented a house in Topanga Canyon, but I had no knowledge of bank accounts or royalties or anything like that. The house I had at that time was three stories, and I had a messy little music room on the top floor filled mostly with beer cans and a keyboard. That's where I wrote "You Don't Remember" on the keyboard. Wally hung out there a good bit, even though I made it clear to him that I, not he, was playing bass on the album. He seemed okay with that, although I suspect he really wanted to play.

From *Marching Out* to *Trilogy* was a quantum leap forward, and everyone who heard it knew that. It was the point at which my career as a totally in-charge composing musician began, because I was determined to let the world know that I was much more than a flashy virtuoso guitarist. I was just twenty-two years old, but I felt so much older than that in terms of my music. I've been told, "Oh, you're an old soul" and stuff like that, which I pay no attention to. But when I look at the kids in bands now who are probably about the age I was then, they're like babies musically—like children just playing around.

When I created *Trilogy*, the musical headspace I was in is hard to describe, but it was really deep. Part of me was crazy and dangerously reckless, but when it came down to the music itself, which was the real deal, I did what I needed to do. The album liner credits state, "Produced, conducted & arranged by Yngwie J. Malmsteen." I also took part in the mixing, so it was the first time I exerted total control over every part of an album. I had a very specific sound in mind when I made *Trilogy*. I was going for an album that didn't sound overprocessed, with a lot of sweetening and reverberation. The guitar sound is really dry, but that's exactly what I wanted.

The recording of *Trilogy* was an exercise in controlled chaos, for a number of reasons. That was back when it cost several thousand dollars a day for the use of a top recording studio. *Trilogy* was completely recorded at the Village Recorder in Santa Monica, California. It was a really nice place, with a very classy lounge that had the ceiling made up to look like the night sky, with little lights for stars.

About that time I decided I wanted to buy a crossbow. I purchased a fully functioning weapon and then decided to use those little twinkly lights for target practice. What probably cost thousands of dollars to create ended up full of holes. It was a horrible thing to do, I know, but at the time I thought nothing of it. I had rented the place for four months, so I thought of it as mine.

Those *Marching Out* and *Trilogy* years were all about excess: how much alcohol you could consume and remain standing, how many chicks you could get into your hotel room after the show, how much damage you could inflict on your surroundings, how fast you could drive your sports car down the freeway, and on and on.

I also bought my first gun during those days, a stainless steel Smith & Wesson .357 Magnum, and it was such an incredible sense of power to feel that huge gun go off in your hand, to feel the kick and hear the loud *boom*.

I had just discovered a recording technique called triggering and sampling (which has nothing to do with the digital sampling that's common today). You could take a very short sound, enhance it, and add it to the mix anywhere you wanted. I got the crazy idea that I would record the blast of my .357 Magnum pistol and then use it to replace the sound of the snare drum. Anytime Anders would hit the snare, it would trigger the .357 Magnum gunshot instead.

We set up a big block of wood in the studio, and I started firing my gun at it, using high-velocity hollow-point bullets. It was absolutely crazy. We miked everything up, and when the tape was rolling I let go. *Blam! Blam! Blam! Blam!* In that enclosed space it sounded like a cannon going off, because that's basically what that gun is, as far as pistols go.

I was really excited to hear what this was going to sound like, but when we played it back, it was just a tiny little click. What happened was that the gunshot was so loud that the diaphragms in all the microphones seized up. I spent two days recording the gun but never could get it right. It was a huge disappointment.

Another bright idea I had was that I would take a long solo segment of about thirty-two bars and double-track it note for note, which was actually impossible because the first solo had been completely improvised, with no preplanning or writing things out beforehand. That didn't stop me from trying and burning up a lot of studio time, though.

I was experimenting. The first song on *Trilogy*, "You Don't Remember, I'll Never Forget," I wrote on the keyboard instead of on the guitar. It's all triads except for some diminished chords, which I thought sounded really cool. The structure of the song is quite simple but very effective. The riff and the chorus are the same thing. That is, the melody is used in different arrangements, but melodically it is the same.

I had an eight-track machine in my house and a small practice drum set on pads. I put microphones on the pads, and it would overdrive them so much it would sound like a full drum. I'd do that and record it back, since I had no drum machine, and then put the keys on using Jens's keyboard. I played it for the guys in the band and told them this was a new song I was working on. They agreed that it had a dramatic opening sound that was exciting, so we got into it right away.

To explode yet another myth, let me say that the lyrics for that song were not based on my own experience. It was my interpretation of what I thought that kind of feeling or situation would be like. Really, it was more like writing a script for a movie.

But I still don't know how we ended up with an album—like I said, it was chaotic. For instance, once Anders and I took the Jaguar to a fast-food place. I went in and told the guy behind the counter, "I want a baked potato with no sour cream on it." Instead, he served me a piping hot potato covered in sour cream, so I decided that it belonged on his face. A big nasty scene ensued. The whole time I was working on *Trilogy*, there was a steady string of full-fledged crazy stuff like that going on. Yet ironically, that album is always hailed as one of the tightest, most controlled, best executed albums I've done. Go figure.

For the recording of *Trilogy*, I had the whole studio on what is called "lockout," which meant that instead of coming in for a few hours or a couple of days to record something in room A while some other band might be in room B doing something else, I had the whole studio at my disposal until I was completely done, which was for about four months. During that time, none of the various recording rooms were available to anyone else. The expense for this was astronomical. When you do something like that, it's pretty much expected that you have every day planned out and that you don't waste your time. I didn't do that, I'm afraid, but I didn't want anybody coming in and taking down the drums or changing the way the mikes were set up so they could set their own stuff up.

When I didn't have a studio on lockout, I would take snapshots of the mixing board to make sure the settings were the same when I came back in after someone else had been using the room. It was very common to record pieces of albums all over the place at several different studios, which could lead to a very haphazard result. Most of my albums were done that way. But *Trilogy* was the one album for which I used one studio for the duration.

People could still come in and hang around, however. In fact, we were distracted by all kinds of people while we were supposed to be working. It was more like a party than work, but somehow that album got done. I remember guys from Ratt being there, as well as Night Ranger, Duran Duran, and Stevie Nicks. It was like one big dangerous party.

My having complete control over the studio and all aspects of the recording also meant that when I wasn't at the studio, no one else could do anything. The studio was in Santa Monica, I was living an hour's drive away. I often slept overnight in the studio, which was a very comfortable place. I'd go in on a Thursday, stay up all night, sleep a little the next day, then stay up all night again, eventually coming back to my house on Sunday. I can't even imagine working like that now.

I hate to say it, but there was just complete disrespect for equipment, for the recording time booked for us, for everything. We'd record a piece of a song and then all go down to Rainbow instead of working, essentially squandering a lot of studio time. That did, in part, lead to "Fire." I very much like the opening riff of that song, with its major-key power chords. It happened like this. I was putting down my guitar tracks, and the rest of the band was trying to get me to go out to Rainbow with them. They were ragging on me to "just put something down so we can go to Rainbow." I did an off-the-wall riff to shut them up, and then later decided to keep it.

The whole process was just very seat-of-the-pants, and it's amazing we ever got anything finished. And, of course, this wasn't true for just me. That was generally the way things worked for a *lot* of bands at that time.

It was an atmosphere tailor-made for Jens and Anders, who loved to play head games with people. At one session, Anders played something wrong, and I told him so. He said I was hearing things, and I told him, "No, what you played there, it's out of time, it's behind the beat." Then he said, as if I were a moron who'd gone deaf, "No, it's not." And Jens agreed with him, saying, "I don't hear it." We went back and forth like that—a total head game.

Recording that album seemed to take forever, but in truth it was because we were so unfocused that we wasted a lot of time and energy doing other things not directly related to recording. We were just as likely to go look at my new car, go make a scene in a guitar store, or do any number of other things instead of working hard in the studio. To this day, I'm very surprised that *Trilogy* actually became an album. I know that it is a big fan favorite, and I agree that it does have some of my best songwriting on it, but it's truly a miracle that it got finished and on the record store shelves.

The album's title, *Trilogy*, obviously referred to the fact that it was my third solo album, so the motif of three is repeated in the cover art. If you look closely, you can see that not only does the dragon have three heads, there are actually three dragons in the scene. The day a photographer came to take pictures for the artist to use in painting the album cover, I had stayed in the studio for a couple of days in a row and was really shaggy and unkempt. That's reflected on the album cover, not by my choice. I didn't feel like posing, but they wanted me in some extreme positions, such as aiming my guitar up at an imaginary attacking dragon. I hammed it up for them, but my mood was pretty surly. Maybe that shows in the picture, too.

I could look back on those days with a bit of nostalgia, but to be honest, they weren't all that much fun. We projected the illusion of fun, of having a wild time, but we were really living in pretty unhealthy conditions. The house in the canyon where I lived for a while was built on a hillside with very strange architecture; it was more like a house and a half. At the top of the hill was my garage, and I walked from there into the kitchen. There were sleeping areas above that, and that's where my room was. But the house continued downward toward the bottom of the hill, where it had another set of bedrooms, and that's where Mark, Jens, and Anders all stayed.

The house was always a total mess. I had bought a waterbed from Jens for about twenty bucks, and it sprang a leak, which pooled and dripped all the way down to the first floor. It seemed like the whole band was living in my house, which might make you wonder where all the money was going, because it wasn't going to me, that's for sure. The guys would bitch to my manager, Andy, but they never bitched directly to me about money. I was just so disconnected from that side of the music business that I didn't ask the kinds of questions I would ask if I were starting out these days.

If I told Andy I needed money, he'd pull a roll of bills from his pocket and give me a couple hundred dollars, assuring me there was a lot more where that came from. It kept me quiet, and as long as I had money to buy booze or another guitar or something else in the moment, I didn't question that he had so much cash on him all the time. When the shit eventually did hit the fan, as it always does, it became clear that he had personally squandered most of the money I was making and that very little of it had actually gone to me. And none of it had been put into any kind of savings account or trust or anything for me to draw from in emergencies, a fact that would have a *huge* effect on my future not too far down the road.

I have to say that Andy Trueman was a bad influence on me in a lot of ways. Not only did he keep me from knowing anything about how much money I was or wasn't making, he also encouraged all kinds of excessive behavior because it contributed to my "bad boy" image, which in turn added to the mystique he wanted to build up around me. It was good press, because nobody wanted to read about a rocker's squeaky-clean lifestyle. People wanted dirt, sordid details of just how decadent you really were. He was no help to me or my career in that way.

But as I said, I was pretty much oblivious to all this at the time. I just went along with the flow and never questioned what I was earning or where it was being spent or by whom. I was not a businessman, and I trusted others to run that side of my career. Big mistake. But, sad to say, it took me years to fully figure that out.

By the time *Trilogy* got finished, we had to make the obligatory music video, because, remember, in those days MTV was *the* major way to promote a band's new album by playing videos made of the singles you were hoping to convince radio stations to put in rotation. There was no YouTube on which to instantly post a video for the entire world to download. The video director for "You Don't

Remember" decided he needed a live audience on the back-lot stage to watch us lip-sync and pretend to play the song, which to me felt ridiculous. And remember, Mark didn't look at all like the typical rock singer.

I was getting ready to do the video shoot, and I saw what I thought was a short girl with long hair in the dressing room. But when this person turned around, it was Mark with a huge wig on. And he was totally vamping, just going totally overboard and saying stuff like "Look at me, I'm a rock star!" It was both hilarious and disturbing at the same time, and it just added to the completely surreal atmosphere of that whole scene. Once the video shoot was done, I drove my Jag roadster around for a couple of hours up and down Hollywood Boulevard, and we were drinking and acting like maniacs.

We survived making the video, but then came the tour, which promised to be even more trouble. Compared to the *Marching Out* tour, which went across Europe to Japan and then to the United States, the *Trilogy* tour was fairly short. We didn't go to Europe at all. And Mark was going through some odd changes in his personality. When he had replaced Jeff for the *Marching Out* tour, he would just go onstage (no wig, no makeup) and sing flawlessly.

But now, when we hit the road for *Trilogy*, he was suddenly showing up onstage shitfaced, playing his rock star persona to the hilt. Somehow he seemed to have gotten a complete personality transplant. Even in that condition he managed to sing, but it was nothing like the note-perfect shows he'd done before. Not that the rest of us were any better behaved, but it just shows you how everything was escalating.

One of the most expensive decisions Andy made was that we should ride only in limos wherever we had to go—no taxis or regular cars. He also insisted that he and I had to fly in a private Lear jet to every gig, even the ones we could have driven to in just a few hours. The rest of the guys would get to the venue on the bus, but Andy and I had to fly. Nowadays, I think flying is a pain, and I love being on the tour bus and hanging out with the band, because you sleep for most of the trip and wake up when you get to the venue; it's very comfortable. But Andy was my manager, and that's how he said things were done when you were a real rock star. As a result, I had to get up very early, take a limo to the airport, board the plane, land, go in another limo, and get to the venue barely in time, sleep-deprived.

Most important, it meant there was very little connection between me and the other guys in the band, which meant that things really started getting out of hand before I would show up, especially with Mark. People in the road crew, the sound guys, and even others in the band would come up to me and ask, "What's with this guy? He's really starting to lose it." He was still wearing the wig and was now wearing expensive rock star clothes, but his singing had diminished to the point that he was off-key, missing his cues, changing lyrics, falling over, and so on. I finally couldn't stand it anymore. And who was available to finish that tour? Jeff. His thing with Rudy Sarzo hadn't worked out, so he was available again. It became a bizarre revolving door with Jeff and Mark.

To set the record straight, Mark and I never became enemies, as was written in a lot of articles after he left the tour. I just basically confronted him with the fact that the situation wasn't working, and he either had to get his shit together ASAP or find another gig. He left, I guess to work out whatever was going on with him, but we were definitely never enemies. In fact, he has worked with me on a number of occasions since then. You know how it is, though: when people don't have all the facts, rumors start, and things get blown way out of proportion. That's what happened there.

It might sound like the *Trilogy* tour was a road trip through hell, but that's not the whole story. A lot of good things happened, too. Sometimes you hook up with some really nice people in spite of the madness. My guitar tech at the time was Ian Ferguson, who had been Ritchie Blackmore's tech during the Purple and Rainbow years. You'd think he would be like a god at what he was doing, but the truth was that he wasn't really that great of a guitar tech. That said, as far as personality goes, he was a real sweetheart. The fact that he'd worked for Blackmore for so long was good enough credentials for me to hire him, but whenever something went wrong, he just turned into a giant question mark.

We played some summer festivals on the *Trilogy* tour, and one in particular was at Foxboro Stadium near Boston, a huge open-air stadium that held thousands of fans. There were a number of bands performing, including Aerosmith. One thing you learn in playing these big festivals is that no matter what happens, you just keep the show going. Sure enough, during this show, my wireless stopped working, and Ian was like a deer in the headlights, having no idea how to deal with it.

I was about to completely lose it, when a guy I didn't know turned up and offered me a wireless, saying, "Here, you can use one of Joe's. Go rock 'em, man, go rock 'em!" And he took one of Joe Perry's wireless sets off his guitar and handed it to me. It turned out that that guy was Steven Tyler himself. I was completely blown away when I found that out. That is a gesture I have never forgotten. The AC/DC guys were like that, too. They were so great to tour with: no jealousy, no backstabbing. They all worked together to make the shows happen, and they were very generous in their support of the opening acts.

When the U.S. dates for the *Trilogy* tour were done, I returned to L.A. and tried to sort out where I wanted to go from there. I moved out of the house I'd been living in, which was totally trashed, and moved into another little house. I hung out with Andy, my manager, a lot, who was living a very rich lifestyle. He had two Rolls-Royce Corniche convertibles, a Cadillac Eldorado, a Range Rover, and a Porsche, and he bought his kid a truck and a Trans Am.

He also had a penthouse in Hollywood, a villa in Calabasas (in the valley), a beachfront office in Malibu, several gold Rolexes, and a five-thousand-dollar-a-week cocaine habit—and I was his only artist. You'd think the explanation for that would be obvious, and I find it hard to convey how detached I was from it. I didn't want to have to handle bank accounts and investments. I didn't want to even know about it. I just wanted to make the music I was driven to make. I did not want to also have to become a businessman.

I was never too inquisitive, but even when I did ask him something about money, he always had an answer. He was really smart about that. It wasn't just me—many other artists were being taken advantage of like that. Unscrupulous managers just seemed to have an instinct for finding people who were more into the music than anything else and who were trusting and willing to let someone else manage the money part of their careers.

And I did trust Andy, because we were friends and spent a lot of time together. After *Trilogy*, I worked by myself on a lot of songs that would eventually end up on *Odyssey*, although at that time the next album wasn't titled yet. I also spent a lot of that time just hanging out with Andy. During one of those times, when we were just kicking around and shooting the shit, I said, "I wonder what Joe Lynn Turner's doing now, since he's not in Rainbow anymore." Andy replied, "Let's call him up."

This was the beginning of a very dark period in my life. The previous couple of years had been one continuous wild and out-of-control party, as I've described, but they were nothing compared to what was coming. It was like getting on the funhouse ride that goes into a dark tunnel. You can't see what's up ahead, but you also can't get out once the car starts moving.

Through Andy, I fell in with an unsavory crowd, worse than any of the people I'd known previously. They were doing drugs, drinking hard, and God knew what else. Joe Lynn Turner was brought into the band during this time, and, boy, did he fit right into that scene. I had never hung out with anyone for any length of time who could routinely abuse substances like that. I knew a lot of people in L.A. who were doing it, but I hadn't encountered it on a regular, daily basis. And the percentage of time spent on music by these people was very small.

Let me clarify how Joe came into the band. Jeff had finished the *Trilogy* tour with me, but even though we were good friends, I didn't want to use him again on the next album because I wanted someone new and different. I started talking to other singers—quite a few, in fact: some big names, some smaller names. At one point I met a guy who lived in L.A. but had some Swedish background, and he had an amazing voice. But the problem was that he had no chromatic sense. By that, I mean that when I showed him a scale or a line of melody, he had a hard time sticking to it. But his voice—the timbre, range, and vibrato—was really very good. I had him do a few demos with me, one of which was "Dreaming" (which at first I called "Tell Me").

Here's how it works in my band. I write the melody and the lyrics, but the singer's voice will give it a certain feel. Take Alcatrazz, for example. Graham Bonnet had not the first clue about how to write songs in terms of structure or melody, but he had a great voice. When I wrote the melodies and choruses for killer songs like "Kree Nakorie" and "Jet to Jet," he had the perfect voice for them. He wrote the words, but the music and vocal melodies were mine.

Or take Mark Boals. His voice was truly an instrument that he could manipulate in any way I showed him. I wrote stuff for him that would have been truly ridiculous, or maybe even impossible, for most other singers. But he didn't have what I would call a true "metal" singer's voice.

As I've said before, I approach the singer's voice as another instrument, which he uses to reproduce the melodies I write. Mozart wrote an opera and hired singers to sing the notes he wrote, not to improvise or add their own melodies. It's the same with me. I don't know why that is so hard for people to understand, but even to this day they just don't get it. When I'm ready to record the vocals for an album, I bring the singer in and play the vocal melody for him on the guitar, and I play the harmonies as well. I put that in his headphones and show him the words so he can hear how to phrase it. It's very accurate and allows him to perform the song the way I want it. It's a lot more work for me, but it's so much more rewarding when I hear the finished product.

The songs that ended up on *Odyssey* were 95 percent finished (if not more) when Joe came on board. Some of them were actually composed while I still lived in Sweden. The riff for "Rising Force" was written when I was fifteen years old. "Riot in the Dungeons" was written and recorded when I was seventeen. The list goes on. Joe did not write the songs *with* me or *for* me, as he has claimed over the years. The melodies and most of the lyrical themes and choruses were already there when he joined the project. What he did was add some words to my existing lyrics, and I gave him full credit for it, which he, to this day, does not appreciate. In his own words in a magazine interview we did at the time, he spoke the truth when he said, "[Yngwie] wrote the tracks. It was 99 percent done when I came in. I came in with lyrics but he had the melodies together."

What he did do was add the radio vibe with his voice and delivery. Joe's addition to the scene skewed the music toward that more commercial sound. I wrote "Heaven Tonight" to be sort of a Van Halen–style, radio-friendly rock song. Everything in the 1980s was so formulaic. One week you had to be like Bon Jovi, the next you had to be like Poison or something. "Heaven Tonight" was an attempt to make a song like that. But I wanted to do it my way. Joe's way was not my way. He is what I call an interesting character. From what I have heard and seen of him recently, he will say nasty things about me to the media, speak of me with such venomous words, which he seems to love to do, then play with all the Yngwie Malmsteen clones and Yngwie Malmsteen cover bands all over the world.

With Joe's vocals, "Heaven Tonight" was a success, the biggest single off that album. The thing is, no matter what kind of song there is, even a heavy death metal song, Joe's voice is going to make it sound commercial. He could sing the fucking phone book and it would sound like a radio song. But the problem was that he would add empty pop-song phrases like *"Oooh,* baby" and "Come on, girl," which made me want to throw up. They're there in some of the songs because my internal turmoil at the time disassociated me from my usual control over every detail.

In fact, on nearly every album I can think of where I let the singer go off on his own and do what he wanted, either with lyrics or melody, I was extremely disappointed in the end. I should have been keeping tabs on my kids, so to speak: my songs, my little babies. But that whole period surrounding *Odyssey* was so bad; I was really lost, and I let others do things in a way I normally wouldn't have allowed.

That period was one of the most vulnerable times in my life. I usually never have anyone else play bass on my albums, but on *Odyssey* I agreed to have Bob Daisley (who'd played for years with Rainbow and Ozzy and who was a total hero to me) play on a couple of tracks. I simply was not exerting complete control over the album. His name came up as someone who might be cool to have on the album, and my response was "Sure, why not?" I just didn't care enough to say no.

I was sleeping all day, existing on junk food and alcohol, with no physical activity and no real life. It all escalated like that without me really paying attention to how bad it had gotten. It was just what we were all doing, and that was that. I rarely saw daylight. And at night there would be one crazy thing after another, running around with my loaded Magnum, shooting it off, and jumping into the swimming pool from the roof of the house.

FAULT LINE

I was also told later that I was clinically dead for nearly a minute—flatlined.

Looking back, it's easy to see how inevitable it was that something really bad was going to happen. On the morning of June 22, 1987, about a week before my twenty-fourth birthday, we'd spent all day drinking. As we got more and more plastered, we did more dangerous and crazy things, like climbing up onto the roof and jumping off into the swimming pool below. At one point, I decided we needed to drive to the store for more beer, so we got into my Jaguar E-Type V12 convertible, which was such a fast car it should have been illegal.

What's amazing is that I was able to back out of my driveway, which was pretty steep, and make it all the way to the store, park the car, get the booze, plow back into traffic at top speed, and navigate all the way back toward my house in Woodland Hills. But just one house away from my house, the car jumped the curb and smashed head-on into a tree. I was airlifted to a hospital with severe head injuries.

I tell all this secondhand, because I have no personal memory of it happening. I vaguely remember leaving the house, and that's it. The next thing I knew, I was waking up and it was dark. I could barely make out a shadow near me. Finally I realized it was Anders standing there. I tried to say something to him, but my voice didn't work right. It was really weird. I was making groaning noises, but no words were coming out. It turned out I had been in a coma for almost a week.

After I came out of the coma, I realized something really bad was going on, but I had no idea what. My only thought was to get out of there, to get away from whatever bad thing this situation was. I tried to fight off the doctors and rip out the intravenous tube in my arm—I really went ballistic. They had to tie me down and sedate me, and the hospital staff started referring to me as the Caveman. I just couldn't believe what everyone was telling me about the accident, because I couldn't remember any of it.

I don't know how fast the car was going when it hit the tree, but I'm told I wasn't braking, so it slammed into the tree trunk at full speed. They told me that the front of the car was so crushed that the engine was accordioned together. I didn't have my seat belt on, so my head hit the steering wheel so hard it broke the wheel in half. I guess when people called me hardheaded, it was literally true. What's really a miracle is that the impact didn't break my neck and leave me paralyzed. I was also told later that I was clinically dead for nearly a minute—flatlined.

The doctors said I had a massive concussion with bleeding inside the brain, so it was hard to tell whether I would ever wake up, and if I did, whether I would be a vegetable or make a recovery of sorts. In any case, the outcome didn't look good. It was the closest to death I'd ever been. Peter was injured pretty badly, too, but not life-threateningly. He broke his jaw, his nose, and his hand. He was in the hospital for a while, but he did eventually recover.

My mother was contacted in Sweden, and she came to the States to see me. I was close to being released and was really glad to see her, but she didn't look too good herself. She had lost a lot of weight, and her skin color wasn't good. I questioned her about it, because she'd been a little overweight the last time I had seen her, which was about a year earlier. She blew it off and said she was on a diet, so I let it pass. I shouldn't have, though, because it turned out she was very ill and just wasn't telling me.

That was in July or August 1987. She stayed for a while and then flew back to Sweden, and we talked on the phone from time to time. But I didn't really know anything about what was going on over there, because apparently nobody had the heart to tell me she was ill. She didn't live long after making that trip to the United States.

I was finally declared well enough to be released from the hospital, and I went home. My picking hand was somewhat impaired from a blood clot on my brain, and again the outcome was in doubt. The doctors told me it might dissolve, in which case I would recover the full use of my hand—or it might not, leaving me without full use of my right arm and hand. I was having none of that, of course, so I started intensive physical therapy to make sure I got the use of my hand back.

Over the years, I've had so many people ask me how I got my technique back after the accident. The major ingredient, I can tell you, was sheer determination. That's part of my DNA: when I want something desperately enough, nothing will keep me from achieving it. Sooner or later, I *will* prevail.

That's how it was with my recovery. The neurosurgeon who treated me in the hospital showed me how the clot was causing a delay in the impulses fired along the neural pathways down to the muscles. He explained to me how blood clots eventually shrink if there's no further trauma to the area. That was encouraging, so I did a lot of reading on brain injuries to learn everything I could about what to expect. I'd been told that I could be cautiously optimistic about regaining limited use of my picking hand. That was totally unacceptable. For me, it was all or nothing.

All I needed to know was that my condition *could* improve in order for me to go all out to make it so. I wouldn't be surprised to discover that by sheer force of will I made the clot shrink and the nerves reconnect and relearned how to fire the muscles in my arm and hand. The physical therapist gave me specific hand-strengthening exercises. I took that ball and ran with it. I forced myself to play, even though the nerves in my fingers weren't functioning properly while the clot was there.

I was pushing myself so hard, forcing the hand to do what it had done before the accident, that when the clot finally dissolved and full function returned, it returned with a vengeance. My picking ability was actually at a higher level than before. Some people may find that hard to believe, but it's true. In ballet, dancers train with weights around their ankles so that when they do the same leaps and jumps without the weights, they actually go higher. It was the same with my hand. Once the obstacle was removed and my brain-hand coordination began to come back, my physical ability took a leap forward.

As my hand gradually improved, I was keeping up a brave front, trying to show everyone around me that I was fine. The truth, though, is that emotionally I was far from okay. I was filled with worries and doubts about my health, my career, my mother's health, and just the day-to-day concerns of how I was going to pay my expenses. While I was in the hospital trying to recover, I found out that the insurance hadn't been paid on my (wrecked) car, which was therefore a loss. When the hospital bills began to mount, it came to light that Andy Trueman had been diverting large portions of my earnings into his own private accounts, leaving me with nothing in the bank and no insurance of any kind. I fired him immediately, but that did nothing to replace all the money he'd clearly siphoned off.

And then, just when you'd think it couldn't get any worse, an earthquake shook the area three months after my car crash. The quake, which became known as the Whittier Narrows earthquake, hit at 7:42 A.M. on October 1, 1987, and reached 6.9 on the Richter scale.

I was awoken from a deep sleep by a piercing noise in my ear. Then I realized the ground was heaving under me. It was terrifying to suddenly be snapped awake with all this going on around me. It was the most frightening moment ever, like the end of the world. The noise was like the screaming of the whole world around me. I've never heard the ground making a grinding, shrieking noise like that. Maybe it was the building foundation or the trees and the buildings nearby, I don't know. It was so loud I couldn't even hear myself, even though I was yelling as loud as I could.

I tried to get up, but the room was swaying, and I kind of fell over as I tried to get out before the whole house collapsed on top of us. The bedroom window overlooked a little pool in the backyard, and I could see trees and power lines moving with a gigantic rippling motion while water was splashing out of the pool. For an instant I had an image of being thrown into the pool with live power lines. I tried to make my way to the front of the house despite the ground bucking up and swaying under me, things crashing and falling, and this terrifying noise all around. I remember being shocked that the shaking sensation was so complete that even my eyeballs were shaking inside my head. I've read since that the main quake lasted a couple of minutes, but it felt like it went on forever.

I scrambled to the front door and saw the pavement of the street move like a tidal wave in the ocean. I mean, the actual street rose and fell maybe seven or eight feet. Cars were being thrown up in the air as the ground bucked, like in some nightmarish cartoon. I figured this was it. It truly felt like the apocalypse, because at first I had no idea what was happening. For all I knew, a spaceship could have landed on the house. It was, without doubt, the most freaky, terrifying experience of my life—ever. This is coming from someone who up until then had never really been totally afraid of anything.

The most horrifying thing about an earthquake is that there's nowhere to go. When the firm ground underneath your feet suddenly turns into a giant trampoline, there's literally no place to hide. And that wasn't the end. Aftershocks kept coming for days. All that, in addition to what I'd just gone through with the accident, was truly the last straw. The message now came to me loud and clear, "You don't belong here. You are turning into something you're not. You should leave—not now, not tomorrow, but *yesterday!*"

I had resumed work on the album *Odyssey* as soon as I started getting range of motion back into my hand. And wouldn't you know it, I fell right back into my bad old ways of party, party, party. I hadn't learned a thing—until the earthquake happened. It stopped me in my tracks and made me take stock of where I really was.

That was when I knew I had to go, and once I'd made the decision in my mind, the act of leaving wasn't hard at all. When I looked at what I had in the way of material possessions, there wasn't all that much: no car, no house, some amps and guitars, a few clothes, and that was about it. Despite three albums that had charted on *Billboard*, huge amounts of press, and constant touring, there was really very little to show for it, thanks in large part to Mr. Trueman. Determined to never live on the West Coast again, I flew to New York, where I had some contacts, and stayed there briefly. I then turned my attention back to *Odyssey*.

With my manager gone, my record company (Polygram) decided to send me and the band (which still included Joe Lynn Turner) to Austin, Texas, where it had booked us into a small studio. As bad as things were in terms of drinking every night, when Joe became part of the scene, we quickly determined that he was the poster boy for heavy partying. Add that to the alcohol haze in which I'd found myself, and you have the hell I lived in for a couple of years.

I had no inspiration, didn't feel engaged with the album under way, didn't think that my playing was up to par, didn't really care whether the album got finished. But the record company cared a lot, because it wanted income to recoup its investment in me. The record company got its money, but the fact that *Odyssey* eventually became my best-selling album in the States meant nothing to me. Those years were the black pit of hell to me, no matter which way I looked at it.

That was why I loosened the reins on the production of that album, which was not normal for me. Usually I would be a total control freak about everything, but at that time I just didn't have the drive to do it. But once the album was done, I didn't much like it. It was too soft, too dreamy, too poppy, too banal, going for the easy hook—not at all the kind of album I would have made if I'd been firing on all cylinders. All the songs had riffs I'd written before Joe had been brought in, so he can't take credit for them. He added words to "Dreaming," "Now Is the Time," and "Heaven

Tonight," but they were my melodies. Certainly his singing style put a commercial spin on the songs.

I also want to mention Jeff Glixman, who was involved in the production side. I really liked him. We got along well and still do. He didn't see eye to eye with Joe, though, and it finally got to the point that Joe flew off to New Jersey to record the rest of his tracks. At one point, Joe argued that his vocals didn't sound as good as the singer on the Kansas albums that Glixman had produced in the 1970s. He implied that Glixman had lost his touch; the fact that Joe was partying a lot supposedly had nothing to do with it.

Glixman had a wicked sense of humor, and he told Joe once in that studio in Austin, "I just can't get the right sound. It just needs something, a more open space, I think. Let's try this, we'll set the mike up in here." And he set the mike up in the men's room. It was totally disgusting in there, but Joe was in there singing, "This could be paradise"—right next to the toilet.

We had recorded the drum tracks in L.A. at Cherokee Studios, and we took the tapes to Austin, where the rest of the album was done. Glixman had some connections there, so that's why we ended up using that studio, which was pretty cheap. I had rented an apartment in Austin, and Jens and Anders had one next door to me. So once again, it was like the three Droogs from *A Clockwork Orange* on the loose. Lots of unwholesome characters were coming by the apartment, dragged up from somewhere by Jens and Anders or Joe.

It seemed like Joe and I would argue about anything, no matter how trivial. It really began to wear on me, because I hated arguing over stuff. That's why I always made myself the boss of the band from the very beginning, even in Sweden, so there wouldn't be any arguing. It's just my way or the highway, or as some said, "There's the right way, the wrong way, and the Yng-way."

Given other circumstances, the *Odyssey* album obviously could have been done differently, but it is what it is, and a lot of people seem to like it. It isn't as close to my heart as the others, though.

We were almost finished with the album by Christmas 1987, so I decided to go back to Sweden for the holidays. When I got there, I discovered that my mother was in the hospital. No one had told me how sick she was. Cancer was killing her. I think that my family and my friends just couldn't bring themselves to do it because they knew I was struggling with having lost everything back in the States already.

I stayed at a hotel in Stockholm while my mother was in the hospital. I remember getting the phone call in January that my mother had passed away. Then there was the funeral to get through. I was completely numb by then, just sleepwalking through all the obligations. I played Tomaso Albinoni's Adagio at the ceremony and felt like my heart had been ripped out. I mean, everyone loves his or her mother, at least on some level, but she was my anchor in this world, my strongest source of support, and suddenly that was all gone. I was barely coping. For the next several years, I felt completely unmoored, like I was drifting out onto the dark ocean with no compass or tiller.

Looking back on it now, I am almost surprised I came out of it—especially because about a year after I lost my mother, my grandmother died, too. And then—it's beyond realistic, almost—a few months after that, my brother, Bjorn, died in a train crash. The whole thing was fucking crazy.

I did anything to numb my reality. At that time, that meant alcohol—I would drink any drink with alcohol in it: mostly beer then, but I would drink vodka, whatever—anything. For about two or three years, I was not sober one day. It was really bad. You could say it was because of what I was going through, but that's not my personality. My personality is "whatever doesn't kill me makes me stronger." I can take some serious hard knocks, but that was just too much in one go.

FASTER THAN
THE SPEED
OF LIGHT

When I moved down to Miami, it was the
same situation as in L.A.: if you wanted to
go anywhere, you had to have a car. So I got
a Ferrari.

When *Odyssey* was finally completed, "Heaven Tonight," with
its schmaltzy lyrics and poppy chorus, got better than decent
airplay, which got the music video airtime on MTV, which sold a lot
of albums. I'm not complaining, it's just that I wish I had been
more in control. I wish it sounded more like what I wanted. Joe's
voice softened the vibe, even when the riffs were heavy. *Odyssey*

was touted as my "comeback" album, and a lot of people were curious to see whether I could still play.

This was a transition phase for me, because Andy Trueman was out and I hadn't signed with a new manager. Polygram brought in Larry Mazer for a while, but he didn't seem to care about anything. However, he definitely knew how to spend money. I don't think he was a crook like Andy had been, but flying to Europe on the Concorde seemed a bit much, and he went way overboard in surrounding an artist with unnecessary personnel.

For the *Odyssey* tour, I had two bodyguards, a tour manager, an assistant tour manager, a tour accountant, a press agent, two stage managers, a guitar tech, a drum tech, a keyboard tech, a bass tech, a monitor guy, two house guys with their own assistant, and, in addition to that, four tour buses and six semi trucks to haul around our own lighting rigs, stage gear, and so on. Unbelievable. We were playing some good-sized venues and probably making a lot of money, but it was all being sucked away by this huge entourage. We had five people doing the job that one person could have done.

Lita Ford was the opening act for those shows. She was really great, so much fun and such a trouper. I was glad to have her with us. She had a big hit single at the time, "Kiss Me Deadly," so we were drawing in both her fans and mine at really big venues. We played some warm-up shows in the United States, then in January 1988 we all flew to Japan—*first-class*. This was a terrible decision for two reasons: the obvious expense of all those first-class tickets, and the outrageous behavior that was guaranteed to happen with Jens and Anders. (This is when the "You have unleashed the fucking fury!" incident happened.)

Somewhere along the way on that very long tour, though, I had a piece of really good luck. Nigel Thomas, a British guy who was a well-known artist manager, caught one of my shows in Japan. We had dinner back in New York, where I had rented a Manhattan apartment, and he told me he'd seen me in Japan and was really keen on becoming my manager. I was kind of wary and held him off a bit, but we stayed in touch.

When the tour was finally over, we all went our separate ways. I headed back to New York and reconnected with Nigel. He asked me about my finances and how my career was being handled, and he actually went with me to visit my accountant. I asked to see how much money was coming in and where it was going. The accountant pulled out the balance sheets, and there it was: eighteen dollars. I had eighteen dollars to my name—no collateral, no assets, no cash, no house, no car, no credit cards, no insurance. This is in spite of the fact that *Odyssey* had gone gold, was climbing the charts and being played on the radio, and I had just toured my ass off across the United States and Japan.

I needed a good stiff drink right about then. It finally dawned on me that all the money I was supposedly making had been paying for the lavish lifestyle we'd all been living, and nothing had been saved. Nigel took one look at the balance and just said, "Don't worry about it." A year later, under his management, I was a millionaire.

It was Nigel's direction and smart management of my income that turned me from a pauper into a very wealthy man. I had gone from being in the blackest state of depression to feeling alive again and actually caring where my career was headed. The tour was supposed to be over by then, but Nigel took me on a very successful follow-up tour of Europe, which further built up my financial security and kept my name out there.

My name was out there even in unexpected places, without Nigel's help or any of our knowledge. Somewhere near the end of 1988, my dad, who is fluent in Russian and had friends in what was then still the Soviet Union, told me that *Trilogy* was number one in that totally insulated communist country.

I hadn't seen my father since my parents' divorce when I was just a little kid, but he came back into my life later, and I'm very close to him now. He was a soldier. The tough guys in movies are wimps compared to him. He is the most badass guy I've ever met in my life. I'm not kidding. He got a Nobel Peace Prize for all the United Nations work he did and was awarded the Swedish equivalent of the Purple Heart in the army.

In the early 1970s, he had decided he was going to become fluent in Russian. And when I say *fluent* in Russian, I mean he spoke it so well that even the Russians thought he was Russian. I know this is going to sound crazy, but it's the truth: You know James Bond? That's what my father was doing. He was a spy. The closest NATO country to the Soviet Union was Norway, and in order to get to Norway, you had to go through Sweden. In the 1960s and 1970s, the Russians were putting submarines in Swedish waters and Russian spies in Sweden. (They didn't have GPS and satellites back then.) They used Sweden as a base. So my father went to the Soviet Union and gathered intelligence for the Swedish government. It was all very secretive. My dad never told me anything; I found out from other sources.

While he was in the Soviet Union at the height of the Cold War, he was shown a record by a guy who said, "Lennart, you must hear this record. It is amazing." My dad replied, "That's my son." The man didn't believe him. "Ha, you're a funny man, Lennart." It turned out that Polygram had sold the rights to *Trilogy* to Melodiya, the Soviet state-run label, for three thousand dollars, and it sold fourteen million copies. I didn't get paid a fucking dollar (or ruble) for it.

The reason I became so big with the Russians was that they actually had an official release. They were selling Deep Purple records and stuff like that on the black market, but they were illegal. Melodiya released *Trilogy* officially, with Russian text and everything. Anyway, my dad told me this, and Nigel said, "Oh, well, we better do a tour in the Soviet Union, then."

This was in January 1989, before the Iron Curtain fell. It was very difficult for Western artists to enter the country and perform. But we managed to do it. I was over there for two months. We did twenty shows, nine at Leningrad SKK Stadium and eleven at the Olympic Stadium in Moscow: eighteen thousand seats, sold out every night for eleven nights in a row. I even recorded a live album, *Trial by Fire*, in Leningrad.

But nobody ever talked about any of that. It was all Mötley Crüe and Bon Jovi, who went there three years later. I'd be lying if I said it didn't piss me off whenever I heard all of the huge press about Bon Jovi's "groundbreaking" trip to play in the tightly guarded Soviet Union *after* the Iron Curtain had come down, when I'd already been there and done that *before*.

Thanks to Nigel, both my career and my financial security were on firm ground for the first time in years. I enjoyed his company and found him quite different from my previous managers. He was very British, with "posh" taste. He owned a castle in England, and I stayed there sometimes. It was really mind-boggling. He was the manager for Joe Cocker, Morrissey, Kingdom Come, the Kinks, and a number of others, and he produced the albums for Saxon. He also managed the filmmaker Ridley Scott and others in the entertainment industry.

Nigel was a very astute businessman and just seemed to have a sixth sense for seeing an opportunity before it was obvious to everyone else. I had a very good run with that guy, from 1988 to 1993, and have much to thank him for. I slowly worked my way out of the emotional black hole that surrounded *Odyssey* and moved into a different phase because of him.

The 1990s were turbulent for me in a lot of ways, but as always, there was both the good and the bad. The decade started off looking good, but then the grunge movement took hold in the United States, and guitar-driven melodic rock took a backseat. But in other places, especially Japan, neoclassical rock and virtuoso guitar playing were still big, and I was very popular there, with a huge fan base. In fact, the record deals I had in Japan during the 1990s carried me through while many other bands and guitarists in the States were struggling or disappeared from the music business altogether.

When I moved to the United States in 1983, I was suddenly an overnight sensation. Because fans and the media became obsessed with me, the whole dynamics of security changed dramatically. Most of it was harmless, like fans who maybe were a little too fixated on me but weren't quite what I'd call serious stalkers. Some of it went over the line, however.

I'm certainly not the only rock musician to have had these kinds things happen, but I was unprepared for it when I hit the States. Occasionally, drunken people have thrown things, and once when we played in Belfast in 1990 there was a bomb threat in the theater. I joked, "Good thing it didn't go off during the show." I've never been a worrier. These days I do have very good security at my shows, though.

A good example of my complete disregard for my personal safety or any sense of danger was once at the end of the 1980s, before I was married. I remember a really weird event involving a very strange chick I hooked up with one night. It's been so many years ago that I don't remember what town this took place in, but it was somewhere on tour in the United States, I think during the *Eclipse* tour. What I do remember, though, was a young woman in full Goth gear—long dark hair, leather, you get the picture—who latched on to me after the show. She came on to me really strong, and we ended up in my hotel room. We started making out and having a good time, then all of a sudden she bit me on the neck. I was kind of pissed, and when I felt the place with my hand, I was shocked to see that she had actually drawn blood.

Then she just went completely crazy, yelling, "I want your blood! I want to drink your blood!" I started fighting her off, but she was determined, screaming, "I have to have your blood!" It was pretty obvious that it wasn't just a stunt with her. She really *believed* that she was a vampire. I think I grabbed her and threw her out somehow, but what's crystal clear in my memory is her biting hard enough to break the skin and then going into a frenzy trying to lick up the blood. She was a total psycho. I had all kinds of outrageous things happen back then with groupies, but that was probably one of the weirdest.

It could be dangerous onstage, too. In the late 1980s, we were playing in a really big venue in Anchorage, Alaska. It was the middle of winter, pitch-black outside, as cold as the coldest day in Sweden. I don't mean to dis any fans in Alaska, but it seemed like the people there, maybe because of the cold environment, liked to hit the bottle pretty hard (not all that different from Sweden, actually). But I digress. This particular venue was a huge sports arena of some kind, probably a hockey arena. I was playing my guitar known as the Duck, and we were doing "Queen in Love" for the encore.

Suddenly I felt a really hard thump, like somebody had kicked me in the chest. At first it didn't really register what had happened, but then I realized that what hit me was a full, large whiskey bottle. It actually landed on the neck of the Duck, on the fifteenth fret, and the impact was so hard that the wood cracked. This was a maple neck, a very hard wood, so you can imagine the force that would be needed to crack the wood. And the fret itself was pushed in at the center so that it was now in a V shape. If my fingers had been there at that moment, I would've been in the hospital with my hand in a cast.

Naturally, I let the audience have it: I said exactly what I thought of this ridiculous behavior from a so-called fan, who had started some fighting down in front and nearly caused a full-scale riot. Not a pretty scene. But I somehow managed to get away unscathed that time. Sometimes drunken people do dangerous things. It's one of the hazards of the job.

In terms of dangerous gigs, Indonesia is one of the most extreme places I think I have ever played. We played at a huge outdoor arena that was like a soccer stadium that could accommodate almost 150,000 people. We were the headlining act and had just gotten set up to play when a drenching monsoon rainstorm blew in, raining sideways into all the equipment, so of course everything died: there was no sound, no wiring, nothing. We had to stop the show, obviously.

But there was a huge unhappy crowd out there that didn't understand what was going on and why it looked like we were getting ready to leave. The backstage crew of locals told us to get out of there quickly, before there was a riot of some kind. They told us, "Get out of here and go hide, don't even go back to the hotel you were in. If the promoters find you, you're dead meat." You can believe we followed his advice and didn't wait around to find out what was happening with the canceled show.

That wasn't my only close call in Indonesia. In 1992, I played a concert in Jakarta at a huge soccer stadium, with more than a hundred thousand people in the stands and filling the entire field in front of the stage. Now, this was during a period of a lot of civil unrest in the country, and the government wasn't stable. In hindsight, we were taking a chance doing such a huge public concert when there was political upheaval going on, but anyway, there we were. For security at this big event, there were two armed groups, the army and the government police force, which were rivals. One side of the stadium was guarded by the police, and the other side was guarded by the army. I found this out later; during the show we had no idea about any of this.

Halfway into the show we heard some loud pops, which I assumed were firecrackers. When I had played in Puerto Rico, for example, the fans were continually setting off firecrackers during the concert to show their excitement and appreciation, so I just assumed it was the same kind of thing.

Suddenly the bass player ran up to me and screamed in my ear, "You wanna stop? We gotta stop!" I was thinking, "What the fuck?" and he pointed out to the sea of people filling the field of the stadium. A huge section of this mass of people had begun to move off to one side like it was being shoved by an invisible force, and then I saw that there were people bleeding and falling down, many of them injured and panicked and getting trampled on as they were trying to get out of the way.

And then I realized what that popping noise was: the army and the police were firing at each other, *across* the crowd of people in the middle. Not only that, my sound guy and my lighting guy were positioned in a tent on scaffolding in the center of the field, right in the line of fire. They managed to get out of there safely, but it was possibly the most surreal concert setting I have ever played in.

Being onstage is sometimes like being a live target. In Puerto Rico, the fans threw firecrackers at us, and in Russia it was coins, which actually hit Joe Lynn Turner in the head. He was so pissed, but nobody in the audience gave a shit—that was just how they behaved, going completely crazy and out of control at a rock show. My father, the big imposing military man, got up on the stage and yelled at them in Russian, and that stopped it right there. We didn't get another thing thrown at us.

All kinds of weird things can happen when you're on tour. I've traveled the world many times over, and I just have to say God bless America. It's always a relief to get back.

On a purely physical level, things began to slowly improve when I moved to Miami in the winter of 1988. There's something about the light and the smell of the ocean and the whole vibe of the place that I found uplifting. I don't think a loss like I experienced when my mother died is something you ever fully get over, but you adjust to it somehow and get on with your life. You distract yourself. Miami was good for that.

Shortly after I settled in Miami, I saw a car dealership on one of the main highways through Miami, Biscayne Boulevard, and there was a row of Ferraris. I was drawn in there like a magnet. I looked the cars over, and it was love at first sight, plain and simple. I wanted a red one, but they didn't have any, so I was about to walk out when the salesman told me to come look at a particular black one, which was the Boxer model Ferrari. I sat in it, and that was that. I bought it on the spot.

Fans often ask me why I'm so obsessed with cars, and especially Ferraris. When I was growing up, my brother had some cool cars, but I didn't really get into them much because my all-consuming passion was my guitars. But when I got to Los Angeles, I quickly discovered that nobody took the subway or train like I'd done in Sweden. If you wanted to go anywhere in L.A., you had to have a car.

The first car I owned in L.A. was a Cadillac Coupe de Ville, a convertible. It was fun to drive around, but it wasn't really what I wanted. What I really wanted was a sports car. The first sports car I had was an MGB, then a Triumph, and eventually a Jaguar XKE, which was a really sick car. That was the one I wrecked in 1987. After I left L.A. I lived in New York and a few other places, and I didn't have a car. But when I moved down to Miami, it was the same situation as in L.A.: if you wanted to go anywhere, you had to have a car. So I got a Ferrari.

That was more than twenty years ago. Eventually I sold the black one and got what I'd really wanted in the first place: a red 308 GT Spider with four twin Weber carburetors, which is such a beautifully designed, amazingly tight machine. I have a total love for perfectly designed precision instruments—which is why I also love Rolex watches—so that once I had driven a Ferrari, everything else was a joke. No comparison. I have several different classic model Ferraris now, and I am totally immersed in their mystique: their history, maintenance, design, and everything else there is to know about them.

I much prefer the classic models, because the brand-new ones are mass-produced by Fiat. Before Enzo Ferrari died in 1988, all the cars were designed and approved by him, which makes them highly exclusive. They're like Picassos—only so many exist. For example, my 1989 red Spider has a vehicle identification number that's only five digits long. Only 710 of that particular model were made. It's a ragtop, rosso corsa red with a tan leather interior in mint condition. It's absolutely gorgeous.

But after Enzo died, they started making cars like hamburgers on an assembly line, and the design became less distinctive, less Ferrari-esque and more like other sports cars, such as Porsche. The newest designs don't look at all like a Ferrari to me. I much prefer the classic models, which have a timeless design. Yes, they are ridiculously fast and amazing to drive, but that's not the only reason to love these cars. To me, it's the whole aura around it—the mystique of the thing—that puts it in a class by itself. I like the

Porsche very much—I have one right now. It's a very nice car—but it is also mass-produced, which immediately takes it out of the class of exclusive GT cars.

History buff that I am, I read everything I could about Enzo Ferrari and how he began his *Scuderia Ferrari* (Ferrari Stable, his racing team). Its history is full of fascinating stories, like how Enzo created the Ferrari emblem, the *cavallino rampante*, or rearing horse. The original emblem belonged to Count Francesco Baracca, who, in World War I, became one of the first flying aces. It was the emblem he put on the sides of his plane. He won thirty-four dogfights before he was shot down, and his mother, Countess Paolina, kept the emblems as a remembrance.

Enzo Ferrari was a race car driver for Alfa Romeo in the early 1900s, and after winning a very famous race held in Ravenna, Italy, in 1923, he met the countess. To reward him, she gave him something unique: the canvas from the plane, a yellow field with a black rearing horse on it, which represented the Italian cavalry. In the 1920s and 1930s, he put this emblem on the side of the Alfa Romeos he was test-driving and racing, and in 1947 it became the official Ferrari emblem, with the letters *S* and *F* added for *Scuderia Ferrari*.

In the early 1960s, Ferruccio Lamborghini, a rich tractor maker from the same farming town (Modena, Italy), bought one of Ferrari's cars and copied it, creating a car that had every feature of the Ferrari—such as the V12 engine, gated gearshift, independent suspension, and disc brakes all around—without actually being one. If you want an analogy from music, it's sort of like the difference between an Ibanez guitar and a Stratocaster. The Ibanez has every feature of the Stratocaster—same double cutaway, tremolo, pick guard, side tuning key, bolt-on maple neck, and so on. The Lamborghini is certainly a beautiful car, but is it original? No. Lamborghini never entered a race with it, unlike Enzo, for whom racing was a passion.

It was with that absolute passion for racing that Enzo developed and produced his cars. He *was* the company: it was his vision, no one else's. He also surrounded himself with the top engineers, designers, and such. When he died, Fiat bought a sizable share of the company and began to make cars differently, with a different assembly process.

In 1993, Fiat came out with a new car called the 355. I have a couple of convertible ones. It's a nice car, no doubt, but in my mind it can't compare to the classics from the early years. If you took all the models from 1947 to 1993, you'd discover that the company made more 355s than all those others put together. As much as I love the Ferrari, if it's later than 1989, it's not pure Enzo.

I was in the Ferrari factory last year. I looked the managers right in the eye and said, "You've really disappointed me. You don't even make a manual Ferrari anymore." I recently bought a 2006 360 Spider, rosso corsa red, of course, with a tan leather interior; it's superb and only slightly less magical than the vintage ones. Mine is one of 10 percent with a manual gearbox. In any other car, an automatic transmission is fine. But a Ferrari *has* to have a stick shift. The ones without a clutch are for pussies.

My mechanic, Tim Stanford, who's like the king of Ferraris, claims that if you drive one of the classics made thirty years ago, you can keep it tuned and running perfectly. But if you tried to drive one of the 1990 or later models, it will not even begin to hold up for thirty years. You'll have to replace every part on it to keep it on the road. And as soon as you buy it, it begins to depreciate in value. But the value only goes up for the ones from the 1980s that are in great shape, because not only does the engineering and assembly make these cars a work of art, they were produced in limited numbers. Very few of each model were built: for the earliest models, only a hundred or at most five hundred were ever made.

I have both the American and the European editions of the 1985 308 QT Spider. They both have a red exterior, a tan interior, and basically the same body shape, but beyond that, they're not the same. I have owned many Ferraris throughout the years—Testarossas, Mondials, Boxers, GTOs, 328s, Dinos, 355s, and, of course, 308s—and I love them all. The other one I have is the 360 Spider (with a manual six-speed transmission!), which is such an amazingly smooth car to drive, even if it's a newer one. All of them have very low mileages, so, in Ferrari terms, they're like new.

These cars are like the Stradivari of violins. I have a real love for something that is beautifully and perfectly designed and engineered, whether it's a car or a watch or a guitar. It's the level of excellence, plus the history behind it, that attracts me.

In 1989, I formed a completely new all-Swedish band and recorded *Eclipse*. The next year, a compilation, *The Yngwie Malmsteen Collection*, was released, finishing out my contract with Polygram. Nigel negotiated a nice contract with Elektra for 1992's *Fire & Ice*. That album was huge in Japan. In fact, it debuted at number one on their charts and went gold and platinum outside the United States. Everything looked like it was on the upswing.

I also got married for the first time in 1990, but it didn't even last a year. In retrospect, I can see why it was doomed to failure from the beginning, but I can also see why I felt the need to be married at that time. Maybe I was trying to fill the hole in my heart left by my mother's death, but there were other reasons, too. I had just moved into an estate I'd bought, and I felt like settling down. I even envisioned having my own little family. Unfortunately, the person I chose wasn't buying into that vision, so of course it didn't last long.

FASTER THAN THE SPEED OF LIGHT

There really wasn't a dominant male figure in my household when I grew up. I don't count my older brother—he was more annoying than anything else, although I loved him, of course. But there were plenty of times when we'd go at it with each other. He made me scrappy and not afraid to defend myself, which I think was a good thing. When he died, it was awful. I really missed him, but that was later, after I'd moved to the United States. In my own household growing up, the dominant personality was my older sister, Lolo.

She was six years older than I was. Most of her friends who came to our house were older, too, and just hanging around them forced me, in a way, to act more mature and serious than I was for my age. And there were my mom and my grandmother, who were very influential in shaping my attitudes and behavior when I was young. They were always there around me, so I learned extreme respect for women. They took care of me, provided for me, and were intellectual and artistic mentors as well.

So I grew up with an expectation of how to treat women—I've always been a one-woman man, always. I've had an extreme reputation for being a party animal in my early days in L.A., but that's not what I'm talking about. In a relationship, I've always wanted to be dedicated to one woman instead of playing around. There were periods, of course, when I wasn't attached to one woman. I mean, when I went on tour with Ted Nugent at nineteen years old, things could be pretty wild.

I didn't take up the guitar to get laid, as many rock musicians will tell you they did, but whenever I was on tour, women were falling all over me. It was quite a contrast to my earlier years. When I was a teenager in Sweden, girls liked me and thought I was cool, but I didn't figure out until I got to L.A. that they'd been hitting on me. I was just so freaking serious as a teenager in Stockholm that I was pretty much oblivious to the fact that they were flirting and stuff like that.

Then I left for the United States, single and available. It was good timing, because Alcatrazz went out on some really big tours with people like Ted Nugent, Eddie Money, Heart, Loverboy, and Triumph, and I saw what the groupie scene was really like. I mean, at that time Nugent was the man, and the audience would always be at least 80 percent screaming girls. Women everywhere. I was a little overwhelmed at first, but it didn't take me long to fit right in.

There were some things I couldn't bring myself to do, like the way certain band members would chat up these groupies, telling each one, "Oh, you're my soul mate, I've never met anyone like you, you're the only one for me" kind of crap. It really turned me off to even think of lying to somebody like that. Stringing somebody along with a phony line like that really disgusted me. I may have sown my wild oats along with the others, but I never did it under false pretenses like that. And whenever I had a steady girl, I didn't screw around—it's just not in my nature to play the field. I've always been single-minded that way. If I'm committed to a relationship, that's it—no fooling around on the side. And I expect my partner to do the same. If not, then that's the end of it right there.

When I first moved to Miami, I went to a huge nightclub called Button South, which isn't there anymore. But at the time, it was the place to be if you were a rocker. I could not believe the number of women who hit on me simply because I had long hair and looked like a rockstar. It still seemed quite bizarre to me, because that wasn't even remotely the reason I had pushed myself so hard to become a musician. I can't say that I chased any of them away, but my preference was always to have one steady girlfriend. I tended to have long-term relationships even though they didn't last.

The first time I decided to get married, I guess it was a desperate attempt to stabilize myself: to create a stable, home-centered life that would offset the craziness of the rock scene I worked in. During the time frame of 1989–1990, which was toward the end of the *Odyssey* tour and during all of the *Eclipse* tour, I was completely wild and out of control, especially where women were concerned. Half the time I didn't know what the hell I was doing. When we were on the *Eclipse* tour, I'd tell the crew that when I got offstage, there had better be some chicks on the bus, or the bus wouldn't take off. It pains me to say this now, because that was so much the opposite of my true nature, but it just shows you how far I'd fallen by then. The only one worse was Joe, with his smarmy lovey-dovey pickup lines.

Eventually, though, I started getting sick of the constant parade of women, which didn't turn me on at all. I thought this behavior was really ridiculous and decided that if I got married, it would settle me down: I could have a family and a stable place to come home to.

But the first girl I married was a fan from Sweden whose place I ended up at one night. I passed out there, or whatever—it's hard to remember now, after so long—but I do remember very clearly waking up and seeing posters of me all over the walls, so I copped a clue that she was a groupie of mine. I stayed in touch with her off and on, and it was about that time, around 1990, that I bought the mansion in Miami. Being a homeowner for the first time made me feel like it was about time I got married and tried to settle down somewhat, and for some reason I chose her.

At the same time, she had aspirations of launching a singing career, and I helped her. She then got a hit single in Sweden and decided she wanted to be a pop singer. Our schedules never coincided, and she really didn't live in the house in Miami, so after eleven months we called it quits. I had had girlfriends in high school for longer. I was disillusioned with her, but I still felt hopeful about eventually finding the right person and having a good marriage.

That first one, you might say, was a "practice" marriage. Then I tried it again, and it was the worst mistake of my life. She was a groupie, too, but ten times worse. I was really doing the whole rock 'n' roll thing. She came on the bus in Arizona during those days when I wouldn't let the bus leave unless there were some groupies on it. Obviously, that's not somebody you marry. I found out the hard way. That was a nightmare altogether.

Emotionally and mentally, life with my second wife was a constant drama from one extreme to the next. I should have known better and followed my instincts that told me not to go through with the marriage. Every time something was bad, I would try harder hoping things would change. I was always hoping that if I was kinder, bought her anything she wanted, take her around the world, things would change. She just became worse. I finally came to the realization I needed to get out of this mess.

She wrecked my cars. Then she wrecked the cars that I kept on buying for her. She would get drunk; the cops arrested her for drunk driving. Each time I would try harder and buy her another new car, she would once again destroy the vehicle while she was drunk and/or high. When she was home, she would create such havoc. One day I had to break down a door to make sure she did not get a gun loaded. God knows what she would fucking do. She tried to put a 9mm clip in a .45, so obviously nothing happened, but still. I had to break the door down to make sure she did not get the right clip in the right gun. To add to my nightmare, I later found out there was not one guy she did not sleep around with behind my back. She cheated and lied all the time, ever since we got together.

I found out lying came natural to her. She would come home at five in the morning drunk and high on something, dressed like the town whore. When I asked her where she had been, she would try to physically attack me, then threaten to call the cops, saying, *"Who do you think they will believe, little me or gigantic you? I will tell them you beat me. You don't want to spend the night in jail, do you?"* This was an ongoing scenario: she would physically attack me, then threaten to call the cops on me. Well, one day, in Los Angeles, that is exactly what happened. In a hotel, shitfaced, she started attacking me, then said *"Watch me call the cops on you,"* and she did. I just sat there shaking my head in disbelief. The police arrived and, the next thing I know, she attacked the cops, and they arrested her. Her threats backfired; she was dragged away kicking and screaming. When she came out of jail the next day she threatened to ruin my reputation, by saying I did bad things to her. Since I was famous and well known, she could spread all the dirt she wanted to, and the media would eat it up. She knew the love-hate relationship the media had with me, and she knew anything bad she had to say would be believed and, most importantly, would put her in the limelight she so craved.

One day while I was recording in Criteria Studios she smashed into two cars, ran in and, without a word, physically attacked me, actually bit my arm. I was rushed to the hospital where I had to get a tetanus shot. To add insult to injury, while we were still married, to my shock and embarrassment, I found out she became a stripper in a well-known club. You could imagine my humiliation when my friends confronted me with the news that they saw my wife stripping naked while I was composing music at home. It all became very clear: I truly was the unhappiest man in the world with this nightmare of a woman. I needed to get out of this hell and fast.

Her mother made things even worse. Many readers will know that she had me arrested for abusing her daughter, which had never happened. I was cleared of all charges, but it was still very bad. I tried to block out a lot of it by staying wasted most of the time. That entire marriage was like a bad dream.

April, my third and current wife, was the one I'd been looking for—it just took us some time to finally get together. When I first met her, it was in England in the 1990s at a disco. She was only fifteen or sixteen then, but I didn't know that. She had such an incredible presence, even for somebody that young, that she just stood out from the crowd. Back then, I was one wild and crazy guy, not very well under control. I tried to hit on her, but she turned me down flat. She wasn't that sort of person. She wouldn't give me her number, but she asked for mine instead. Eventually she called me and I asked her out to dinner. I figured that one date would be the last time I would see her.

Six years later, by sheer coincidence, we met again in London. April was hanging out with A-listers, attending a private opening at a hotel art gallery. She was in the modeling industry—a whole different world. The event happened to be at the same hotel I was staying in. I was in London for that one day only, and she apparently decided to attend the event at the very last second. The way the story goes, she was at the event, got bored and decided to look out of the window. At that very moment, I happened to be walking in to the hotel. She walks out and says, "Hello stranger—it has been a long time, hasn't it?" The attraction between us was very clear. What are the odds of that happening? I guess we were meant to be, because we've been together ever since.

In January 1993, Nigel died very suddenly of a heart attack. At the time of his death, Nigel had complete control over the business end of my career: my music companies, record deals, bank accounts, and all my expenses. He made sure my bills were paid and the house maintained—I mean, he took care of everything. With him gone, I realized that I didn't know how to manage any of that stuff. Shortly afterward, I got dropped from Elektra (as did a number of other rock musicians when the grunge craze moved in).

Once again, I had no manager and no record deal. And then an old friend from my Polygram days showed up on my doorstep.

Jim Lewis came to see me at my house in Miami. He just showed up on my doorstep unannounced and proceeded to make himself available to me. He had heard about Nigel's death, and we talked about the possibility of him becoming my manager. He knew all of my history, of course, and was quite aware that in terms of business, I was more than willing to turn complete management of my affairs over to someone else and never pay attention to what he was doing.

Jim was there at the right time, offering to help me sort out my affairs and everything else Nigel had been doing. I'd known Jim since I was twenty years old, so I trusted him. I was more than happy to let him take charge of the business side of things. In fact, I thought he was the perfect choice to take over for me.

I didn't change the way anything was done, in terms of financial control, I just shifted it all from Nigel to Jim. And as much as I didn't want to see it then, I realize now that all of his efforts at making me successful were just so he could steal more money. I don't believe he really ever had my best interests at heart, such as whether a particular deal would be good for my long-term career or whether there was any investment being made in my future. Although I was glad to see him when he reappeared in my life after Nigel's death, I honestly don't believe that he came with any good intentions.

When Jim took over as my manager, the American market was very slow for melodic or guitar-based rock. In fact, I didn't have a U.S. deal for most of the 1990s (but all the albums I recorded during that time were eventually released in the States on Spitfire Records in 2000). Japan was a huge market for that kind of thing then, and especially for me. To his credit, Jim negotiated a very lucrative multirecord deal for me with Pony Canyon, which was part of Fuji. Not to his credit, however, he set things up so that the enormous sums of money were paid not to me, the artist, but directly to him. I didn't know this, of course, until years later.

Jim was always looking for a new angle that would bring in more money. I was already getting paid major sums per album from my Japanese label, but he'd say something like "Let's put out an EP [extended play, a recording that's longer than a single but shorter than an album]; that's another couple hundred grand" or "Let's go do a tour in Japan; that's another [so-and-so]."

It was ridiculous how much money was to be made in Japan at that time, while there was really nothing in the United States. The market for music in the States was all downer grunge stuff, anti-guitar skills, anti-stage presence, anti-everything that the 1980s had been. But in Japan it was a whole different scene. My biggest-selling album ever was the Japanese release of *Fire & Ice*, which went double-platinum in one day, and *The Seventh Sign* and *Magnum Opus*, which were multiplatinum sellers as well.

Those last two albums and other deals, like EPs and compilations, were negotiated by Jim with Pony Canyon. He also used to take advances from the publishing companies that held the rights to the sheet music, often in the hundreds of thousands of dollars. There was an amazing amount of money being made, and once again, I was only dimly aware of just *how* much and *where* it was all going.

A number of people warned me about him after I let him take over, but I wasn't seeing him from an outsider's perspective. I was still thinking of him from the perspective of when I was twenty years old and with Polygram. I mean, I knew that in general, managers in the music industry had a bad reputation for being slimeballs and for screwing people over—hell, I'd had my own version of that with Andy Trueman—but I didn't think Jim would treat me that way, because he was an old friend.

Little did I know how much he used that friendship and trust to cheat me out of millions that I earned from record deals, royalties, publishing rights, touring—you name it. The longer he was my manager, the more the people around me tried to tell me something wasn't right, because he held the purse strings and access to the credit cards and bank accounts.

I'm sure now that part of what convinced him he could get away with stealing from me so blatantly was that he had seen how Andy had done it to me so easily years ago. Managers like that can spot a target a mile away. They think, "This kid can only play the guitar and doesn't know shit about how the business works—it'd be very easy to rob a naive artist like that blind." As with Andy, it nagged at the back of my mind that Jim seemed to be living very high off the hog—again, I was his only big artist—but I never called him on it until six or seven years later, when I found out directly from the Japanese industry people exactly how much they'd been paying out and to whom—not me, apparently. A lot of that money had been hidden in bank accounts abroad or had been sheltered in other ways, but by then I had no hope of recovering it all.

The first album Jim was involved with was *The Seventh Sign*, which came out in early 1994, shortly after my second marriage. Jim was highly opposed to me getting married again, and, as it turned out, for once he was right. Again, I'd made a wrong choice, and the emotional toll it took on everyone involved was pretty high.

At that same time, though, my career was moving ahead, and I was just starting to get the construction of a state-of-the-art studio in my house under way. It was a large investment of money, but it was intended to save on the cost of recording once it was in place. At first I just created a place where all my guitars could be recorded. The drums were done at Criteria, the overdubs were done at my own studio, and the mixing was done back at Criteria.

That was a weird period for me, in terms of making the album. I had to put the drums down afterward instead of first, which is backward from what I was used to doing. I recorded the guitars and bass to a click track (a kind of metronome), then put the drums on. I also didn't click with what Glixman was doing then, so I suggested he maybe take a hike for a while. Looking back, I have nothing bad to say about the guy, because I think the problems were more with me and the shit I was going through at the time.

The album turned out all right and has a couple of winners on it, like "Never Die" and the title track. And while I think there were a handful of really strong songs on this album, they definitely weren't what the guys from Elektra were expecting as my follow-up to *Fire & Ice*. The grunge era was taking hold about that time, and having a grittier, grungier sound was all the rage.

Facing the Animal, which I did in 1997 with the late, great Cozy Powell, was basically created the same way as *The Seventh Sign*. That was the last rock album Cozy played on before his death in a car crash, and I wish I'd been able to do that album with him in my current studio—what a monster that would have been. In 1998, I added a 64-fader fully automated mixing console, so all my albums were mixed there from that point on.

Facing the Animal was kind of a turning point for me. To put it into perspective a little, I had just finished a huge tour promoting the *Inspiration* album, going to a lot of different places all over the world, like Thailand, all of Europe, all over the United States, and Japan. The last leg of the tour was in Britain. I was scheduled to play with my own band at a club called Mean Fiddler/Astoria 2 in London and then the following night in the Wembley Arena with a pickup band of some big names, including Cozy, Neil Murray of Whitesnake, and Spike England, who was playing keyboard for Queen. I went to Mean Fiddler/Astoria 2 for a rehearsal and was really excited to be in the company of Cozy, who was like a god to me on the drums. We hit it right off, and were laughing and sharing all the interests we had in common, like Rolexes. The sound check for the Wembley show was great, all kinds of well-known players were there, and the vibe with Cozy was just really good.

We played the show, which was fantastic, and the legendary Hank Marvin came into the dressing room after the show and said to me in his laid-back way, "Nice job, son." Hank Marvin, for those who don't know, was an amazing Stratocaster master from the early 1960s, and for him to take the trouble to do that for me meant a lot.

I was hanging out with Cozy, and the camaraderie was just great. I asked him whether he was interested in coming back to Miami to record some tracks for my next album, and he immediately agreed. It took me a few minutes for the gravity of that request to sink in, but once I realized that the great Cozy Powell had just agreed to play on my album, I can tell you, I was pretty damn excited.

I got back to Miami and soon had a bunch of songs and ideas for more songs under way. Jim brought in Chris Tsangarides to engineer the album. I had a couple of instrumentals I was thinking of putting on the album, but Chris said no, there shouldn't be any instrumentals on this one because the next album, *Concerto Suite*, would be the ultimate instrumental. I agreed that he had a point.

When Cozy got there and listened to the demo for *Facing the Animal*, he was all over the slower stuff and raving about the ballads. He kept telling me, "You got to do the slow stuff, man." People may not believe it, but he was very much responsible for the song choices for that album. And I wasn't about to tell him he was full of crap for wanting it that way. I actually was pleased that here was my hero getting so into my music that he was thinking about which songs should be on the album.

There was a song called "Another Time," which was a really commercial track that had a riff I had come up with in 1989; it ended up becoming one of the tracks because of him. I allowed

Cozy to really influence a lot of the shape and spacing of that album. I'm sure that's one of the reasons that album had such commercial success. He also persuaded me to write two ballads for that album.

The actual making of that album went very smoothly and took no time at all, compared to a lot of the others. We were just in and out of the studio in no time, it seemed. It was very professionally made, and a lot of hooky riffs gave it a more commercial vibe. It had some of my best ballad writing—for example, "Like an Angel," which was written for April. That's another reason I mark this as a transition album, because that's when she came into my life and started to wake me up and rescue me. It was also the last album for which I didn't write *all* the lyrics.

Facing the Animal also had a couple of songs that revealed in a nutshell what I felt about the whole record industry. "Casting Pearls before Swine" pretty much says it all, because that's what I'd been doing for most of my career. I'd pour my heart and soul, my blood, sweat, and tears, into an album, only to have the record company put it on the back burner or at the bottom of its list. Just make the album and shelve it, thanks. I was very bitter about that for many years.

Thank God I don't have those kinds of worries now. But earlier, especially in the 1990s, when the rock scene was so bad, I felt very angry and frustrated and screwed over a lot of the time—and even before that, too. I still believe that albums like *Trilogy* and *Odyssey* should have been number one hits, but they got really sidelined by Polygram, which was interested only in heavily promoting the two or three top acts.

I'll never forget this. *Odyssey* had just been released, and we had one single out. I was sitting in a meeting with some of the record company guys, and the top guy says to me, "So when are you going back to the studio to make another album?" My jaw dropped, because here they had this very commercial rock album with at least half a dozen very radio-friendly cuts that with just a little bit of promotion could have easily become hits on the radio and on MTV. I yelled at him, "What are you, a fucking musical retard?"

That outburst might have had something to do with the way the company treated me later on. Case in point: *Trial by Fire*, the live album that came out of my tour of the Soviet Union, went virtually unnoticed, even though I had played to more crazy, rabid fans than any rock act that had ever been allowed in that country. I was very disgusted with Polygram, and when Nigel took over as my manager, I told him that he had to get me on a different label that would give me better support. That situation led to a sort of latency where shit would happen and then my disgust would show up later in a couple of songs.

As most people know, shortly before the tour for *Facing the Animal*, Cozy was killed in a car accident in England. That was a huge shock, because the night after we'd finished recording the album, we sat together in my kitchen, and I said, "Coz, I'm not asking you, I'm *telling* you to go out on the road with me." And much to my surprise, he said, "Yeah, I'll do it." He was so cool—I loved him. So the album was released, and we were setting up the rehearsal space for the upcoming tour. His tech was there, his drums were all set up, and I got a phone call. It was Cozy, and he was crying into the phone, apologizing profusely.

What had happened was that he'd flown into Miami, and while he was still at the airport he had gotten a call from his girlfriend. I don't know what they said, but he turned around and got right back on a plane to London. So it was a letdown, but you know, shit happens. The expectation was that when he had worked through whatever his problems were, he'd fly out and rejoin the tour. But the next phone call I got concerning Cozy was that he'd been killed.

When Cozy died, I felt like a light had gone out, but you know how it is: the show must go on.

Japan wasn't my only fan base in the 1990s. The first time I played in South America was in 1996 for the *Inspiration* tour, and I hadn't really known what to expect. But *oh my God*, when we got there, I could not believe the reception that was waiting for me. I truly had no idea there was such a large and fanatical fan base there.

The best way for me to describe what sets the South American fans apart is to compare them to a soccer crowd. They're so enthusiastic: they go totally crazy, dancing and jumping around, really over the top. When you play for a live audience you expect people to make some noise, but these fans were deafening. And they sang along—loudly—to all the songs, *even the instrumentals*. It was totally mad. There's a similar feeling you get when you go to Spain, but Rio de Janeiro, São Paulo, and Curitiba, Brazil; Santiago, Chile; and Buenos Aires, Argentina—those places were insane.

So I thought at the time, "If I do another live album, I'm recording it here." Energy from the crowd is crucial for a live album. When we went to Brazil in 1988 for *Facing the Animal*, making those shows into a live album was a no-brainer. The result was a double CD-DVD album called *Live!*

As live albums go, this one was way better than the one from Leningrad, from a production standpoint. The Russian fans were just as over the top, but the recording was much, much better in Brazil. We filmed one night, which is on the DVD, and recorded two nights. Occasionally there will be nights at concerts when you have to work hard with a crowd to get it to give something back, but believe me, that never happened at any of the South American shows. If anything, it was just the opposite. I was wondering whether the audiences were ever going to slow down. All in all it turned out very good with the exception of the complete lack of stage presence of the singer of the time.

I ended the 1990s with *Alchemy*. It was the last album I did under Jim Lewis' management, and in many ways it marked the end of an era for me. I was starting to move away from some of my bad old ways, and I was changing my pattern of putting an album together.

Sad to say, *Alchemy* was done in a really haphazard way. I hired Chris Tsangarides again to engineer the album, but he developed some personal problems I never understood, so I had to let him go right after the drums were tracked. Then I hired someone else to be the engineer and Tom Fletcher to do the mix, and eventually I think we ended up with a satisfactory album in spite of its shaky start.

The mind-set I brought into that album was to make the heaviest sledgehammer of a record possible. I told everybody I didn't want anything remotely commercial. It was intended to be a heavy metal shred-fest of unrelenting, over-the-top playing, and I think that was well accomplished. It also had some great lyrics taken from historical events and characters. I made a lot of effort and did a lot of research to write the lyrics for *Alchemy*, especially on songs like "Leonardo," and I was very adamant that I didn't want anyone but me writing any of the lyrics this time around.

Looking back, I realize that a lot of that decade was a dark time for me. I went through two divorces, my manager Nigel Thomas died, and then Jim Lewis came nosing around. I should have had my guard up, but at the time I just wanted to turn everything over to somebody else and immerse myself in my music. In hindsight, that wasn't such a good idea. I was still drinking like a fish, which didn't help anything, of course. During that period it seemed like everything I did was just digging a deeper hole for myself than I could ever get out of.

It's a funny thing about the 1990s: I'd been living in the United States for more than a decade, but I probably spent as much time in Japan as anywhere else during those years. I was in Japan at least two or three times a year, on tour or doing some other kind of publicity event, like promoting the theme song I wrote for Takada, a very famous wrestler over there. Japan was the place to be for melodic rock and guitar-based heavy metal, because the United States was busy being sidetracked by people who couldn't even tune their guitars and who looked like they were utterly miserable, with socks pulled down over their eyes. I wasn't about to change my style for that kind of crap, so I concentrated my efforts in a country where the fans were crazy about the kind of music I was playing.

ICARUS DREAM

Do you want to be a famous rock star, or do you want to be a great musician? To be a rock star often doesn't take any talent at all—it just takes being lucky.

In 2000, I built a bigger studio a couple of miles away from my house, in addition to Studio 308, the state-of-the-art recording/mixing facility I had built in 1995, where I could record drums. It had a control room and a sound stage, so from that point on I stopped using Criteria. I never had a guitar sound I was satisfied with until I built my own studio. The guitar sound I have now is just monstrous. It's like a jet plane taking off, a very big sound. I remember when I recorded *Fire & Ice*, a lot of those songs were meant to be built on a big guitar rig—songs like "All I Want Is Everything"—but when I listen to it now, it sounds like a little scratchy bumblebee or something.

That was also when I fired Jim and his accountants and started gathering evidence against them for a lawsuit.

Here's just one example of the kind of deception that had been going on. The last album I made while Jim was my manager was *Alchemy* in 1999. The idea was that it would be some kind of anniversary album and I would get a signing bonus for it. I later found out that the actual budget for the album was exorbitant and that the signing bonus was on top. Of course, the astronomical sum of that bonus was paid to accounts I didn't have access to and, in fact, didn't even know about until I hired some people to officially look into it. A lot of the money I made was spent on Jim's mansion up north and on his yachts, Lamborghinis, and lavish travel—just as Andy Trueman had done a decade earlier.

I did eventually manage to get some satisfaction, though. In 2009, I won my suit against the accountant who had set up the exclusive account that only he and Jim could access. My suit against Jim is still pending, but we believe the evidence shows that the number of dollars they'd embezzled is in the millions.

These days, my wife, April, manages everything. She has a great mind for business and is very creative in looking for ways to enhance my career. It's also impossible to intimidate her, so she's had no trouble interacting with music industry people on a daily basis. It's an enormous relief to have all of my finances and business dealings brought completely in-house, so together we know exactly where our money is, how it's invested, and so on. On that level, it's now a family business.

Here's the bottom line: when somebody else, no matter how well-intentioned he or she starts out, has control over all of your money, the devil will get into it one way or another. And if the person you allow to have this control has dubious intentions from the very beginning, then it's all over. You will lose everything until you put a stop to it. Almost all the managers and financial consultants I've had to deal with in the music business have been a little shady.

Artists, who are mostly not business-minded, are really easy marks for these predators, because if their goal is to become a really great musician, it's going to take all of their time and focus to perfect their art. And predatory managers and industry people can spot them a mile away—they always do. I don't think it's possible to be a brilliant businessperson *and* a brilliant musician at the same time. There are people who are less brilliant as artists but are really smart with money, and they don't get ripped off.

I'm often asked for advice on how to get started in the music business, and my answer is always another question: Do you want to be a famous rock star, or do you want to be a great musician? To be a rock star often doesn't take any talent at all—it just takes being lucky. But to become an amazing musician takes sacrifice and dedication, which means you must have someone else to run the business end of your career.

As bad as my financial situation was with Jim as my manager, some extraordinary music was produced during that time. Albums like *The Seventh Sign*, *Magnum Opus*, and *Facing the Animal* had some really good songs, but it wasn't rock music that made this period of my life so significant musically.

About the time I started to conceive of *Concerto Suite*, I was stepping out of the poisonous atmosphere of my second marriage and had started seeing April. Around that time I began to get a different kind of inspiration. Pieces of purely classical measures and themes were flowing into my mind in a continuous stream, and I felt an undercurrent of excitement, a feeling that something really big was ahead, although I couldn't imagine at the time exactly how groundbreaking it was going to be.

Before I talk about *Concerto Suite*, there's a distinction that needs to be made. *Concerto Suite* is not rock music with an orchestra added in the background, it's not rock songs rearranged for classical instruments, and it's not a classical theme played by a rock band. Many bands—Deep Purple, Kiss, Scorpions, Metallica, and a lot of others—have done all those approaches. I have nothing against that, and in fact I have done some of that myself, like performing a brief version of Bach's *Badinerie* on the *Fire & Ice* album. But as cool as all those styles are, they were never in my mind when I conceived the idea of *Concerto Suite*.

With *Concerto Suite*, I composed music completely in the classical mode, with the guitar taking the role of the classical solo instrument, just as if it were a violin—no rock rhythms or arrangements, no rock percussion, no rock lyrics. In other words, it was a very orthodox approach to a very unorthodox concept. I stepped totally into the world of classical music and created my own concerto. I knew it was risky—it was an act of bravery to do something like that, knowing I could be seen as a rock musician with very little official classical training who was invading the classical world on his own terms, a presumptuous move that was fairly unheard of.

The two biggest challenges were these: first, could I actually compose such a piece, and second, could it be performed so that it worked as purely classical music? I was really putting myself out there on both counts. Once I got started and was fully engaged in creating the music, I realized that this was a completely different kettle of fish from making music that was just classically influenced. There were no easy structures like an opening verse, a catchy riff, and a cool chorus. Not at all. The way I composed the movements for the concerto was that I had melodies and themes in my head that were designed to be performed with the guitar as the lead instrument. It was a good start. But what really came home to me once I got into it was that the orchestration and instrumentation for the various sections of the orchestra that surround the solo instrument are just as important, and in some cases more so.

For months I worked out the orchestration, the arrangement of every instrument in the orchestra. I must have immersed myself for ten months solid, at the very least, just composing and arranging. The process I used was fairly painstaking: I wrote note for note the lines for all the string, percussion, and wind instruments and the choirs in each movement of the concerto, and Mats Olausson, my keyboard player, sat with me in the studio, recording those lines with a patch for each instrument onto the multitrack recorder. We might, for example, spend an entire night working on just the oboes in a single section of one piece. I'd show Mats the theme, we'd put it on tape, I'd listen to it and alter it slightly, then I'd listen to it again and maybe add a counterpoint to that, and so on.

I spent a lot of time on the counterpoint of all the instruments, such as the woodwinds and the contrabass lines running underneath each section. And I really worked on the cadenzas, the free-form solos in which the lead solo instrument gets the chance to shine. Composers who were also performers would always improvise their cadenzas and a cappella parts while the rest of the musicians, the orchestra, had their parts scored out for them. That's what they did in those days. The spaces allotted for the soloist weren't always carved in stone.

That's why I always say, "Improvisation is the genesis of composition." To compose, you must be able to improvise. Bach, Mozart, Beethoven, Liszt, Paganini—all of them in performance would go into lengthy improvisations. We know this from looking at the written scores, where the space for the soloist is indicated but not written out. Sometimes a certain number of bars are shown, and sometimes not.

This was very common back then, but unfortunately most people don't know that. People think that classical music was carved in stone note for note by the composer. But the fact is that so-called classical music was *popular* music when it was written, and it was open to a lot of variation in performance. (This fact has driven my own performance style throughout my career as well.)

The actual orchestration of my entire suite—the *arrangement*—was done like this, long before the score for the piece was written down by someone else. Every instrument, every part in its complete form, was put on separate channels on a multitrack tape, so it was exactly what you heard on the album, but with sampled orchestral sounds. Obviously, however, the live orchestra members would need the printed score in front of them before they could record it, so David Rosenthal was hired to transcribe my arrangement, which is very different from creating the arrangement itself.

The reason I make such a big deal of this is that many people got the impression that Dave was brought in to arrange the orchestra around my guitar solos, and that is absolutely not the case. Everything from counterpoints to trills was written first by me, synthesized by Mats, and then transcribed to print by Dave. This process took a very long time, but finally we had a full orchestral score that I could take to Prague for the recording with the live orchestra, the Czech Philharmonic.

I was very lucky to have the conducting services of Yoel Levi, who at that time was the conductor of the Atlanta Symphony Orchestra and whose son was a big fan of mine. When I played for Yoel some of the sections I had recorded in my studio, he was pretty amazed, and it wasn't hard to convince him to join the project. I was glad I had someone of his experience, because when we got to Prague, we were told we would have just three days with the

Czech Philharmonic to record the whole thing. We had three hours in the morning, from nine to noon, then a break for lunch, and then we resumed from one to four. That's just eighteen hours all together to record everything, including the choir. If you think that sounds daunting, you don't know the half of it.

A lot of time was spent trying to figure out how to prevent my electric guitar from overwhelming the orchestral instruments in the hall where the recording was to take place, and finally it was decided to record all the orchestral parts with me playing live but not miked, then overdubbing my guitar parts back in the studio in Miami for the actual album. We got that sorted out, and then we began the first dry run with the orchestra. It was an utter disaster. Everyone was nervous and tense, and these classically trained, old-school musicians from one of the oldest and most prestigious European orchestras simply did not know what to make of me. They were complaining that the lines I'd written were too fast or too difficult, had too many flats, or whatever.

I was thinking, oh my God, here my life's work is going to be utterly demolished in front of my eyes. It got so bad at a couple of points that it was turning into the comedy hour or something. I was utterly freaking because this was it; there wasn't going to be a second chance. I thought, "If we can't make it work, and it bombs, I won't be given the chance to try it again later. The whole idea will just be written off as an ambitious mistake."

Yoel was trying to calm me down, telling me, "Don't worry, they're still getting used to the piece, just give it a little time," and I was saying, "We don't *have* fucking time." We had to rewrite some of the violin parts because the arpeggios were just too fast for them. They weren't used to playing like that for a whole movement. Yoel pretty much kept it together and let me do the freaking out. Even though this event was during a period when I was still drinking, at that particular moment I was stone-cold sober.

I didn't want to appear in front of all those musicians impaired in any way.

We broke for lunch, and the musicians all went down to a little pub in the cellar of the hall. I followed them down there and discovered that they were knocking back huge steins of beer one after the other, as though they were done with the job. I mean, their drinking was putting *me* to shame. I started freaking even more, thinking, "What the hell? No, you're *not* done yet." I was panicking, because I was sure that whatever they would do when we started up again would sound like total shit.

Instead, they returned for the afternoon session and nailed everything. Once they got loosened up and had decided that I was okay, we had smooth sailing. You know how when orchestra members want to applaud after a session, they will tap their bows on their music stands in unison? When that afternoon session was over, they did that for me. I was overwhelmed. I can't tell you what an immense relief it was. I was at last one of them and not some madman outsider.

By the time we were done, we had several takes of each movement, and the recording technicians there in Prague edited the best ones together into a single seamless recording of the orchestra for the entire concerto, which is how they routinely produce classical records. Then I took that master tape back to Miami to add my guitar to it. And believe me, I took my time doing it, because I had no intention of rushing that part of it. I would spend a couple of days just getting one movement perfected by playing it over and over, getting really familiar with every nuance of it. I do read music, from having taken piano and cornet lessons as a kid, but I prefer to play by ear and improvise, so sight reading isn't something I do very often. But I could follow the score and tell where I was in each section.

I must admit that I was exhausted, mentally and physically, by the time we'd recorded *Concerto Suite*, because playing with a ninety-piece symphony as a soloist is an overwhelming experience. It was almost like you have to be out of body in your concentration, because if you start to think about what you're doing and worrying about making a misstep, that's it—you will.

In composing and recording this album, it was critical for me to re-create the pulse and feel of the Baroque era, including the shimmering beauty of Antonio Vivaldi, the precision of Mozart and the Classical era, and the grandeur of Ludwig van Beethoven and the Romantic era. This is how I turned a very orthodox art form into an unorthodox final product: I accessed an array of different periods of classical music, which was not done by Bach, Vivaldi, or even Pyotr Tchaikovsky, for example. Those composers wrote music typical of the eras in which they lived and worked. In addition, they wrote for the instrumentation common to them, by which I mean Bach didn't have the full symphony orchestra that we expect to hear from the Romantic period onward, and in Tchaikovsky's day composers didn't often use the small stripped-down chamber orchestra of the previous centuries.

I designed the instrumentation and arrangement for *Concerto Suite* to be appropriate to the style within each section, yet with an overall Malmsteen vibe that would meld all the sections into a unified whole. The Sarabande, for example, is in the Baroque style, whereas the Fanfare is more symphonic and large, but both fit into the greater scheme of the suite.

Composing this music also gave me the opportunity to make use of a classical choir, a sound I've loved since I was a child because my mother sang in the famous Scola Cantorum, a choir founded centuries ago and still going strong today. Hearing the massive sound of those voices performing at high festivals like Christmas and Easter was a major influence that has been with me ever since. I was greatly moved by all those voices and the pipe organ filling the rafters of the church or the performance hall. The experience was very powerful and overwhelming, as it was meant to be in earlier times when villagers and townsfolk came to the cathedrals. It was very important for me to have real live voices for the choral parts of my concerto, not a synthesized chorus. This added yet another layer of complexity onto the project when it was time to record the album in Prague, because the choir could come in on just one day: the last one we were there.

Several years later, the record label, Pony Canyon, minus Jim Lewis, wanted to bring out a live recording of *Concerto Suite* with me and the New Japan Philharmonic, performing two nights in the Shibuya Orchard Hall in Tokyo. I agreed to do it as long as we could film both nights, essentially giving us two takes that we could use for the final product.

That turned out to be a hasty decision, and here's why. Once I make an album, I move on from it and never listen to it again. I just don't listen to my own stuff. This meant that I hadn't listened to *Concerto Suite* in at least three years. To be able to perfectly perform the whole suite in front of a live audience would mean relearning each movement practically from scratch, which wasn't going to be possible, since I was completely focused on the release of my next album, *War to End All Wars*, and was in the midst of a world tour for it.

In any event, the record label moved ahead with the project and lined up the New Japan Philharmonic, with conductor Taizo Takemoto (who turned out to be a miracle worker), and the orchestra obtained a copy of the printed score. Work was proceeding in Japan on the logistics for such a concert while I was completing the American part of the *War to End All Wars* tour and was doing the European stint.

By the time we got to Britain, the scheduled date for the live *Concerto Suite* performances was fast approaching, and I still had not been able to take adequate time to prepare for it. The last show of that tour was in Nottingham, England, only a few days away from the performance in Japan. As soon as the Nottingham show was done, I went straight to the airport, got on a plane, and headed for Japan. Anyone who's flown from England to Japan knows that it's a very long flight and you are in for some serious jet lag. I've done it enough to know that you don't even know who you are for a day or two after you land in Tokyo—it's that bad.

I got off the plane in Tokyo, stopped just long enough to drop my bags off at the hotel, and went straight to the concert hall for a couple of hours of rehearsal. This already was jet-lag hell, but it was nothing compared to what followed. I met Takemoto, the conductor, who turned out to be extremely good and very talented, but he didn't speak any English. Somehow I managed to convey my wishes to him, and I think he did an amazing job. He was just a really remarkable conductor who fully embraced the music and understood what needed to happen to bring his orchestra and me together.

That said, the enormity of what I was about to undertake was starting to feel like I was facing a firing squad. Here's what I was up against. Not only had I not even played the CD of *Concerto Suite* all the way through since its release, I had no idea how the New Japan Philharmonic had interpreted the score during its rehearsals without me. I had listened to the CD as carefully as I could on the flight over, but that was hardly enough. You might compare it to showing somebody a video of how to fly a plane and then putting him behind the controls and telling him to take off. Now I was faced with performing all twelve movements straight through with ninety-six other people, with virtually no rehearsals together, *and* being filmed playing it with them for the first time in front of an audience, all the while jet-lagged and sleep-deprived.

I told the representatives from the Japanese label that they absolutely must film both nights so we'd be assured of at least one good take for each movement, and they assured me that this would happen. Then I found out that they had arranged orchestral versions of my signature rock pieces, "Black Star," "Trilogy Suite," "Brothers," "Blitzkrieg," and "Far beyond the Sun," to also be played as encores during the performance. I decided that these guys must have infinite faith in me or else they must have been drinking way too much sake to expect all this with no rehearsals. Even in the best of circumstances, with *no* jet lag, this would have been a formidable challenge—especially when I heard the way they'd scored the rock songs for the orchestra.

The arrangements for these songs were all wrong. And as first-rate as the New Japan Philharmonic is, some of those passages were just too much for them and had to be rewritten. I especially remember the problems with "Blitzkrieg." The concertmaster (and arranger) had listened to my recording of it off the *Alchemy* album but couldn't pick out all the notes of the long arpeggios in order to write them down for the score. I was almost ready to lose it.

I told him, "Look, this arpeggio is an A-minor scale. It's not chromatic from C down to A; it's within the scale, and that's how it should be played." And they had the percussion all wrong for "Trilogy Suite"—the beat was completely different. Clearly, it was time to go back to the drawing board.

The concert hall in which this event was to take place was extremely elegant, and my dressing room had a grand piano in it. I sat at the piano with the concertmaster and played the tempo and the scales for him, and he made revisions all over the score. Poor guy, I really put him through the wringer. I had an interpreter there, but even so, my head was in outer space.

Maybe that was a good thing, because it prevented me from worrying to the point of paralysis. Instead, my mind just stopped trying to process what was going on and went into some weird kind of automatic pilot, totally focused on each detail in front of me. You need to have this fixed here, to play this there, to do this here, to not do this there, and to not question whether it will work—that kind of thing. With a rock show, anything goes, and you kind of expect to have an occasional fuck-up. But with a classical concert, the people who go to those shows expect perfection.

That's especially true for my lengthy cadenzas, in which the soloist improvises as the orchestra maintains the background, waiting for the score to resume—in those passages there is absolutely nothing to hide behind. But at the same time, if you try too hard not to screw up, you run the risk of becoming too careful and safe. I decided to throw caution to the wind and really go for it. No holding back. I was thinking, "If the stars align and it all falls together, I rule. If not, end of my classical career."

The concertmaster rewrote the score for all the encore pieces, staying up all night to do it. The next day, we assembled for rehearsal, and he had a handwritten copy of the revised score for all ninety-six members of the orchestra. My mind was blown yet again. We did some preliminary rehearsals on parts of the concerto, working things out and getting used to the revisions to the score. All the New Japan Philharmonic musicians were extremely good, and they caught on quickly to the changes.

My pieces also required a five-string contrabass that goes down to B-flat (the normal bass is tuned to E). The contrabass player was superb, and he cracked me up during rehearsal, because he was playing superfast arpeggios up and down, and then he stopped and said, "You know, I should get more money, because this is so many notes and too many flats. It's a lot more notes than I normally play." That was too funny.

Then we began serious rehearsals, playing the concerto straight through as if it were the real show. I said to myself, "Okay, this is it. Somehow this thing is going to happen." I had a music stand in front of me, and I'd made a couple of notes on the score during our morning rehearsal, like where there were an uneven number of bars in certain places, where there were key changes, and where there were certain types of segments.

Once again, Takemoto, the conductor, just rose to the occasion completely; for instance, at a *colla parte* segment, which means "follow the soloist," he had it down, totally. He had an uncanny ability to connect with me and transmit to the orchestra members the instructions they needed. He followed me like a hawk, and the ninety-six members of the orchestra followed him, and we all just flew together like one mind. I still get goose bumps thinking about it. You want to talk magic? That was it. It was the most surreal, wonderful, scary, and completely insane experience I've ever had.

I recall walking out on the stage of the concert hall for the first time just hours after getting off the plane and thinking, "How can I do this? How can I fucking remember the original arrangements and all the key changes and improvised cadenzas, on top of being nearly delirious from no sleep?" But even more unbelievable was the moment after the performance, when the audience gave me a standing ovation and I realized that in spite of all odds, I'd pulled this thing off, and it had been stupendous. And as I found out later, only one night had been filmed, so thank God it had all worked.

In my rock shows now, I frequently add the Fugue from the *Concerto Suite* to the playlist. I use the backing track from the Czech Philharmonic and play my part live. I insert it into my long solo segment after I've done a bunch of my wild playing: bouncing around the stage doing my dives and rock 'n' roll moves. Then I suddenly shift gears into the full-on classical shit. I love watching the audience when that happens. The fans' faces run a gamut of expressions: perplexed, shock, awe, amazement. I love it.

After the event in Tokyo, I played *Concerto Suite* live with the Taipei Symphony in Taiwan as part of a continuing rock tour. I performed the concerto one night in a big concert hall, and the next night in the same venue I played a rock concert with my band.

The concerto performance in Taipei went really well, too. That conductor had gone to the show in Tokyo so he could get familiar with the piece and how I played it. He was an extremely cool guy, a bit more laid-back than the Japanese conductor, and we had a lot of fun at the performance in Taipei. I did a dress rehearsal with the orchestra, and then we just went for it.

Perhaps I will do more live performances like that, but it would require scheduling the show a year or two in advance, because that's the lead time required to book a major orchestra. And I would have to learn the piece all over again. I won't say it would be easier to do now that I know what to expect, because it's a different adventure every time. But I am able to say with confidence, "I *can* do this."

As for ever doing an all-classical album again, I've written some sections and other pieces for guitar and orchestra that may turn into another album like that; but then again, they may show up on a rock album instead.

I have a lot of extremely classical bombastic stuff, with double bass drums, Carl Orff–type choruses, and such. Right now, I feel like that's something I can do later—it's not where my heart is right now. I'm very much in rock mode these days, and I will probably stay that way for some time to come. These days I feel very good—mentally and physically, very together—and I just really want to rock out.

There's no hurry to do another completely classical album. You can't rush that kind of composing. Writing and performing *Concerto Suite* was an overwhelming experience on many levels, but I was totally driven to do it at the time, to the exclusion of everything else. Let me just say that there's plenty of material waiting for me when I decide to go back into that mode.

LOOK AT YOU NOW

My music—contrary to those who may have
thought I was a flash in the pan—has staying
power. I believe that there will always be a
taste for music that's a challenge, that is complex
and has depth, and that can blow your mind
over and over again.

W hen I started out in my music career, things were done old-
school: you had to get on a big record label, and you needed
big management to get anywhere. Radio play ruled whether your
music lived or died, MTV video airtime was a must, and so on.
Now all that's gone.

In the 1970s and especially the 1980s, there was a required
sound, an expected style, and a formula you had to fit into. In
1991, the formula changed drastically when Nirvana became

popular. It you didn't fit *that* formula, you were out of luck. But get this: when the grunge formula played itself out, nothing else definitive took over. After the so-called Seattle Sound faded, there was nothing pushing it out of the way. Right now, there isn't a "sound" that everyone has to adhere to. And guess why? These days, radio play isn't required because there's YouTube and the Internet, and MTV is irrelevant: it doesn't focus on music videos the way it used to.

It used to work like this. You'd write a song like "Heaven Tonight" because that's what would get airplay on commercial rock radio. Your management would book a tour with a big-name band whose record company could afford to mount a big expensive tour. And you'd carefully craft a certain look and image, because that's what the record-buying public wanted to see.

These days, all that's out the window. Anything goes, and because there's no formula driving the rock music industry, just about anything has a chance of catching people's interest.

The entire 1990s was a wasteland for electric guitar players in the United States. If you knew how to tune your guitar, you were already too good. Maybe I exaggerate a little, but not much. Now, post-2000, things have changed. Anything goes, but also, what goes around comes around. A lot of what I'm hearing now on the rock scene is not new, although it may sound new to younger listeners who weren't even born when it was first hitting the airwaves.

Only now the airwaves are digital and everyone's listening to the music on their handheld devices connected to the Internet. It's a whole new ball game that has actually given new life to many styles and musicians who are being rediscovered. Of course, games like Guitar Hero and Rock Band have had a lot to do with that, which I find both gratifying and a little odd, because while these games give young kids the sensation of being an instant rock star, a lot of the music on these things is old. But it sounds cutting edge because it's new to the kids.

It used to be that when I'd go out, people would ask me, "Hey, dude, what band are you with?" But now they say, "Yngwie! Yeah!" That's all because of April's amazing knack for marketing, as well as YouTube, Guitar Hero, and Rock Band. Instead of just listening to whatever was served up on the radio, as in the bad old days, fans can now listen to whatever grabs their interest, and they're grabbing on to me in numbers I've never seen before. YouTube videos of me, legit and otherwise, get millions of hits daily. You couldn't buy that kind of mass exposure when you were depending on record companies to get promos of your stuff out to the public. Thank God those days are long gone.

I started to notice this transition during the 3G tour with Joe Satriani and Steve Vai several years ago, but it has escalated way beyond that now. Kids come right up to me and know who I am, and they want to show off licks to me. It's great.

I'm realistic, though. I know these things go in cycles. I remember being totally skeptical when the Internet first started to play a role in people getting their music out to their fans. I admit I fought it tooth and nail for a while, but now I recognize that it's the best thing that could have happened to me. I can't tell you how many times people come up to me with their cell phones, showing me a clip from some show I recently played, and within hours it's all over the Internet. I could never have dreamed in my wildest imagination that this kind of thing would happen. Needless to say, record companies don't have the same role as before. They are more like distributors now rather than totally molding an artist's career, from music to image to promotion, as they once did.

I guess this is a good thing in many ways, but it does feel weird to me that there's currently no well-defined sound that rules the airwaves and determines what record labels are looking for. It's all over the map. And let me tell you, quantity is not always better. This newfound freedom has resulted in a flood of noise glutting the Internet—I guess some of it is music. But there's a lack of filtering now, which the record companies used to do. I can't even come up with the name of a new band that has ushered in the next new sound. An analogy is the publishing industry: it's now very easy for anyone to self-publish a book, regardless of whether he or she can write anything worthwhile. The mechanisms are in place for an individual to do it. Same with music.

The freedom of access that everybody has now to anything that's digital has connected me to a whole new audience. It includes kids whose parents know me from the old days, but the kids are watching videos of me on their cell phones. Instant access. My music—contrary to those who may have thought I was a flash in the pan—has staying power. I believe that there will always be a taste for music that's a challenge, that is complex and has depth, and that can blow your mind over and over again. My music is real, it's from the heart, not manufactured as just a commercial venture. Fans have always said that they connect to it on a deeper emotional level. I can't tell you how many times fans have written to me or told me that when they were going through tough times, my music was what helped to pull them through.

With the Internet, I'm instantly connected to my fans, and new ones are finding me all the time. Whichever way the winds of change blow, you have to stand at the helm of the ship, so to speak, and stay the course. I've stayed true to my muse, regardless of what the critics have said I should do. I've heard it all before: "Oh, you'd better change what you're doing, because you'll become outdated." I've pretty much proved that my music is timeless, because lo and behold, after all these years, my fan base is growing, not shrinking. My music is all over the Internet, and I have no doubt that it will be played and copied for a long time to come.

I find it very cool that I have very young kids in my fan base who are just now discovering the style of music I play as well as my very dedicated approach to musicianship. They have very little knowledge of my history or how I developed the neoclassical style, so they approach what I do from a very different angle. In a way, you could say that it was to my benefit to be out of the spotlight during the 1990s in the United States. That is, the first type of guitar playing these kids probably grew up with is the very basic, unchallenging type of playing. To suddenly encounter my "Arpeggios from Hell" then blew their minds.

This illustrates another thing that's very different these days. Fans aren't pigeonholed the way they used to be. For instance, if you were labeled a heavy-metal fan, it meant you didn't listen to anything else, and record companies marketed to you as a very specific niche. That kind of thing doesn't exist anymore; there is so much out there, equally available to music fans, that there's no need to create rigid marketing cubbyholes. Everything blends into everything else on the Internet, which is now the major marketing tool for anyone in the business. I never thought I'd say that, but now it's true.

For me to give advice to someone trying to start a music career is pretty difficult. I can tell you what I went through to get where I am, but the whole career machine from the 1980s and 1990s is obsolete. It's gone. Today you can record a song on your home equipment and put it on the Internet for millions of people to download without ever having a manager or a record deal.

For someone like me, it's a new golden age. I can set up my own companies to record and distribute my music and market it any way I want—there's no right or wrong way anymore. And the freedom an artist has to follow his or her own path is pretty much unlimited. Distributors in the old mold have found that they must be much more flexible in dealing with clients and artists. In fact, their days are numbered. Physical music stores with racks and racks of CDs have been phased out all over the country, and online sources like Amazon and iTunes are now the major sources for music sales.

And you don't have to buy the whole album anymore. If you like just a few songs on an album, you can buy them and download them in seconds. That might work for other musicians, but it doesn't work for me. My albums are so versatile—there might be a song that's really bluesy followed by something that's all neoclassical—that by buying one song, you're really missing out on the flow of a whole musical work.

Probably the best advice I can give someone is to persevere in reaching higher levels for your own ability. For example, you can become a successful artist without being good—that's not hard to do. But if you want to become an extremely good musician, there's no shortcut for that. Do you want celebrity, or do you want respect? Perhaps you can have both, but it takes work, determination, and belief in yourself—and maybe some luck along the way.

There are two things you can't buy or manufacture: genuine charisma and talent. And both are essential if you hope to make the leap from so-so player or average musician to someone people instantly recognize and aspire to become like. By "charisma," I don't mean wearing makeup and flashy stage clothes; I mean "presence." When I think back to the 1980s and the whole "glam rock" look, I think, "Jeez, how corny." For a time, you could call yourself a rock star if you just looked the part. But that was a flash in the pan—there was nothing under the glam to sustain a career. Looking back, you can see that it's bedrock talent and ability that have allowed long-term careers for me and other musicians who were launched in the 1980s.

This current lack of a formula is good in one way and bad in another. The good part is that there's more allowance for creativity and the freedom to do what you want. But the downside is there's no direction at all, no music industry guidelines, nothing specific to aim for. Instead of being so intensely focused on a specific goal, as I was as a teenager, you run the risk of just going in circles, not doing much of anything.

What's important is to stick to your guns if you believe in what you're doing. I know I would not be where I am today if I had tried to change myself according to all the advice I got from critics and managers over the years. I knew what I wanted to do, in my own way, and that was that. I've been called arrogant for that attitude, but there's no point in trying to excuse yourself to anybody when you know that what you're doing is genuine. To try to change it would be phony.

In terms of where the music industry is headed, it seems like it will be even more fragmented in the future, with no definable style or fashion as it had in the past. I think it will be completely indefinable. I also wonder if the majority of music will even be made by what we think of as real musicians. It might become mostly electronic: not just sampling, but even the source may not be organic. So much manipulation is done electronically; you can speed up the tempo without changing the pitch, and vice versa, and you hear it all the time these days, sometimes without realizing it. A lot of it is showing up in video game soundtracks and YouTube videos.

It's everywhere, and I don't see that trend stopping. Will we get to a point where some music can't be performed live because it wasn't produced that way to start with? I fondly remember my

Studer analog two-inch tape machine that cost a fortune when I bought it; it now seems like a dinosaur. But that's change—you have to take it for what it is.

When I think about how things used to be in the music industry, about twenty years ago, it was all so simple. You made a recording and tried to have at least one song, maybe two, that would be acceptable for radio airplay: good solid songs with catchy hooks and glued-to-the-brain choruses. For promotional videos, you knew that MTV was the only outlet. There weren't hundreds or thousands of sites playing your video; there was just MTV, on television. You knew that every rock station had a certain format, and when you were touring in that city, you'd do an interview on the air with the disc jockey. That's the format every record launch followed. You made an album, and you toured on *that* album only, to publicize the hell out of it and sell copies of the album at every show.

While on the promotional tour, you would basically go wherever the record company and the tour agency booked you, and you would keep doing that until they stopped booking you. Then you'd come back home, maybe take a little time off, regroup, book studio time, and start working on your next record, which would come out roughly a year after the previous one. As for reviewing your album, whatever *Kerrang!*, *Guitar World*, and a couple of other magazines said was it. The album's fate might depend on whether they gave it two stars or five. If you were lucky and your record label had some pull with the magazine, you got a cover story that would appear in print close to the time your new album was released.

All of this was very well understood by everyone in the business: artists, managers, labels, press, and fans. It was the music industry album cycle. These days, *none* of it applies.

That game plan changed somewhat for me once I got my own studio set up, because then I didn't have to be dependent on the schedules and costs of booking an outside studio. Studio time is very expensive, so the schedules were quite rigid: this week it's drums, next week it's guitars and bass, the week after that it's vocals and other overdubs, and so on. Having my own studio really made a huge difference for me in terms of getting an album made. It meant that both the creative inspiration *and* the pressure came from myself alone. But the real quantum change in album making came with the Internet.

Instead of a music magazine giving your next album one of its coveted slots for a review or a feature story with an on-staff music journalist, now everybody with a blog can assume the role of reviewer and write anything, regardless of whether he or she knows anything about the subject. You know the old saying "Everyone's a critic"? These days it's true, literally.

Even though my view of the critics of old was not always the most flattering, at least they were paid to listen attentively to records, to evaluate them with some knowledge of what was involved in making them, and to display some ability to evaluate the skills of the artist in context. They had usually been in the journalism business long enough to be able to write somewhat intelligently about the subject of music, and they had the skills of their publications' editors and fact-checkers to screen the articles before they were printed. Not anymore. These days, anybody with access to the Internet can set him- or herself up with a blog or a website and call him- or herself a music critic. And this person can post a video clip of you without your permission or even your knowledge.

But there's an upside that goes hand in hand with that. I happen to have a clip that somebody posted on YouTube that was shot back in 2000, and it has now reached twelve million hits—and probably many more by the time this book is published. I did nothing to promote that little video clip to make people check it out. And there are other, similar clips of me with ten million hits and climbing. That popularity made the Guitar Hero game developers decide they wanted to have that clip included in their program. There are good things that have come out of the Internet revolution.

But on the downside, what's really sad about the way things are being done now is that in one sense it's harder for young kids to break into the music business. They have to compete with a zillion others for attention, and even though they may be talented, the likelihood of a record label picking them up is even slimmer than it once was. They can post their music on YouTube and hope to gain a following, but the Internet is so saturated with thousands of others just like them that it's virtually impossible to rise above the noise level.

I used to think I was lost in the shuffle way back in the beginning because I was on the same label as Bon Jovi and Def Leppard, who got much more promotion than I did. But I really wasn't, because there were maybe just five or six bands competing with one another on that label, compared to a billion on the Internet. Everybody there wants to be the next big thing, but the very structured filtering process of the old music industry is gone now, so the next big thing on the Internet may last only a week, if that long.

Again, this is both a blessing and a curse. In a lot of ways, musicians are no longer at the mercy of record labels and station programmers, but at the same time, when you were on a label you could count on a certain amount of publicity through channels otherwise not available to you. These days, if you want to watch a video of Ronnie James Dio (God bless him) or Iron Maiden or Judas Priest or me, you just type in the name and take your pick. But for someone trying to break into the business, it's a challenge just to make people know you're there.

One thing I don't miss about the old structure is the belief that you had to make at least one or two videos to go with each potential hit single off your new album. For me personally, making these promotional videos was pure hell. They were totally phony, often just lip-synched and guitar-synched with the track off the album, so you weren't really playing at all. In addition, you might have to act out some silly script of some sort that was equally as phony. For me, the best promotional videos are actual clips from live shows.

For example, today I can go out to a National Association of Music Merchants trade show and put on a short demonstration concert. It is posted on the Internet and gets four million hits overnight. Now that's the kind of promo video I like. But making MTV videos to promote a new album—I hated it with a passion. Being told, "Just pretend to play" simply did not compute in my head. I at least wanted to match the movement of my fingers with the song itself. In my not-so-humble opinion, music videos amounted to a lot of money spent on a fake image that probably didn't sell that many albums, anyway.

There are considerable advantages to having my own music company and label. Twenty-five years ago, I wouldn't even have dreamed of doing such a thing, but now it makes perfect sense. These days, the whole music industry has virtually imploded. There is no record label out there looking for new bands and new artists the way it was doing when I started in this business. Most of the traditional music labels have been swallowed up into megacorporations, like Universal, that handle movies and video games along with music. Many of the actual exclusive *music* labels are now gone.

What filled the void were a number of smaller, more limited companies in Germany, England, and the United States that produced the stuff the former big companies had let go of or ignored. These smaller companies put out a lot of rock albums and carried the weight for a little while. They were mostly signing bands that had already released albums, offering a small advance and cheap production values to get a back catalog, but rarely developing new artists in the way the old companies had done. I worked with some of these labels during what I call the dark ages (i.e., the 1990s), when 1980s' rock music was in decline and grunge was moving in. There was very little money and progress to be made.

April and I talked a lot about how it would make much more sense to take out the middleman and market my music directly to my fan base ourselves. Now, the fact remains that if you want to have a label and produce records, you must have a distributor who takes your products and makes sure they get into the stores, get set up for digital downloading, and all that. Luckily we were able to sign up with a major distributor, which of course makes all the difference.

It costs a lot of money to make an album, but guess what? Instead of the money from each sale going into the pockets of another record label, it comes to me. Before, after all the people in the middle got their cuts, there was not much left for the artist. Royalties on each sale are not that big, so you have to sell thousands of copies to make a decent amount. Obviously, once we owned the company and produced the CDs ourselves, the income was increased.

It's not just about the money, though. Having my own company allows me to set my own timetable and determine all the things about an album that I didn't have control over before. I feel very lucky that I am now in a position in my career where I am able to do this. The chances for new bands to get signed with a record company and get their careers launched properly are slim to none. If you want to play your own brand of music that doesn't produce instant hits that fuel the big conglomerate machines, tough shit.

LIVE TO FIGHT
(ANOTHER DAY)

I'm finally now living the life I always dreamed of
when I was an ambitious, driven teenager back
in Sweden. I wake up feeling great; I look in the
mirror and like the person I see instead of being
scared shitless.

My wife April is very important to where I am now in my life. If
it weren't for her, I would not have opened my eyes and gotten
rid of the bad people around me: the bad accountants, bad managers, the hanger-on acquaintances, and so-called friends who would
turn around and stab you in the back at a drop of a hat—the leeches
that come with this industry. I probably would not have stopped
drinking, probably wouldn't have gained a healthy outlook on life,

and probably would not have become financially secure—I could go on and on. When we got together, I felt like I was born again.

"Like an Angel" was written about her: "Like an angel you came to me, and now I see the stranger in me is finally free to feel true love." And I mean every word and every musical note I play on that song. She is unlike anyone else I'd ever become close to. Not only is she stunningly beautiful, but also spiritual, nurturing, and extremely intelligent. Her knowledge of and education on the world is mind-boggling, and on top of that she is an amazing mother and a wonderful life partner and companion and, yes, I can keep going on. She just beams with that certain energy and light.

April is a very proper person. She expects you to behave properly and take care of yourself and others. She does not drink or smoke and believes a good positive outlook in life mixed with creativity, productiveness, and a good workout is what you really need throughout the day. April has always been a good influence on me and has introduced me to a lot of new things. She reads poetry, listens to music from around the world, goes to Broadway shows. She goes to fashion shows and educates me on fashion designers, the latest trends, and so on. Funny, I know.

One of the most important qualities April has is she is very understanding. She understands me and where I came from and where I had been. April's parents, my in-laws, are wonderful, caring people, too; they have been married for forty-two years, and I actually really like hanging out with them. April understands music and the entertainment industry. In fact, she was the creative mind behind the acoustic album *Angels of Love*. I do not know if I have ever met anyone that works harder than she does, and I believe that anyone in the industry who works with her would say the same. When she puts her mind to something, there is nothing that could stop her from achieving her goals. She will find a creative way, or a more difficult way if she has to.

When she first came to our house, April said, *"I just want you to know, I love serenity, and peace; no craziness, no weird people turning up in middle of the night."* She filled the house with white candles and white flowers, and the house was always immaculately neat. She decluttered the entire house, and that is unfortunately when our maid accidentally threw out my stage clothes from the *Trilogy* era. (The incredible thing is, three years later, someone left them on the front gate of our house, with a note saying, "I believe these belong to you.")

Literally the second day she was at our home April said, "Hey, that tennis court—is that yours? Why don't we gear up and go use it?" She got me a coach and a trainer, and now I play tennis every day. (I've used the same coach since 1998; his name is Mike Melanefy. Everything that I've done in my life, I've always been the boss. I've always been the leader, the one who says "Do it like this" or "Do it like that." To actually take lessons and learn something, where you're definitely the disciple and not the teacher, is very humbling. It's very good for me. I've got a big serve, but there are always things I can learn from Mike.)

The really good thing that came from it was that I emerged clear, focused, and sharper in some ways than I had been before. It was a little bit like when I had my car accident. You go through a period of trying to function with a severe handicap, and then suddenly when that handicap is removed, you can go even further than you did before. In the months of physical therapy that followed my car accident, I pushed myself so hard to regain my skills that when the nerves going to my hand finally healed and the clot on my brain dissolved, I was like a race car off the starting line.

The same thing was true when I woke up from the fog I'd been living in for years and felt acutely aware of everything around me. In all those years of unhealthy living, I had to work a little bit harder to function and stay on top of my game. With the fog gone and the demons banished, I'm working on an entirely different level. Of course, maturity has something to do with it. You don't have the experience and insight at twenty that you do at forty-five—you just don't. When you're in your early twenties, you may have advanced technique, but you don't have life experience. These days I know how much that counts in artistic development.

April helped me to change everything for the better. I don't mean just my health, although that was a big part of it. From day one, when she met Jim Lewis, she instantly saw him for what he was. She told me, "He's ripping you off." Of course, at first I refused to listen, because he'd been my friend from the bad old days in L.A. when I first came to the United States. But she was convinced and started looking into the finances a lot more closely.

For example, she started finding out the exact figure we had taken in at the concerts in Japan, plus all the merchandise that was sold, plus the money actually paid from my Japanese record company. It was well over a million dollars each year, and she would ask Jim, "Where's the money?" He'd always have some cover-up answer, and the most common one was "Expenses." She refused to take that at face value and started trying to account for all these alleged expenses, at which point we decided to get legal help.

She was clearly a threat to him and his cushy little situation as my manager. And once our son, Antonio, was born, Jim must have realized it was all over for him, because now I had a family to support. I couldn't afford to let him manage everything and just blow it all away. I worked very hard to make the money he was squandering, and finally it all just hit the fan, as they say.

April has a very sharp business mind—she had run her own modeling agency in London before we got together—and she knew instantly that the accounting wasn't right. Once Jim was gone and she took over the business end of my career, things began to turn around in a hurry. We uncovered so many ways that money had been diverted and covered up. While Jim kept telling me we were hurting for funds, I had in fact been making millions over the years and seeing very little of it.

It's such a change for me to be in the loop on everything that happens careerwise, whereas before I never was. April runs the day-to-day business, but I know everything that's going on and can provide input. A few years ago we set up our own label, called Rising Force Records, and that was another leap forward in freeing me from the leeches who just wanted to suck up my money. That was one of the smartest moves we've made yet. April has an instinct for these things. I'm convinced that keeping the business in the family is the best option a musician can have. Stewart Copeland's brother, for example, managed the Police. When I look at how things used to be and how they are now, there's no comparison—it's like night and day.

The way we cut deals and hire people, April has taken the whole thing forward. She doesn't rely on the industry standard. She'll come up with an idea for a way to promote something or find a new opportunity that leaves people scratching their heads, wondering why they never thought of it. She is absolutely not intimidated by anybody, and the first time somebody tries to take advantage of her, she puts a stop to it. Really, it's been very smooth working with the recording and distribution companies. She continually comes up with great marketing ideas. She's very creative, so it's a natural fit for her.

And, of course, now that the finances are all in the family, there is no outsider who might be likely to rip us off. I know that a large part of my previous problems with untrustworthy managers was my fault, but that still doesn't make it right. I had always put my energy and focus totally into the music and not the business side of my career, which made me a very easy mark—I'm sure anyone could see it a mile away. But no one is going to pull a fast one on April. It's simply amazing how good her business instincts are.

I clearly remember the first time I ever took a drink of alcohol. It was New Year's Eve, and I was seventeen years old. My cousin had a small bottle of vodka and gave me a sip. I can't say that I liked it, particularly, although the effects were pretty instant since I'd never had any before. My friends and I would go to parties where there would be a lot of alcohol, especially in the summer when the weather was warm. We'd go up on a hill near my grandmother's apartment in Stockholm and drink for fun. I and the guys I hung out with during my teenage years in Sweden were definitely "bad guys" in our leather jackets, with beer cans in our hands, generally making a scene to annoy people. We partied a lot and got into fights and shit like that.

I think a couple of those guys were definitely what you'd call budding alcoholics. They'd go to the liquor store regularly, every weekday (in Sweden, liquor stores are owned and run by the government and are closed on weekends), and spend every cent in their pockets for a "mixed bag": a combination of beer, wine, vodka, and whatever else they could afford. They didn't have jobs and didn't make any money playing music, so I assume they were on welfare and that's where all their money went. I wasn't drinking that much, but occasionally I'd wake up with a hangover and swear

I would never drink again. Obviously I didn't stick to that. But most of the drinking I did in Sweden was at parties.

That wasn't my real introduction to the demon alcohol, though. That started a few years later, probably the year I left Sweden and definitely after I got to the United States. Once I was in the States, my alcohol consumption continued, but the vibe was different. There were serious drinkers at all the parties and clubs, and it was expected that you would get plastered to the limit.

In the mid-1980s in L.A., the party scene was nonstop, which meant the drinking was also nonstop. We thought nothing of driving, or doing any number of other dangerous things, in a complete drunken blur. That ended, predictably, in my famous car crash. But that didn't really end anything, because once I had recovered and been released from the hospital, I slipped back into my bad habits pretty quickly.

It's a little hard for me to remember how it felt to play onstage totally wasted because I've moved so far beyond that now, and I love the way it feels to be totally clear and alert to everything around me. But I do remember that in the late 1980s and throughout the 1990s, I'd start out with beer before the show and move to hard liquor by the end of the show. So when I would lie down on the stage and play "Purple Haze," it was probably because I couldn't stand up straight. I would set up the playlist so that there was nothing difficult to play toward the end of the show. That was during some of the worst of my drinking—I knew that things were seriously fucked up, but at the time I didn't have the genuine desire to stop it. So it just went on like that.

If you come to a point where you drink because you know that if you *don't* have a drink, you're going to feel terrible, then you have a real problem. Your body gets used to it, expects it, and craves it. It gets so that every part of your daily routine is a trigger for it. I would drink even on the tennis court—not so good for my game, for sure, but while that might seem comical, it was also socially acceptable, because I certainly wasn't the only person doing that.

Think about it this way. If you're a bus driver, an office worker, or doing any kind of responsible job, you can't drink on the job. You can't start drinking the moment you wake up and head off to work and drink all day. But if you're a rock 'n' roller, you're supposed to do that. And I did. It was all part of the image. It wasn't a party, let me tell you. At the worst of it, there wasn't anything I did that wasn't fueled by alcohol. My surface brain just told me that this was the way business was carried on for rock stars. We were glamorous to others and were expected to have our excesses.

I think I finally hit bottom sometime in 2002, around the time *Attack!!* was released. I don't think we gave any bad shows, per se, because I could play most anything with my eyes closed and in a coma if I had to. But it certainly was not a good time for me. The next year, I seriously decided that I'd had enough of living like that, and the internal desire to be free of it took hold.

From that point on, it was a steady struggle toward getting unaddicted. I had a couple of slips—not too many, but they were severe enough to remind me why I needed to get this monkey off my back. Each time it happened it was just horrible—for me and everyone around me. And it's a fact that if I hadn't had April there supporting me all the way, the outcome could have been very different.

When I took the first steps to clean up and get rid of my bad habit, I was really motivated to do it. I really was. But the minute I tried to stop, I felt like there was a physical hole in me somewhere. I didn't think I could function, mentally or physically, because of my craving to fill up this hole. I'd try to drink just a little to fill up the hole, but then I'd very quickly be back where I started. Then I'd try again to stop, because I genuinely wanted this addiction to go away. And around it would go, for most of that first year.

When I started touring again, I was hyperaware of every single thing that was happening, so for a while, everything became an issue for me. This wasn't good, because suddenly the joy of playing live was gone. I was so self-critical and critical of the show that I couldn't just relax and enjoy it. In spite of that, there were a couple of shows, one in Stockholm and one in Barcelona that were so near perfection that I knew this was the way it should be and I just had to give myself time to adjust to my new awareness of my surroundings.

After coming back from a long stint in Europe, we went on a very lengthy tour across the United States. By then, things had started to change completely for me. When we did the American tour that year, it was beautiful. That was the point at which I began to really kick back and totally enjoy the shows. They were immensely satisfying in ways that had been lost to me when I was walking around in a drunken haze. I started to really groove on all the details of getting the sound just right, of playing the perfect solo, and of so many other aspects of the show. I felt certain at that point that I was over my old ways and that it would be smooth sailing from there on. Then a short tour in Japan.

Then back to the States for another round of shows at the beginning of 2006, where I leveled out again and got back into the groove I'd found before I'd left for Japan. Again, I began to play shows with the crystal clarity that was so amazing. Then we went to Southeast Asia and Australia. The show in Taipei, Taiwan, was beyond amazing because I was totally firing on all cylinders, completely in control of my music, totally aware of what was going on.

From that point on, I never touched a drop and have remained clean ever since. When I play now, it's the way it was always supposed to be, before I got so totally fucked up. When I look at footage from those bad old days, I have to shake my head at how lost I was.

The people around you are crucial if you really intend to stop drinking. But in the end, or course, it all comes down to you. For me, it was realizing that the devil alcohol might make you feel good, but it's still the devil and will eventually take everything away from you, including your soul. You'll lose your talent and your abilities, it'll take your family away, and if you push it far enough, it'll take your life. Of course, your health will suffer, but when you're in that state, you don't give a shit about something like that. I can remember how that felt, but I don't really dwell on it anymore. What I focus on is the fact that every time I wake up in the morning I feel like a million bucks.

I think the biggest relief was to discover that my ability to think clearly had returned, that I hadn't come out of that experience permanently brain-damaged. I became hyperfocused on everything, but in a good way. In the beginning of sobriety, it feels like everything around you is too clear, too loud, too bright, and too intense. But once you get used to it, you realize that that's how life is supposed to be. Now I appreciate every detail of the water and the sky and the palm trees, almost like I'd never really seen them before. I would never give this up again in order to sit in a bar and drink myself into oblivion. *Never.* It sounds trite to say I feel reborn, but it's the truth. I don't mean in the religious sense, like reincarnation or anything, but just in the sense of getting my real life back.

I told myself, "You can do this," and I did.

I'm not trying to preach, because I certainly know that preaching didn't work on me. I'm just telling it like I see it from the other side. And my reality on that side is totally amazing. Why would I ever want to go back to something that's the opposite of what I have now? I don't envy anyone. I'm finally now living the life I always dreamed of when I was an ambitious, driven teenager back in Sweden. I wake up feeling great; I look in the mirror and like the person I see instead of being scared shitless. I like everything around me, I have the most beautiful and loving wife in the world, we have a beautiful son, and I make a living doing what I love most in the world: making music. This is my reward for choosing to stop taking the poison.

You would think that after all these years I might lose my excitement at getting up in the morning, going into my studio, and seeing what I can come up with now, in the clear light of day. The answer is *no*. I am as enthusiastic as ever about being a musician, about having the freedom to create new music, and about doing it with a completely sharp, clear focus and inspiration. That is my joy, not something I have gotten tired of over the years.

The fact that I've reclaimed my life, with the help of my family, just makes it sweeter, because what I have now is beyond my wildest dreams of what I thought I could do when I was first starting out. Driven at such a young age to excel beyond everyone's expectations, I really wasn't ever thinking in terms of money or fame. It's hard to explain in words what was pushing me so relentlessly. It was the music itself, and it still is.

Once I became sober, the change was really amazing. I don't know how to explain this very well. It was like a caterpillar turning into a butterfly. I look back at my drinking days, and it's like all that misery and insane behavior happened to a different person. I know that sounds like a cliché, but that's exactly how it feels. And even stranger, my years in Sweden feel like they happened to a totally different person, too. I've gone through the larva stage, then the cocoon stage, and I finally made it to the butterfly stage.

These days I enjoy life so much: I'm clearheaded, I play tennis regularly, my music flows effortlessly, and I have a beautiful family. Life is good. I think I was always more or less heading in the direction of the life I wanted, but I went through so many detours to get here that at one point it didn't seem possible. But here I am.

April's constant love and support for me was obviously a very big part of my being able to change the way I did. The greatest challenge is to look at yourself in the mirror and confront who you are. Scary thought, eh? There were a few times when I was still having doubts. But now, years later, I see someone who's alive and well and who looks forward to every day with new enthusiasm. I wouldn't trade that for anything.

After I got myself free of the poison and totally cleaned up my act, touring and playing shows was an entirely new experience. It meant that I had to deal with the band and the crew in a completely different way, especially those who did want to do some drinking. At first I was a bit offended when they drank in front of me, but these days I don't care who drinks in front of me, because I am totally not interested in it.

These days, though, no one in my band or my crew has a drinking problem. Everyone is sober and clean. We run a tight ship, totally focused on our jobs, with no alcohol distraction—we're like a precision instrument, like a perfectly tuned-up Ferrari. It's a whole different scene, and I won't have it any other way. Back in the 1980s and 1990s and up to 2003, it was so bad that I had bandmates and crew members who were sometimes in worse shape than I was, and I wonder now how they kept standing, much less put on a show.

It was like the objective was to get as shitfaced as possible and then see if we could do the show. But now I expect anyone who works for me to be clean and sober, period. To show up drunk or high and expect to be part of my show is unprofessional, and everything suffers for it. If you have to drink or get high to perform, there are plenty of other bands you can join and do that.

But everything you do in life—all the experiences, even the bad ones—count for something, because they give you a better appreciation of how lucky you are when things turn around. I thank God every day for April, because I know, having had two bad marriages before, just how lucky I am to have her.

April and I have a son named Antonio. He was born in 1998. He's my best pal. But I have to admit that it took me a couple of years to come to grips with being a father. The first year, it was strange to have this new creature around who needed to be tended and fed, but once he began to vocalize and clearly become a real person, then I was completely won over.

That being said, I feel like I have a natural fathering vibe. Having children was something I always wanted at some point in my life—it just had to be at the right time and with the right woman. I was there in the delivery room when my son was born. I cut the umbilical cord. Our doctor had prepared me for what would happen if I wanted to be there. I remember her handing me the medical scissors and saying, "Cut here." I did it, but I was about to faint.

All went well, however, and in no time we were taking the little guy home. The hard part was that just three weeks later we were supposed to get on a plane and fly to Japan to start touring. Antonio got a passport and took his first airline flight before he was even a month old. By the time he was a year old, he'd been to Australia and Europe. He was turning into a road dog, just like his dad.

April and I took him everywhere with us, which was our intention from the very beginning. I decided the moment he was born that I was in it all the way: taking care of him, diapering and feeding him, carrying him around with us, the whole nine yards. Obviously, he couldn't be at the shows or sound checks, where it was loud. As a father, I think I've spent more time with him than the average father spends with his kids.

Now I take him to school every day and pick him up. We go places together all the time, sometimes just driving around in one of the Ferraris, hanging out. He's definitely my best bud. His personality is his own, of course, but he does remind me of myself in a lot of ways. His artwork has a very similar, detailed style, and he's quite musical—he plays guitar and sings quite well—but we haven't forced music lessons on him or anything. Of course, I'm willing to show him anything he wants to learn, but that's totally up to him. He's interested in it all, but he's not driven like a maniac the way I was. Now he's fifteen, completely dedicated to his guitar, and runs his band with an iron fist. (Sounds familiar. . . . Hmmm.)

The most important thing is that we're pals. My son says to me, "You're such a dad!" I love him—he's my best friend, and I want the best for him. But April and I don't let him run wild, we make sure he knows how to behave properly, and so on. He's always well looked after, no matter where we are. Because I'm a public figure, my first instinct is to want to protect him from public exposure, but at the same time he travels everywhere with us when he can. It's a fine line, but so far we've managed to make it work.

Antonio recently played his first gig at school. I'm quite pleased and proud of him, but I want to emphasize that playing guitar is all his choice. I never tried to push him toward it. We've encouraged him in all his artistic and musical endeavors, but we have never tried to deliberately steer him one way or another. I've always been willing to teach him things about music, but at his request. I've shown him the major and minor scales and demonstrated vibrato.

He'll ask to learn a song, so I'll teach it to him. Sometimes I'll record a backing track for him, and then he can play over it in the studio and we'll make a little CD out of it that he can share with his friends at school. Not long ago he asked if he could take one of his guitars to school. I used to routinely take my guitar to school when I was a kid, so I figured, "Why not?"

When I picked him up that afternoon after school, he said, "Hey, Dad, you know what happened to me?" I said I hoped he hadn't gotten in trouble or anything. He's a very well-behaved kid, so I didn't really expect that, but you never know. Instead, he said, "All these girls came up and started hanging out when I was playing my guitar." I really had to laugh, and I reminded him that I had said that might happen.

Then he told me he had decided to audition for the school's talent show. As you might predict, he took the really cool backing track I'd made for him, played his own guitar live over it, and blew everybody away.

The next day he asked again if he could take his guitar with him to school. It's okay with me as long as his teachers don't mind. His pals are starting to think that maybe playing rock music for real is more fun than doing it as a video game like Rock Band or Guitar Hero. And now I have found out that he's getting them to play with him like a band, and it's like déjà vu as I see all these pieces falling into place that are just like how I started out.

But there are differences, of course. When I recruited my first band, I just assigned roles to the kids I knew, and that was that, even though they protested. I decided that one kid would be my drummer, and I told him that. He protested, "But I don't play drums," and I just said, "Now you do." Then he argued, "But I don't have a drum set," and I countered, "Well, I do." No further questions.

Antonio is much more diplomatic than I was, so in that respect we are different. He said to me, "Dad, I think I need a roadie." And I told him that roadies usually get paid to schlep your stuff around for you. He thought about that and replied, "I can tell them that their reward is that they get to hang out around really cool people." I can see that he's got that musician's vibe happening now, and it's really interesting to see where he is taking it.

As far as teaching him things, I make sure that he starts out right, that he has a good understanding of basic music theory, and that he develops a good clean technique. He can throw it out the window later if he wants to, but at least he will know how to play with good technique from the start. He sometimes asks me, "Hey, how does this sound?" And I'm always honest with him: I tell him what I think is good and where he needs some work. And I've shown him alternate picking and how to use all four fingers on the left hand.

I'm really adamant that if Antonio wants to play guitar, he starts out right. We started out with the building blocks: notes and scales. I showed him, for instance, that you can play an E here, here, and here. What happens is you start to see patterns and the light dawns. Once that makes sense to you, you can do things that are much more exciting. He even figured out where the arpeggios are on the keyboard without me showing him, so I guess my tutoring skills aren't too bad. I play with him a little when I'm showing him things, which is also fun. Of course, he can play on anything he wants in the studio, but he does have a couple of guitars that belong to him.

Antonio does have talents similar to mine, both musical and artistic. He draws very detailed and precise images, with a lot of shading and accurate perspective, much the way I did when I was in school. He doesn't draw the same subjects I did, because he's a gentler soul, but the talent is clearly there. He has a lot of interests; much of the time he just wants to be a kid and ride his bike, and that's fine. I'm not about to try to make a prodigy out of him and tell him he has to play guitar until his fingers bleed—that was my own obsession, not his.

When Antonio was born, it was such an incredible event that I really couldn't wrap my head around it. I knew from that moment onward, life was not going to ever be the same. And I'm sure this is true for most new parents, but it felt very surreal at first. You feel totally out of your depth. It's easy to feel that way because you really don't know what to do. This little creature doesn't come with an operator's manual.

PLAY LOUD

When you turn the volume down, as far as I'm concerned, you can't play.

Back when I started playing guitar, what most aspiring electric guitarists did was to buy a Strat, chop a big hole in it, and put a double-coil pickup in it, known as a humbucker. The humbucker gives so much more power with no noise. The sound has all the harmonics, and beautiful things happen when you plug in one of those guitars. But, for some reason, I thought that using a humbucker was like cheating, and I didn't like the way it looked.

I asked the guys at the music store what else they had in the way of pickups, and they showed me an FS-1, which stands for Fat Strat 1, made by DiMarzio. I put that sucker into my Fender and was blown away—the sound was awesome. I was sold. I stayed with that configuration—FS-1 DiMarzio pickups in a Strato-caster—until my Alcatrazz days.

The FS-1 is a standard single-coil pickup, which, like the Fender, has a sixty-cycle hum, which is extremely annoying. That hum goes away when you turn the volume down, but when you turn the volume down, as far as I'm concerned, you can't play. It was a terrible dilemma for a guitarist such as myself. When I was in Steeler, I was introduced to Larry DiMarzio, and I told him, "I can't stand this fucking hum," which was even worse in the United States than in Sweden because of the quality of the electrical current being generated by U.S. power stations. The effect for me was that when I held a long sustained note, the buzz would suddenly take over the note.

I told the DiMarzio people that I had a great idea, which was to take two coils and instead of putting them side by side, put them one on top of the other, inside the same space as a Stratocaster pickup. They liked the idea and made me a prototype, which they called the HS-1, which stands for Humbucking Strat 1. I tried it for a while and told them, "No, it still sounds like shit."

Then they came out with a refinement called the HS-2, which was closer but still not good enough. They kept trying and came up with the HS-3, which was close enough, and I used it for years. I have to confess that I compromised my ideal sound so much just to get rid of that noise. Basically, I got half of the great sound and half of the power. By putting the coils one on top of the other, the DiMarzio people effectively cut the FS-1 in half.

I finally just gave up on it. I couldn't put up with that noise any longer, so I had to sacrifice the sound to get rid of the hum. For the record, I was never completely happy with the HS-3, although I used it for years. It was simply the best compromise at the time. But in my heart of hearts, I never truly abandoned my desire for the perfect pickup.

I would look for ways to get around it, like putting a little extra on the DOD. But by doing that, I gathered more background noise by having the gain from the overdrive, so now I had a hiss instead of a hum. Anybody who knows anything about electric guitars knows that if you don't have sustain, if you don't have gain, you don't have anything. Sustain is like your violin bow. Then I discovered something called the noise gate. If you listen to my 1985 recording *Live in Japan*, the hiss sounds like the entire ocean coming out of the Marshall amps. That was because it was the only way I could get the sound I wanted for those shows.

When you pick up a Gibson, or any guitar with the standard humbucker pickup in it, everything in the sound is doubled because of the humbucker. But I didn't want to put that in my Stratocaster. I labored for years with half the sound I was looking for. And I did pretty well with that compromise, I guess, given the number of people continually trying to duplicate my sound exactly. In a way that's kind of funny: here they were, trying to copy my sound, while I was trying to change it because it wasn't good enough.

Then in 2009 the folks from Seymour Duncan came to me, and we discussed possible endorsements for various things. They said, "We know you use DiMarzio pickups, so we won't even ask you about that. But we make other things as well, which might interest you." My response was "Let's go back and talk about pickups." And that started a yearlong saga of microscopically dissecting why, when a string vibrates, the pickup acts a certain way, taking into account its interaction with the fret board during a small vibration, a high vibration, legato, staccato, you name it. We asked questions like what exact combination of metals should be used and should the windings be 75 percent more or 75 percent less. The research these people put into engineering pickups was practically at the molecular level. I'd never seen anything like it in my life.

I've always been very involved with these issues, but the level to which I delved into the physics of sound for these pickups with the Seymour Duncan technicians was insane. Part of what was so gratifying about the Seymour Duncan experience was being able to do hands-on work in the lab with the technicians and engineers. I think they were a little leery at first of letting me do some of the work, but when they saw that I knew what was going on, it freed us up to work together in a much better way than simply as artist and engineers.

Somewhere around revision number twenty-one of this pickup, I was finally closing in on what I wanted. In order to get the fluidity and the power that I didn't have before, the tolerances were on an extremely fine line. By the end it felt like we were inventing the freaking lightbulb or something. What it all boiled down to was this: How do you make something that's half of something else 100 percent as powerful? I know that seems like a contradiction, but that's been my sound dilemma all these years.

This pickup had to be more powerful than the DiMarzios I'd been using, which were wimps in terms of power but had been the only way to get rid of the noise. At the same time, the note coming from the instrument had to be pure. That pure tone is shaped by the pickup position, the coil winds, the magnets, and the magnet wire. Then it's ghosted with overdrive going to the preamp of the Marshall, where it's sort of boosted, and then here's the clincher. When the sound comes out of the speaker, a lot of people think it's done, but that's wrong, because now you've got to get distortion back to the cone. In a nutshell, you have to start with a completely pure signal and end with a completely pure signal. In other words, you have to use the three-hundred-watt Marshall four-by-twelve with Celestions, which gives you a complete reproduction of what comes out of the Marshall, so there's no coloring of the speaker. The pickup is the first part of the sound chain, the speaker is the last part, and in between is where you put the distortion.

The result is an extremely customized pickup called the YJM Fury. Each pickup in each position is uniquely designed (that is, the neck pickup has different magnet staggers and winds than do the middle and lead pickups). It's the closest thing that has ever been created to a perfect transference of sound plus power. Period. The engineers even designed the cover to look exactly like the vintage pickups, down to the exact shade of the color, with a matte finish. My plan is to replace all the DiMarzios in my two hundred or more guitars with the Fury.

I've also got forty to fifty Marshall amplifiers, and they're all individual—not one of them sounds exactly like another. They could have all been made on the same day, and each would still have a unique sound. You have to factor that as well into the quest for the perfect sound reproduction.

I've been working with the Marshall designers for a couple of years to create an amplifier that was like the 1970s vintage ones I've used for years, only better. I told them, "I want it to look exactly like a vintage two-hundred-watt head, like the ones I've used for years." On the front, this new model looks exactly like my old ones: no extra knobs, no cluttered design, very plain and simple. On the back, it's another story entirely. A number of modern technology essentials are built in: an overdrive, a noise gate, a digital reverb, a special effects loop, and a half-power switch that can shift from fifty to one hundred watts (essentially from two to four tubes).

It's also got a master volume on the back that's nothing like any master volume control ever placed on a Marshall. The problem with master volumes in the past is that you'd have a preamp and a power amp. The volume control decided how loud the sound would be so that you would only overdrive the preamp, not the power amp. What I asked Marshall to do was put the actual volume after the power station, so that even though you play at one decibel, the entire amp works at full sound. That is a unique configuration, even though it's based on the 1959 Plexi head.

This new amp was built ground up for me, just like the Seymour Duncan pickup. It's the most exciting technology I've ever been involved with. And the sound is amazing. In the past, I always felt that I had compromised with what I was using, but this is as close as I ever dreamed of coming to that perfect violin-like sound that I hear in my head. The versatility of this new equipment is just totally amazing.

The way the new Marshall came about was this. I was at the National Association of Music Merchants (NAMM) trade show several years ago. Everybody knows I'm a very loyal user of Marshall equipment, and Marshall has been very good to me over the years. We've always had a great relationship. I was looking at the Marshall display at NAMM and talking to the people standing around, including a couple of guys who looked like company representatives. I said, half joking, to the guy next to me that instead of whoever was on the cardboard stand in the display now, next year it's going to be me, introducing *my* model Marshall. Little did I know that the guy I was talking to was Paul Marshall, the founder Jim Marshall's son. And he nodded, like okay, cool. I was mostly just joking around, like I do sometimes, never thinking I had set something in motion.

A few months later, when I was in Frankfurt, Germany, doing a big event for Fender, I had requested that I have a wall of Marshalls instead of Fender amps. I ended up with a huge setup of thirty Marshalls that dwarfed the drums—it was ridiculous over-kill, and I loved it. We invited the Marshall representatives to come over and check it out, and when they saw it, their eyes nearly popped out.

Shortly after that, I was invited to play at a London guitar show just a week or two before my own tour of the United States was to kick off. I flew to London to do that one event and went to the Marshall factory while I was there. After a few days, I went back to Miami to rehearse for the tour, but then a week later I made another quick trip back to London at Marshall's request before the tour started. Plane hopping like that is definitely not my favorite thing to do, but I had a feeling it was going to lead to something.

That meeting basically consisted of the Marshall guys saying, "Tell us what you want." I was sitting in the conference room with these guys, and I just decided that instead of trying to not push too hard or scare them away, I would simply lay out, like a checklist, exactly what I wanted for a new Malmsteen model stack of amps. I figured there was no reason to pull any punches. If it didn't happen, it didn't happen. But instead, I got exactly what I asked for. I was completely stoked, and the result was truly amazing, not to mention my enjoyment of eventually seeing *my* stand at the Marshall NAMM exhibit, just as I'd predicted. Every amplifier company you want to name—Peavey, Carvin, Randall, Mesa Boogie—has courted me over the years to endorse its stuff, but I've turned them all down, saying, "No, Marshalls are my only choice." That loyalty eventually paid off in spades.

When I was at the Seymour Duncan factory to work on developing my new pickup, I was explaining to the engineers how I record in my own studio. One of the things I did when I was remodeling my studio was to gut the servants' quarters of the house I live in and put all my Marshall amps in there; I call it the Room of Doom. The engineers laughed and asked if the pickups could tell me if anything had been moved around in there. They were joking, but I assured them that if somebody moved even one thing, I would know.

That actually happened just recently. Somebody had stored a box in there, and I could hear it. You can't see that room from the studio because it's not connected to the house, but I can totally tell if the sound dynamics coming from there are different in even the tiniest degree. I tell this incident to emphasize how critical the entire sound chain is to me and, in turn, how important finding the right equipment is.

Over the years, in my quest for the perfect tone, I have worked with the equipment I had to the point that I sometimes altered the way I did things. Through years of trial and error, I've figured out how to string my guitars so that they stay in tune no matter how I play or what I do onstage. People are baffled by that and ask me what the trick is. But that's my own little trade secret—I have altered my way of doing things in order to make the equipment I have perform the way I want.

With everything I've ever used, I've attempted to figure out how I can make it better, how I can alter something, to get closer to the quality sound that's in my head. It's been a lifelong pursuit, and I keep inching closer to it as the years go by. I've done things to the guitar like cut the tone knobs off because that makes a little bit less resistance—granted, it's minuscule, but it makes a slight difference. What your fingers do on the strings is a very minute movement that gets amplified into a huge movement, so the sound has to start out pure. All this experimentation means that sometimes I have discovered things by accident. I guess you could say my improvisational skills aren't confined to just playing the music.

Here's where I think many people make a mistake. They have a crappy tone to start with, but they think they have to have a hot pickup with really high output because it will distort anything. The problem with this is that it's like painting a car a vibrant color, but underneath the car is rusted. You have to have a pure sound at the very origin of the note, way back at the very *beginning* of the sound chain. That's why the pickup is so important.

Here's another problem. Some people think that twenty-five-watt speakers are better for a certain distortion. I hate that, so I put three-hundred-watt speakers in, and they have no distortion. This means that the beginning of the note and the end of the note are clean and pure. The "dirt" comes from the amp and the over-drive pedal. The system is no different from anybody else's. For instance, Jimi Hendrix had a fuzz pedal in front, and he used one-hundred-watt heads through a twenty-five-watt speaker, so he got distortion from start to finish. That was great for him, but not so much for me.

The thing with having a clear, pure tone from the beginning is that it doesn't hide anything. It forces you to be more accurate, to make every note count. You're basically naked—you can't hide your mistakes under a layer of distortion. When I first started out, people used to think that I played without any distortion in the sound chain, which is wrong, because I had so much gain in my chain it was ridiculous. If someone picked up my guitar and tried to play, he'd get a roar like an elephant that was completely uncontrollable (and also very funny, I might add).

It's all about how you play it. There are a lot of opinions about distortion. Allan Holdsworth, who has the greatest sound and technique, says distortion is a necessary evil. He hardly uses the pick and needs distortion to get a legato response. I don't think it's necessarily evil. When you play a power chord, it definitely sounds cool. Very metal.

Distortion has different contours. If you play a chord with just the root and the fifth notes, it distorts in a harmonic way that everyone recognizes as a power chord. But when you play a single note, it shouldn't have a distorted sound or feel—it should be a smooth, singing note. You can't have that with all the high-output stuff and racks pedals and whatever. It's just a different philosophy about tone that I have. Audio technology is vastly different now from what it was when I started out in my career. It's tempting for people to rely on all these effects, so often what you hear isn't real playing at all.

You need to hear the guitar's voice. You need to hear its vibrato.

Vibrato can be produced many different ways. If you bend the string, you will bend it up to pitch, and then the vibrato that you produce with the bent string will go flat and sharp. If you just do one set of notes, like on the high E string, the vibrato will only go sharp. Different conditions produce a different quality of vibrato. If I'm onstage, for example, running around and such, moving really fast up the neck, I might go up to a B but actually be hitting a B-flat. Without thinking, without any effort, I just bring the note to the right pitch.

The vibrato is a method of expression that the musician can make with the instrument. I've always preferred a slower vibrato, because an extremely fast vibrato starts to sound like a goat bleating. It's not a pleasing sound. Also, when you bend a string to pitch, it has to be done perfectly. I am extremely pitch-conscious, and nothing makes me grit my teeth more that hearing somebody's vibrato that's not done well. It doesn't matter whether it's guitar, violin, or singing—it's painful.

Using a device to produce the vibrato, like a vibrato bar (which is also called a whammy) or a slide (which a blues player might use), is fine. But to me the true skill lies in the actual ability of your fingers on the strings—it's an intimate, personal way of coloring the note that expresses an emotion.

The amount of pressure I put on a string varies—it depends on the sound I'm trying to achieve. To be honest, I've never tried to break it down into discrete movements. I just do what I need to do to produce the sound I want to hear. Over so many years, I just know without thinking about it how to get the sound I want. The vibrato I prefer is a singer's kind of tone, a more "vocal" kind of vibrato. It's definitely more the way a violinist would produce it. It's a wide, slow vibrato that sometimes matches the tempo of the song, although a fast song does *not* equate to a fast vibrato.

I've been asked many times how to practice making a good vibrato, but all I can say is that I never practiced over and over to get that kind of vibrato—my fingers just did what I needed them to do to produce the sound I wanted to hear. I really think that sitting down to methodically practice making a vibrato over and over will make it sound just like that: something unemotional and practiced instead of a sound that organically arises from the music itself. This is very difficult for me to explain because I've rarely tried to break it down into a technique described in words.

What makes an amazing musician or an amazing tennis player? No matter what activity you're doing, you have to be totally dedicated. You cannot do a little bit of this and a little bit of that. You have to be extremely serious all the time. You have to have a full set of skills. A lot of people have demonized technique, but you have to have that to build on. It's just a tool. It's what you create with it that matters.

I was asked in an interview recently, "So when did you decide that you were good?" This took me a little aback. I never *decided* I was good. I was just driven to play at a level that would blow my own mind every single day. Nothing less was good enough. I didn't aim to be better tomorrow, the next day, or next week. I had to be better *now*, in that moment. I can't tell you where this insane drive to excel came from, but it was there from the beginning—that much I know. I never accepted the idea that I could figure something out later or work on getting better next week. Once I started trying to play the guitar, in my mind I was performing. I wasn't practicing the way I had on the other instruments I'd taken lessons with. I was performing.

I didn't want to just pick up the guitar and play scales or even riffs that I'd played the day before. I wanted to have something happen that would blow me away, which I know is really insane. And I wouldn't stop until I could make that happen. That led to playing for twelve- to eighteen-hour sessions and then falling asleep on my bed with the guitar on top of me. The next day I'd wake up and start again. I was truly obsessed in those early days.

I've often wondered what made me do this, because there was no carrot, no reward or payoff, like if you play at this level you will get rich or be famous or have chicks or whatever. When I came to the United States, I kept hearing people say that they took up playing guitar in order to get laid. That was an alien concept to me. I'd never even heard of such a thing. I just had this burning, internal drive to surpass myself, every single day. I was driven to see how far I could push this thing, to discover what level of skill I could get to if I kept on trying.

One of the things that has always taken me by surprise is the desire on the part of the fans to analyze my playing technique piece by piece. This really blew my mind when I first did interviews in Japan, because they wanted to know every detail of how I did what I did. I was forever getting questions like "How do you hold your pick, at what angle and how tightly?" and "How big is your reach on the fret board, and do you mute strings with your palm?" I truly had no idea what I did, in some cases. I just played the best way I could to produce the notes I heard in my head. I wasn't paying that much attention to my fingering or the angle of the pick. I found those kinds of interviews a little exasperating. But here's a funny thing: I *love* doing guitar clinics.

One of my most pleasant clinic experiences was at Berklee College in Boston. Everyone there was so responsive and appreciative. I was able to joke around with people and get a good, relaxed vibe going. One student asked me something like "So, you've done so much with the neoclassical style—where are you going next?" And I said, "Philadelphia, I think." The room exploded into laughter. We had a great time. I live for those moments.

I do a lot of clinics these days. It's a way of interacting with my fans that's much more suited to me than trying to do the meet-and-greet scene after a long concert on tour. My fans are so obsessive about uncovering the secrets of the "Malmsteen sound." It's amazing to me when I talk to some of them how much they home in on every little detail. They can't seem to accept that the sound comes from just a Strat and a stack of Marshall amps cranked to eleven. Of course, there's more to it than that, but I've always been a no-frills kind of guy in the equipment department. Very early in my career, I found the perfect combination of guitar and amplifier, and I've seen no reason to make any major changes over the years.

Sometimes I get asked how to do sweep picking. Let me be clear: I don't do sweep picking. Maybe when I play extremely fast arpeggios it sounds like sweep picking to some people, but that is definitely not what I'm doing. Sweep picking would be playing down through the strings, and if you do that it will sound like a chord, but that's exactly what you *don't* want it to sound like. What you want is for the motion to produce a sound of completely separate notes. It's much more difficult to play articulated individual notes in a properly executed arpeggio. Sweep picking produces a telltale merging or mushing of the notes together. Believe me, you can definitely hear the difference if you train your ears to listen. There's no set rule for playing legato, staccato, or whatever, but the goal is to play so that it's not sloppy, so that the notes are distinct.

Fans get so hung up on speed, as though they must somehow reach the holy grail of sixty-fourth notes, which is stupid. Who cares how fast you're playing if the articulation of the notes is crap? They've totally missed the point. The issue of vibrato is somewhat similar. I've been asked in interviews exactly how I do it, as though it's something you can measure. The question should not be how do you do it, but what do you hear and feel when you use the vibrato? The ability to hear pitch and the execution of the vibrato in your hand are tied together—it's very individualistic, like a fingerprint. People ask me how they can copy my vibrato, and the answer is they can't. It's just not some physical trick of the wrist that you can learn, like paint by numbers.

And it isn't just speed—you must use your ears. Is the note coming out too flat or too sharp? Is the interval too wide or too short? It is smooth, like a nice violin bow pull? Is it expressive so that it complements the notes being played? A good example is the opening to Bach's "Air," which I love to play live, in which the vibrato can be altered (slowed down and speeded up) to match the singing sound of those opening notes. That's *rubato*, which is Italian for "stolen time." It's all about phrasing, slightly speeding the tempo up and then slowing it down to add expression or color to your interpretation of the piece. This may take years of experience to cultivate, and it separates the talented from the typists.

Think about it this way. On a piano, you can play a note only on a piano key that is tuned to that note. You can't make a regular note go sharp or flat on the same key. Playing a trill is sort of an approximation of that, but the actual note (the key) itself cannot be changed. On a stringed instrument, like a violin or a cello, this is not the case. That, to me, is why the violin or the guitar is the most expressive of instruments.

That's why it's ludicrous to simply be obsessed with speed. Do you want to sound like a tuneless typewriter? Of course not. If you have speed with fluidity and expressiveness, fine. But it's not an end in itself. Having said that, I will admit that I really like the flash—the splendor, if you will—of a lightning-fast ripple of notes; it's exciting. But it must be in conjunction with the more expressive components of playing. Expression is as important to me as execution. They must go together.

RELENTLESS

I have always been a one-man show. It's just a
fact. I'm not a team player. I'm a tennis player, a
boxer, a fencer. I don't participate as a member of
a team.

Sometimes I get the feeling that I was born in the wrong century,
because I think of my band more as a hired orchestra with
myself as the composer and conductor. I hire people I consider the
best players for the album I'm making. Sometimes a certain player
continually fulfills the role the way I want, so that person has longevity in my "orchestra." Also, I compose for the voice the same
way I compose for all the other instruments. In my band, the singer
is not the front man; he is another instrument that expresses my
music in the specific way that I dictate. In fact, I've been called a
musical dictator. It's my way or the highway.

Imagine Mozart rehearsing a new ensemble. Do you think the second violinist or some other member of the group would stop him and say, "I think we should play it like this"? Of course not. The musicians are hired to play the music written by the composer in the way he dictates. The same applies to me. I have always, even as a teenager, been in search of the perfect ensemble to play my music, and that ensemble includes the singer. I expect the singer to perform my melody and my lyrics, because as a composer, I am expressing myself in words and music. The members of my ensemble have to be consummate musicians, and they have to be able to follow my directions to perform what I hear in my head and what I want to hear with my ears.

It's that simple. In the past, perhaps I didn't make this concept clear to everyone, so certain members of the band were maybe expecting to be collaborators or contribute their own material for the band to play. My name is on the record; it was never a band's name. I still don't know where a lot of people got the idea that Yngwie Malmsteen was a band. I have hired so many different musicians for so many different projects that I had created over so many years, I am surprised that people are still shocked when I hire someone new and give them the opportunity to show their musicianship on one of my new projects. On second thought, it probably is because I hired singers to sing my compositions, and then hired them to go on tour and kind of be like the front man. It is what people are used to. It is more usual to have the singer in a band as the front man rather than a guitar player, so in a way what I was doing was quite unusual for a solo artist. This is how it has been for nearly thirty years. But when an album is being made, I am the composer, the orchestrator, the arranger, and the conductor—period. My instructions are so specific that I will, for instance, go behind the drum set and actually play the part myself. I'm orchestrating the music just as a Tchaikovsky symphony would be orchestrated.

When I go out on tour, the dynamics are somewhat different, because we play as a cohesive unit. In that sense, we are all performers together onstage, making the music happen. In that sense, we are more like what people think of as a traditional rock band. On the road, I like to be one of the guys and hang out with the others—no special treatment. I sleep cramped on the bus like everyone else. I don't aim to be the prima donna while on tour. We all pull our weight equally to make the shows the best they can be. I'm talking about the way it works now, realizing that back in the bad old days, things might not have gone that smoothly.

But when it comes to the creation, production, and direction of the music itself, it's my baby. I released a DVD called *Raw*, which is a documentary of my career onstage that spans almost thirty years and contains some very early footage of me onstage. It's clear all through the years how consistent my sound and vision have been, from almost day one to where I am now. I'm sure that even now, some people just won't get it, but that's the best I can explain my band ethic. It's not a democratic situation—it's a hired ensemble that is paid to play my music. Their talent and skill obviously contribute to the overall product (that's why I hired them, of course), but the person in the driver's seat is me.

There have been a few times in my career when I've compromised on that ideal, mostly because I was lazy or was going through personal problems. But I can say unequivocally that I was never satisfied with the results of those compromises. They may have been somebody else's vision of the album at the time, but they weren't mine. *Odyssey* is an example: I wrote all the melody lines, but I let Joe Lynn Turner do some of the lyrics. On

Trilogy, I wrote everything, and guess what? To this day that album remains a fan favorite. I must have been doing something right.

These days, I spend a huge amount of time working on lyrics and melodies. I like the sound and weight of certain words, and I like building lyrics around them. Sometimes I'll use certain words because of their sound in the lyrics as well as their meanings. I'm composing music with words as well as notes. I think people are still figuring that out.

Most of my problems with band members have been with singers. At some point, they have all begun to think that they should be leading the band, writing the lyrics to the songs, or writing their own melodies. That's usually the point at which I start looking for their replacement.

Mark Boals came close to being the kind of singer I wanted, and for the most part he was also quite good to work with. He obviously had the range and ability to sing my melodies, and I think he quite understood what the deal was with being in my band. We did a lot of good work together.

Graham Bonnet had his moments, before we had our falling out. He couldn't come up with melodies, which was great for me because I was still pretty new to the rock scene, yet I was able to write all the music, which he then put words to. Some of his lyrics were pretty weird and funny, but they still worked. In that sense, we were a good team.

Now, when I say that the singer is just another instrument in the band, this doesn't mean that when we play live he should hide in the background. Absolutely not. The singer needs to have confidence and connect with the audience while he's singing my songs the way I want him to.

When I'm invited to play on other people's albums, that's a different situation. It's their show, their gig, so I ask them what they want me to play, and I deliver. Sometimes they'll just say, "Do it your way," so that's what I do. Or they might ask whether I can play a jazzier run, and my response is "No problem," because in that particular situation, I'm an instrument in *their* ensemble. Sometimes what they want is a challenge, and that's fun, too.

I give these examples to point out that I'm not inflexible at all. In fact, I'm quite adaptable to any given style, if that's what's needed. The point is that on other people's albums, I give them what they ask for, and the same applies to my own band: my ensemble gives me what I demand of it. I pay all the bills, so, yes, I get to dictate how things should go. This is the way I've chosen to work. In more typical band setups, the members might share the expenses as well as the decisions about how the band is run, what is played, and who does what. In my experience, though, that leads to continual arguments and conflicts and often breakups, which I just don't want to put up with.

That's basically what my band situation is all about. I suppose on some level I would like to be able to have the same group of guys in the ensemble for years, keeping the same vibe and group dynamics, but so far, that hasn't happened. Many times over the years people have said I should collaborate more, change the kind of music I play to be more bluesy or more something else, or let other people contribute more. I do believe that the reason I am still here, still making a living by making music—and, in fact, doing better than ever—is that I have refused to compromise on these basic rules. I've done it my way, and I'm still here.

One of the things I learned about composition is that you must let it move at the speed it wants to instead of trying to force it to happen. It's like a river; I jump in and flow with it, not knowing exactly where it's going. For example, when I relax in front of the TV with my guitar, just noodling around, occasionally a really good riff, melody, theme, or even a full-blown passage will materialize. I run upstairs to my studio and put it into my ProTools software program before I lose it. That way, I have it recorded and filed away, and I can come back to it later. I've amassed a data bank of countless song ideas this way.

Sometimes, when I go into the song bank and listen to things, I find passages that make me think, "Whoa, where did that come from?" If I were a spiritualist, I might think that I was channeling something. This happened a lot when I was working on *Spellbound*. I got into improvisation mode and just let the recording roll, and fully formed, fully structured pieces emerged right there on the spot.

A case in point is "Knight of the Vasa Order," from my *Relentless* album. If I had sat down and deliberately plotted out such a distinctly neoclassical piece, it would probably work okay, but it wouldn't have that spark of imagination and spontaneity that came from the improvised piece. As I've said many times, my aim is always to blow myself away. If I can't impress myself, then it's not good enough. I've always had that approach, but it's never been as easy to catch those moments of "divine" inspiration as it is now, with ProTools added to my state-of-the-art recording facility.

The way I work nowadays is so much easier than when I was at the mercy of having to rent studio space. I have everything I need right there in my own studio, and I have my own rehearsal space when I need it. There's no need to have a whole album ready to record in a certain week because that's all the studio time we have booked. Instead, I may drive around in my Ferrari writing songs in my head, then I'll call up my drummer, he'll come over, and we'll lay down a basic track for the song. Then I'll think about it some more and flesh it out further. The songs often develop like that, in stages and over time, whereas before I had to make it happen *now* because the meter was running. That always diminishes creativity; the pressure to rush things simply kills the joy, and it's not spontaneous.

It's very hard to be creative on demand, as was required with the old system. Quite often the best music comes from just thinking about riffs and songs and letting them kind of stew around in your head. Or sometimes, like with "Knight of the Vasa Order," they just come out of nowhere and strike when you least expect it. When that happens, I just run up to the studio and grab it while it's still fresh in my mind. I get the gist of the song down, then work on it and expand it at my leisure. Now both my vocal songs and my instrumentals are much more complete and fully realized than a lot of the tracks that were done under the time constraints of the old studio rental system. That may be the greatest difference in how I create music today.

A few years ago, I used to do a lot of writing and composing with other people in the room. Even though they didn't contribute directly, the work was necessarily filtered through them as I was putting it together. For example, Mats Olausson would sit at the keyboard, and I'd say, "Listen to this. Play this." I'd show him a bass line or a chord progression, and then, as he played it back, I'd improvise something on top of that, which would develop into something else.

To his credit, Mats never tried to inject his own influence into those sessions. He just played what I asked and let me worry about how to change it or enhance it, which is probably why he lasted so long. Then I'd have somebody program the drums, and it worked pretty well to build the songs in layers. I used that method for many years and was fairly satisfied with it.

After about twelve years of doing it that way, I just decided to clean house. I fired the whole band, intending to start with a completely clean slate. This was right before the *Attack!!* album in 2002. I got myself a guitar synthesizer, which allowed me to record various tracks (such as for voices and violins) and try them out, much as I'd previously done with Mats. I also decided that I didn't need someone to come in and program the drums—I realized I could do that myself. There was a bit of a learning curve, but being a drummer myself, I didn't need a long time to get the hang of it. Out of that process came some of my most innovative and strong songs, such as "Stronghold," "Valhalla," "Ship of Fools," "Exile," and "Baroque 'n' Roll."

I was a little concerned about how I was going to work on making a new album without a keyboardist or a drummer on site to lay down the preliminary tracks, but it turned out to be better for me once I figured out how to do what I needed myself. I simply had to be in total control. Over the years, people have asked me why I don't collaborate with this songwriter or that producer. If I wanted any of those people, I would certainly have them on board. It would certainly be less work for me if I gave some of the responsibility to other people.

But every time I've done that, I've been disappointed with the results. For one thing, they would inject their own style into mine, diluting what I intended with their own vision of how the lyrics, arrangements, or production should go. That isn't what I'm trying to accomplish in my career. I have always been a one-man show. It's just a fact. I'm not a team player. I'm a tennis player, a boxer, a fencer. I don't participate as a member of a team. Think of me as a painter. I paint the complete canvas: the main objects, the foreground, and the background—everything. I don't do half of it and leave the rest to my assistants. I even frame the picture.

Sometimes I'll write lyrics without having the music in mind, like writing poetry, and then come back to them for the right musical setting. That's what I did for "Razor Eater," which was inspired by the author Clive Barker. The lyrics to "I Am a Viking" were written on a drink napkin on the plane from Tulsa, Oklahoma, after my fateful last night in Alcatrazz. I found the perfect riff for it later that really expressed the aggression I wanted to convey.

Sometimes the lyrics don't have a deeper meaning, although they may sound mystical and mysterious. "I'll See the Light Tonight" is one of those. The words don't really mean anything; they're just there to express the melody, which I really loved. Sometimes I like to use a certain set of images to set the vibe of a song. I still like to use occult imagery in my lyrics, but not all the time. I sometimes write about history (I often get inspiration from watching the History Channel), like on *Alchemy* or *War to End All Wars*, or current events like I did on *Attack!!* Songs like "Bad Reputation" and "The Wild One" are about myself. "Miracle of Life" is about my son. On *Relentless*, I have a song called "Caged Animal," which is about how much I hate hotel rooms.

My lyric writing has become broader, and anything can spark an idea for a song. One thing I don't do is use songs as a political soapbox, because I don't think music and politics mix very well, at least for me. I don't try to preach my own political ideas or convictions through my music. Of course if you listen carefully, you could draw your own conclusion from songs like "Enemy Within" and "Poisoned Minds" from *Spellbound*.

I do think my songwriting has matured. I'm much more aware of writing lyrics as poetry. It was a chore for me when I was younger, but it's been gradually improving over the years, mostly in stages. An important period of change occurred when I started working with no one in the studio but me. Without the distraction of another person, I am much more focused and have a lot of time to sift through the files of ideas I have stored on my computer and see what strikes me as something I want to work with. I might come up with a great line or two but nothing else, so I just file it away and figure that eventually it will find a home in a song. "All I Want Is Everything" used lyrics I'd written long before the melody of the song came together. I wish now I'd put it to a better riff. The lyrics are good, but now I think they deserved a better setting.

I'm always extremely excited about an album right after it's released. It always feels like my best work yet, and it takes a while for the newness to wear off before I get itching to do something else. I've been asked how I decide whether a piece I'm working on needs lyrics or should remain an instrumental, and that's a tough call. Sometimes there's a melody line so good that the piece kind of "sings" by itself, and I know it's good just the way it is. At other times, vocals might come to me later, after I've finished a song that was originally an instrumental. It varies. These days, with digital software, it's so easy so add or remove vocals that the process is very different from the way I used to decide about adding lyrics to a song. A perfect example is the song "Shot across the Bow." I first played the melody on the guitar, intending it to be the vocal line, but then I decided it sounded better as an instrumental. *Spellbound* is full of melodies played on the guitar that could just as well been sung. That's the beauty of being in total creative control without having some producer breathing down your neck.

Arranging a song is like taking all the gold nuggets and creating a piece of jewelry with them. I like to arrange songs in a fairly traditional way: intro riffs, verse, chorus, bridge, solo, and so on. But not always. "Icarus Dream," from my first album, is made up of three different movements. I do like to mix things up a bit to see what effect I can create. In writing rock songs, there are traditional parts that you have to work with, and they have a typical structure. Classical music has its own, very different structure: you have a musical theme or motif and its variations, and these are spread out over the different instrument sections of the orchestra, which pick up the theme and carry it in a different way from its first statement. In a sense, it takes logic, like solving a math equation, to create baroque arrangements.

I started out listening to the very tightly made songs of Deep Purple, contrasted with those of Genesis, which were all over the place in terms of arrangement. I think it was important to hear how something catchy and simple in structure could be very effective while at the other end of the spectrum there were songs that were so complex they were impossible to predict. I've gone through phases of creating both kinds of arrangements and of putting those elements in unexpected places in a song.

Very early, I was concerned with not only which part goes where but also which instrument plays what. In most rock songs, the bass plays the root note, anchoring the song in a certain key, while the other instruments play over it. In many of my songs, the bass lines are not like that. I like the bass parts to be integrated into the melodic structure of the song, so, for example, instead of holding the root, the bass line might play an inversion of the main melody riff. When you play that two-note inversion up and down the neck, you suddenly have a pattern similar to Bach's. A great example of this is the arpeggio section on "Never Die"—the bass doesn't play the root note even once.

These underlying bass structures from baroque classical music are etched in my brain, and they tend to take precedence over the simple bass notes used in most rock songs. What I also like to do is have the bass hold the same note and have the chords change under it, or have the bass line echo the guitar in counterpoint, which sounds really heavy. This is why I insist on playing bass myself on my recordings. When I play bass, the guitar is almost always drop-tuned so that the low E-flat is tuned to a D-flat formation, which gives a heavier sound. You have to rethink the pattern and pay attention until it becomes second nature, which it is for me now.

Anyone who knows me knows I've never been a computer kind of guy. I much prefer the hands-on feel of wood and wire. But at the same time, and this may seem contradictory to some, I've always loved electronics, especially knowing how things work. Put those together and you have my love for scalloping my own guitars, wiring my own pickups, creating precision tapes from the big Studer analog multitrack recorder in my studio, and so on. But I've never much cared for computers or computer-generated music. I basically stayed away from computer technology until I couldn't avoid it any longer.

Eventually, I remodeled my home studio from my analog tape setup to accommodate computerized mixing and digital recording, but I still wasn't using state-of-the-art software to create the actual tracks. Keith Rose, my engineer for decades, kept badgering me to learn ProTools, and I kept resisting. But in 2010, with the release of my album *Relentless*, I took the leap and have never looked back. Keith upgraded my system and installed the latest version of ProTools, and I set out to learn what it could do for me. I use ProTools as I would a tape recorder—my recording chain is an AKG 414 in front of the Marshalls; the mike signal goes through a focusrite EQ, a Summit audio tube compressor, then into the digidesign interface, into ProTools, and then out of ProTools into the 64-fader mixing console with API equalizers. Voila! There's my sound.

Much to my surprise, it came very quickly to me, and soon I was using it seamlessly to instantly capture new musical ideas the moment they struck me. I couldn't get over how effortlessly I could also deal with works that were already in progress. The amazing array of options for what could be done on the fly or at a later time opened a new door for me. I consider *Relentless* a milestone album because I was able to take control over my music in ways that I hadn't done before. With *Spellbound* I took it even further, as it was created entirely with this method.

When I went from having to rent a studio to having a studio in my home, that was a big step in a lot of ways. But even once I had built my own place, it was still somewhat limited in the sense that I remained stuck with having to put down ideas as sketches. I didn't have the capacity to take a fresh idea that had just come to me from nowhere and actually use that for an album. With the equipment I had, it just wasn't possible. Moving from that type of studio to what I have now is a dramatic difference. Now I can put a musical idea into reality on the spur of the moment, instead of having to sketch it out and show it to the drummer or keyboardist and then rerecord it to get it into a usable format. By then, a lot of the spontaneity of the original idea would be lost.

Some songs on *Spellbound* are completely spontaneous results of my improvising while I was sitting on the couch and the few minutes it took me to go up to the studio and create it right there.

In the old way of making song tracks, I couldn't put something down and then do the drums later—it wasn't possible. In the old way, I would have had to put the click track down, mike up the drum set, teach the drummer the part, and so on. By the time the idea got redone for the actual album track, it was hard to replicate that initial spark of inspiration. But with the switch to ProTools, all that went out the window.

A good example of what I'm talking about is the brief overture to *Relentless*. We were near the end of mixing the album, about a day or two before the album files had to be delivered. I was sitting by myself on the couch in front of the TV with ideas running through my head, and I started to hear a measure with a very dramatic C-sharp minor chord sequence, with a punctuated beat. So I ran upstairs, fired up ProTools, and put down all the parts—guitars, bass, cellos, drums—exactly as I was hearing them on the spot. I added a layered overdub of the guitars, and it was all done.

And that overture is exactly what's on the album. The ease with which I was able to create this piece and have it finished and ready for the album, within just minutes of conceiving it, is a quantum leap, like going from analog to digital. It was a magical moment.

For all the albums I recorded before *Relentless* and *Spellbound*, I used a "scratch" guitar track with a drummer, which means you play just the bare arrangement on the guitar (like for a demo), and the drummer puts his part down, then you add the more complex guitar playing and the bass afterward. That's the way most albums were done in the past, but it's not ideal, especially not for the way I want to work now.

The further I get into my career, the less I feel like what the typical rock 'n' roll musician used to be: writing an album, recording it, going on tour, coming home, then writing the next one, and so on, ad nauseam. I can't stand that. More and more, I want to be a musician, an artist, who works in the moment, on my own schedule—not what I'm told to do by a record company that just wants to make money and doesn't care anything about my musical process. I need to blow my own mind when I create something. Otherwise, what's the point?

Overcoming my reluctance to get with the cutting-edge music production software was the smartest thing I did in 2010. Since then I have been incredibly inspired, like never before. Once I began to master the program and understand everything it could do, it totally freed my imagination. For example, for one song on *Relentless* that I sing on, I have a mike that stays connected, so if I want to add some backing vocals, I can. Everything is always switched on, so the artistic flow isn't interrupted. Whatever I want to do at any given moment is immediately done. It made such a difference in recording *Relentless* and even more so on *Spellbound.*

In "Knight of the Vasa Order," that whole theme and the D-minor chord progression happened all at once. I had done it as a demo, as I described above. But after I got my new studio setup, I was listening to the song and I thought, "What if I wanted to take that baroque-sounding middle part and put it at the beginning?" One click and it was done.

Here's an interesting aside about "Knight of the Vasa Order." My uncle, who is very much into genealogy, did some extensive research into our family tree as far back as the 1500s. He was especially interested in the fact that nobility was bestowed on the family in the seventeenth century, and he wanted to know what the precise title was. According to what he discovered, "Knight of the Vasa Order" is the exact wording of the title. As a direct descendant of that family, I too am a knight of the Vasa Order. That's what inspired me to use it for the song title. You can visit the House of Knights in Stockholm right next to the royal palace and see the coats of arms of all the noble families, including my family.

During the creation of *Relentless*, I was in the studio just messing around with some ideas. I jotted down some lyrics on a guitar string packet and started singing them into the mike right there in the control room, with no headphones, and saved the file. Later I went back and listened to it, and it sounded pretty darn good, so we decided to use it. In the old way of writing songs, you wouldn't write the lyrics until you had the right number of bars. I used to hate that, but I don't have to worry about that anymore.

I have to laugh at myself, because formerly I would have been the last person in the world to use this kind of production editing software. I really scoffed at people who did. But now that I understand how it can free the creative process and make your job so much easier, I can't believe I waited so long to get a clue. I still use the big mixing console and such, but I use ProTools as the recorder.

True art, for me, is what comes straight from the artist without any afterthought or concern about what other people will think or what they want you to do. If you're into making a product, that's one thing—then you have to please the consumers of that product. But if you want to do true art, you can't be concerned with that. You have to let flow what's in your soul.

RELENTLESS

When I was sixteen, spending hours alone in the basement studio of my grandmother's apartment building, being completely surrounded with just music coming out of my own mind and fingertips, that was the realm of what I mean by true art. My focus was hard, cold, and real, with no aberrations. My musical vision and intention was like a laser beam, sharp and totally precise.

I got away from that somewhat in the decades that followed, as my career was developing and I became fully immersed in the music industry. For many years, I seemed to be living slightly out of focus. The lens I was looking through was distorted by so many demands and influences coming from outside.

I have reclaimed that focus now. It's hard to describe to other people, but I know exactly how that feels. I find myself thinking and doing things much more like I used to do when I was in my teens. Now, many years later, I find myself in the position once again of making *pure* art. Things have come full circle.

At this writing, I am just just about to finish my latest album, *Spellbound*, and it was created from the start on ProTools.

But it's not just with music that this has happened. I've also regained my love of building things, figuring out how things work or don't work, fixing things, and coming up with solutions—problem-solving. That's a talent I've regained after living so many years in a blur. I made some great music during those years, but the state of my mind and my body back then was troubled a lot of the time. It was like "Just point me toward the stage and I'll play another gig." Sometimes I didn't even know where I was. I feel like I've woken up after years in a dream state.

I know a lot of people feel nostalgic for those years, but let me tell you, I don't miss them. None of it. And as I've said before, it doesn't feel like it was me. It feels like it was someone else. I truly believe I was reborn a few years ago. I know that sounds like a cliché, but it's the truth. Unless you've gone through it yourself, you can't really know what it's like to live in the dark for so long and then step out into the light again. The desire to change, to genuinely reclaim your life, has to come from inside yourself. It helps to have strong people around you who believe in you, but unless you really want things to be different deep inside yourself, it won't happen. I don't want to sound like I'm preaching—it's just a fact.

At this point in my life, I believe that I'm creating the most inspired art I've ever done. *Trilogy* was a really inspired album, in the sense that it was my first record in the United States, where I had my own controlled studio space to write in. It was just a little room full of beer cans, but it was my space and allowed my focus on the music to stay true. But after that, the albums became more unfocused in a general sense. Each one had its gems that stood out, but overall there was a trend away from the focus I had started with.

Many of the songs on *War to End All Wars* are some of the best songs I've ever written, even though the album itself has compromises in terms of sound and production that make it less than perfect. It's very possible that I'll remix that album in the near future. *Relentless* and *Spellbound*, as I've already explained, were definitely game-changers in terms of how I create and produce music.

RELENTLESS

It really is mind blowing to me that after all these years, I can find myself newly inspired to this level. Through my music, I've connected to those fans who have been loyal to me and to new fans who have just discovered me. They understand what I am about, and they connect to the energy and vision given by my compositions and my playing. They know what I do is real, and they feel it. God bless them.

Index

INDEX

INDEX

CPSIA information can be obtained
at www.ICGtesting.com
Printed in the USA
LVHW031627020421
683319LV00001B/12

BIO MALMSTEEN
Malmsteen, Yngwie J.
Relentless :the memoir
04/07/2021